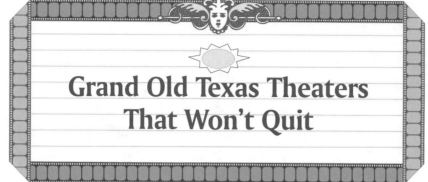

Grand Old Texas Theaters
That Won't Quit

Joan Upton Hall

and

Stacey Hasbrook

T0168365

Republic of Texas Press
Plano, Texas

Library of Congress Cataloging-in-Publication Data

Hall, Joan Upton.
Grand old Texas theaters that won't quit / Joan Upton Hall and Stacey Hasbrook.
     p. cm.
   Includes index.
   ISBN 1-55622-884-8 (pbk.)
   1. Theaters—Texas—Directories. I. Stacey, Hasbrook. II. Title.

PN2275.T4 H35   2001
792'.025'764—dc21   2001530657
                                      CIP

Republic of Texas Press is an imprint of Wordware Publishing, Inc.
No part of this book may be reproduced in any form or by
any means without permission in writing from
Wordware Publishing, Inc.

Printed in the United States of America

ISBN 1-55622-884-8
10 9 8 7 6 5 4 3 2 1
0112

Product names mentioned in this book are for identification purposes only and may be trademarks of their respective companies.

All inquiries for volume purchases of this book should be addressed to Wordware Publishing, Inc., at 2320 Los Rios Boulevard, Plano, Texas 75074. Telephone inquiries may be made by calling:

(972) 423-0090

Dedications

Stacey:

I dedicate this book to my parents, Barbara Carroll and James Richard Hasbrook, both of whom are gone now. To my mother, for her quiet strength and independence, and my father for unwavering belief in my abilities. Also to my children, Jeffrey and Brettne, for their love and taking care of everything while I was "on the road." And last, to my other friends and loved ones who continually make me believe.

Joan:

I dedicate this book to my family who have always cheered me on even when supper wasn't on the table on time, especially to my husband, Don, without whose support I would have had to either quit the project or him! I hope he, my son David, and my daughter Diane, along with their families who have made life worth living, will deem the book worth it when they see it. Last of all, I thank my parents, James and May Bell Upton, for bringing me up to realize that books will outlast us all. I only wish they had lived long enough to see *Grand Old Texas Theaters That Won't Quit*.

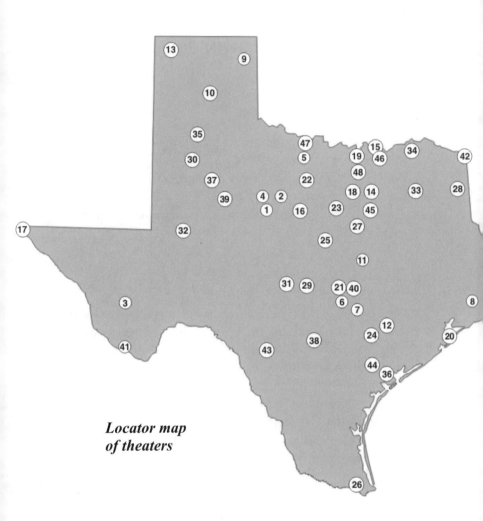

Locator map of theaters

Contents

Acknowledgments

We wish to thank all the people who shared their theaters with us—in touring, photographs, stories, facts, and written accounts—as well as boosting our enthusiasm with their own. To name everyone of these people would take an encyclopedia. We don't have room for that, but we do want them to know we now count them among our friends.

Special thanks go to those who notified us about theaters other than their own, especially to Ed. Allcorn, who provided information and photos for several theaters across the state. Thanks go also to Carol Menchu for saving us many hours of research work on contact sources, city attractions, etc.

The photographic assistance of Melinda Doster and Ernest Upton was much appreciated as well. To Pamela Robison, whom I've never even met, for offering to "shoot" any Dallas theater pictures I lacked "one artist to another."

Without the computer wizardry of Ashley Keith, we would have piles of useless digital images we couldn't open due to incompatibility of systems (and our technical ignorance). She answered all our questions and gave us hope when we weren't sure our computers could "talk" to those of Republic of Texas Press at all.

Introduction

NOTICE: The spelling of the word "theater" has another variation, which many prefer. In this book we have used the "-er" spelling except in chapters where the name of the institution is spelled "theatre."

Texans, whether native or born-again, don't stint when it comes to historical pride and preservation. Any other vintage building might find its salvation in new functions (i.e., an old bank becoming a museum, boutique, or bed & breakfast). But mess with a theater, and you hit a nerve. Something about a theater hates to give up the ghost—sometimes literally.

People have a sense of ownership about the place where they first saw *Gone with the Wind* or perhaps a silent Rudolf Valentino in *The Sheik* (1921). Where they shared popcorn or held hands with their first love. It's as if memories of larger-than-life characters have taken up residence in the bricks and mortar, and judging by the audiences and managers, even young people crave to share that nostalgia.

Traveling shows once brought "culture" to the outlying areas in the form of musical shows, plays, and even prizefights. Ironically, most theaters that showed movies enjoyed their heyday in the twenties and thirties when money was most scarce. Theatergoers during the Depression somehow scraped up their pennies (as few as five) to pay for a ticket and maybe even popcorn and a Coke. Well into the forties old movie serials used to bring kids back every Saturday to find out how their hero or heroine escaped certain death, only to have them jeopardized again with the words "To be continued" flashed on the screen.

During World War II, ten-cent tickets went to nine cents because anything ten cents or over was subject to a "defense tax," and managers found it easier to drop the price than do the math. What a blessing it must have been to escape into a palatial building and be carried away to other worlds. And wouldn't we still want to escape from modern stresses in an exotic setting?

Today vintage theaters all over the state are struggling to survive although many couldn't make it into millennium 2000. Some of the survivors continue to reel out celluloid, delightful anachronisms competing against modern giants with multi-screens, surround sound®, and stadium seating. Others have found new life as stages for the performing arts, utilizing local talent and road show professionals.

At the impersonal multiplex cinema, we buy a ticket to see a movie. At the grand old playhouses and picture shows, we invest in an experience. Yet in only a few cases did we find information about a city's theater in its web site. Often the town's tourist brochure failed to list it as an "attraction" as well. Discovering the people whose passion has kept the old showplaces alive was often difficult, and the authors of this book commend those cities that recognize what a treasure they possess.

It saddened us to be told, "There used to be a theater..."; to see an old movie house gutted, painted road-sign yellow, and turned into a dollar store; or to hear the crunch of bricks and smell old wood splintering under a wrecking ball. But preservation requires public interest.

Some of Texas's few surviving metropolitan theaters compare favorably with those I've seen in New York City. Small town ones range from slick sophisticates to cozy or rustic. A few are in sad need of repair, but the structure's there—an opportunity waiting for an entrepreneur. One thing became clear to us in our travels. Success for a theater depends on a three-way partnership: creative visionaries, business-minded managers, and eager public patrons (who will come if the first two fill a need). It's about pleasure, not desperation or guilt.

Next time you're looking for something special to do or a fun bit of history to show your kids, we hope you'll open your copy of *Grand Old Texas Theaters That Won't Quit* to locate one of these treasures and contact the management for what's playing. Indulge yourself in a bygone era where each building had its own personality. The show will ensconce itself in your memory instead of just passing through as a consumed two or three hours.

A General Historical Overview

As we visited theaters, a pattern emerged of success-to-hard-times-to-revival, and all but a few theaters bore this out. Consider the following:

1880s - late 1920s: Variety/vaudeville skits came between acts of a play or at saloons. Sometimes vaudeville became the whole show.

1880s: With experiments to produce "moving pictures," Thomas Edison succeeded in 1889 after Hannibal Goodwin developed transparent film and George Eastman manufactured it. "Kinetoscope" parlors opened in New York, London, and Paris.

1896 - 1900s: Edison realized the potential and gave the first exhibitions. Motion pictures (no stories) became popular attractions at amusement arcades, novelties between vaudeville acts in many countries. In 1897 Dallas led Texas into the motion picture age, less than a year after New York City had. Stores set up nickelodeons (5-cent movies) wherever space allowed. Short films often supplemented live acts.

1903: As novelty wore off, storytelling saved movies. The first important narrative film was *The Great Train Robbery* (Edwin Porter, director). Air domes (open-air theaters) became popular, opera houses started showing silent movies (accompanied by piano or organ and sound effects), and stars were born.

1915 - '16: D.W. Griffith turned movies into an art form with changing camera angles, long shots, and closeups in *Birth of a Nation* and *Intolerance.*

Late 1920s: Silent film gave way to "talkies" and became social gathering points. Many of our grandest theaters were built before the thirties. Vaudeville was getting crowded out.

1941 - '45: The U.S. became involved in World War II, and movies and newsreels united citizens at home. People gathered for cheap entertainment or just human companionship in downtown around movie and opera houses. Sometimes theaters were built in clusters. Promotional gimmicks added to the fun.

1950s - '70s: Two world wars had taught manufacturers mass production of cars. "A car in every garage" became possible. Car culture brought about urban flight and general deterioration of inner cities. Drive-in movies, shopping malls, and TV took over. (Car-chases in today's movies continue to provide popular special effects.) Thousands of old theaters were torn down to make new, efficient business space; others just stood vacant. Notice how few large cities kept their theaters. (Kudos to those that did!) The theater industry tried to bring patrons back with novelty innovations like Cinemascope®, Todd-a-O®, and even the faddish 3-D. New anti-trust laws broke up the control of chains and changed the way movies were distributed.

1980s - '90s: In or near malls, multiplex theaters dominated the industry, showing first-run movies, using state-of-the-art technology, capitalizing on the public's flight from the inner cities.

Late 1990s - ?: Interest in reviving downtown areas began. High-rises and loft apartments (in restored business buildings) provide city workers with chic alternatives to long commutes to suburbs. "Main Street Projects" encourage citizen interest in downtowns as fun places to go, an adrenaline shot for many historic theaters. Some have upgraded equipment and show first-run movies while others thrive on classic films and/or live entertainment.

1
Abilene: Paramount (1930)

Ernest Upton photographer

At first sight, heraldic shields backing Abilene's Paramount sign hint at aristocracy. The impression on entering heightens with trappings of old gold and Spanish opulence. In 1986 the theatre was restored to the original 1930 grandeur that builder H. O. Wooten intended—and more. I admired the ornately carved pillars and a brass marquee rescued from New York City's now demolished Helen Hayes Theatre. Attention to detail shows in newer, hand-painted Pueblo Deco designs (Southwestern influence) that adorn the lobby's two-story-high ceiling.

Stairways at right and left lead up to mezzanine balconies all around that provide an upper lobby area. I had been told to look for actor Spencer Tracy's portrait at the head of one stairway, a prop from his movie *Broken Lance*, and there he sat on horseback, a commanding figure in western attire. But I was even more intrigued by another painting, directly opposite at the head of the other stairs. It portrayed a beautiful young woman in a white dress. I climbed the stairs to take a closer look, expecting to identify some famous actress but couldn't. I made a note to ask who it was later.

Elegance and grace emanates from the chandeliers, classical statues, and paintings. However, I learned from founding member and past president of the Paramount Board Robert Holladay that only the chandeliers are originals. All else had to be replaced after a dark event in the early seventies. "One day at high noon, Interstate Theatres, financially troubled owners of the theatre at that time, came in unannounced. They stripped out the original properties to sell at auction."

Frank Sheffield, Paramount manager at the time, remembers the details. Interstate had asked for an inventory of their properties "for insurance purposes." Thus they knew what valuable pieces their flagship theatres across the state possessed. "I imagine the same thing happened to other Paramounts at Amarillo, El Paso, Austin—who knows how many." Sheffield even had to help them load up and haul the goods to Dallas, but he managed to take a couple of things home that had escaped inventory, an ornate mirror and two of the front doors, which later served as a pattern in the renovation.

Public disinterest in the theatre led to further decline. Only the completely volunteer Paramount Committee of the Abilene Preservation League was able to save it from destruction. They presented a classic film series, but by 1979 Interstate had to close the doors. Indicative of the area's demise was the fact that Wooten's other building, the Wooten Hotel next door, had become low-income housing (but it's now slated for renovation).

Ed. Allcorn, who later became the Paramount manager (now at Eastland's Majestic), came on the scene then as a "follow spot" operator for a country music operation that was attempting to buy the building and fix it up. He stayed on through a succession of this and other failed ventures before the building suffered bank foreclosure.

Hopes for the Paramount's future soared in 1984 when an anonymous benefactor bought it, turning over business management to a nonprofit corporation, the Dodge-Jones Foundation. When 1999 rolled over to 2000, the newspaper revealed the benefactor, Julia Jones Matthews, naming her "Abilenian of the Millennium." So much for anonymity.

While present executive director Barry Smoot toured me through the theatre, he said the Paramount had been called "the most atmospheric theatre in the Southwest." I knew what that meant when I entered the auditorium and had to catch my breath. Golden domed towers flank the stage on either side like Moorish castles, backlit with evening blue. Softly lit alcoves extend back toward the lobby, giving the effect of a Spanish plaza, just as designer David Castle had intended. And when the house lights go down, stars twinkle on the ceiling. Atmospheric indeed!

Killis Almond, restoration architect, did a superb job of keeping the original look. The Paramount is now a member of the League of Historic American Theatres and is listed in the National Register of Historic Places. Technical improvements far surpass those of the old days though. No musty old museum, this building is occupied over 200 days a year, accommodating an estimated 50,000 people. Professional lighting, sound, and rigging equipment enhance live theatre done by Paramount Productions, which utilizes the wealth of talent in and around Abilene.

With comfortable seating for 1,200, the facility has provided a venue for other groups too, showing concerts, opera, dance, and school performances. Free self-guided tours of the building are offered every afternoon from 1:00 to 5:00. The Paramount is an integral part of the city's life and has impacted surrounding downtown businesses. It has also fostered the development of such organizations as the Abilene Ballet Theatre, the Abilene Opera Association, and the Abilene Christian University Children's Theatre.

As for movies, classical films are shown every other weekend that might, as the website says, "sweep you back to bygone days," but they do it in DTS® Digital Stereo Sound®.

Robert Holladay grew up here viewing films before they became classics, and he had some stories to tell. During the restoration, the curtain somehow caught fire and might have set them back to point zero had they been unable to put it out. He also remembered various managers.

The most colorful one, Wally Akin, served in the early days. He presented all sorts of social gatherings and benefits for kids, and he went to great lengths to promote the shows. For the movie *The Greatest Show on*

photo courtesy of Paramount Theatre archives

Earth, he brought an elephant to town. For the movie *Hell's Angels* (starring Jean Harlow), he adorned the marquee with a crashed airplane.

Famous people visited the Paramount too. In 1927 Charles (Buddy) Rodgers came in honor of his wife, Mary Pickford, for a showing of *Wings*, the only silent movie ever to win an Academy Award (for Best Picture).

Frank Sheffield, who still lives in Abilene, served the longest managerial tenure, 1952-78. He recalled the world premiere of *Take Her, She's Mine* in 1963. Stars James Stewart and Sandra Dee attended, and 35,000 people came to see them in a parade. Also making an appearance in the sixties were Natalie Wood and Robert Wagner. Ben Johnson visited several times, and Harry Carrey Jr. came three. When *Gone with the Wind* was shown as a classic, Butterfly "I don't know nothin' about birthin' babies" McQueen graced the theatre.

"In those days," Sheffield said, "going to the movies was an event. Men wore ties and women, their Sunday dresses." Soldiers who were stationed at the base nearby still come back from all over the United States to share the nostalgia with friends and family.

Ed. Allcorn photographer

Weddings, dinner parties, business gatherings, and whatever people can imagine take place here too. Barry Smoot recalled a favorite incident. A young man reserved the theatre for a private dinner for two, his friends acting as waiters. Then he brought his lady love in for the surprise of her life. He proposed, and how could she resist that?

The stories and dazzling sights almost made me forget to ask Smoot about the mystery woman in the mezzanine portrait, but when I did, he gave a quizzical smile. "We don't know who she was. We just inherited her. Some think our Lady in White might be the source of eerie feelings they've experienced. All I know is that her picture won't stay straight—and it's the only one that doesn't."

Later I asked Robert Holladay about ghost rumors and he said, "Well, every Halloween we show *The Changeling* (starring George C. Scott), and every time strange things happen. Like once on a still day, a freak wind suddenly ripped the letters off the marquee." He was quiet for a moment. "And there's the Lady in White people claim to see."

Could it be that the Lady in White objects to the Halloween movie?

Frank Sheffield has his own ideas about theatrical hauntings. He had only been at the Paramount a few months and was working late in the office alone one night. He kept hearing an irregular thumping noise in the balcony. He checked several times and finally turned up the house lights before he figured out the weakened springs couldn't hold the folded-up seats in the balcony. One by one, they were falling open. So he didn't worry about the sounds anymore. "I think we unconsciously replay memories of our old experiences here. The first date. The first kiss. What we said to each other. These are the things we hear and feel."

Perhaps he's right that theatergoers simultaneously leave a slice of their lives and take a slice of the theatre with them. Still, I remembered a conversation with Ed. Allcorn when I had asked him if his theatre was haunted.

"Aren't they all?" he answered.

I was to discover only some are, depending on who you ask. After all, every emotion known to humankind has been played out in these buildings, sometimes in real life by the staff and patrons. Of course, old buildings tend to creak and groan from the effects of heating and cooling, and maybe that's answer enough. *—Joan Upton Hall*

 For information:

The Paramount Theatre
352 Cypress
Abilene, TX 79601
(915) 676-9620
theatre@paramount-abilene.org
www.paramount-abilene.org

Other attractions:

Abilene State Park
Abilene Zoo
Buffalo Gap
Center for Contemporary Arts
Dyess Air Force Base
Fort Phantom Hill
Grace Museum
Lakes, golf

Annual events:

West Texas Fair
Western Heritage Classic
Celebrate Abilene

For details and accommodations:

Visitor Information Center
1101 North First
Abilene, TX 79601
(915) 676-2556 or
1-800-727-7704
visitors@abilene.com
www.abilene.com/visitors/

2

Albany: Aztec (1927)

Clifton Caldwell photographer

Watt Matthews always said Albany was a little town with big city ways. I guess what he meant was that nobody ever told them "You can't do that." Matthews was a rancher whose efforts to preserve western heritage is legendary in the area. Recipient of numerous awards for his generosity and vision, he must have led the town by example during his ninety-eight years, because Albany seems to have more than its share per capita of strong leaders.

When Frank Whitney built the Aztec movie theater in 1927, he could have blended it into the same architectural style as the older downtown buildings, but he didn't. It stood out as a Spanish hacienda with stucco walls and a red clay tile roof—a handsome style, but odd against the other buildings of brick, stone, and wood. In 1939 the next owner, H.S. Lion, transformed the plain interior to resemble a Spanish courtyard, similar to that of the atmospheric Abilene Paramount. Turrets stood guard at each side of the stage, and faux windows along the sides showed painted landscapes. Cove lights and stars in the "sky" provided soft lighting. He added new carpet and a color scheme of silver, royal blue, maroon, and beiges.

During the fifties and sixties, the theater suffered a loss of movie-going audience, changing hands several times. A group of citizens even pooled their money and bought the theater in 1971, trying to operate it on weekends in an effort to provide entertainment at home especially for youth, but by '77 they had to close. They couldn't compete with the mall movies in nearby Abilene.

In 1974 the Shackelford County Courthouse Historic District had been listed on the National Register of Historic Places, prompting most owners to renovate. By default Aztec was part of the award, but it had been getting steadily more run-down, and in '85 it went on the market. Though they didn't live in Albany, two members of the Brittingham branch of the Matthews family, Sally Wallace and Dotsie Brittingham, bought the Aztec. They had the roof repaired to halt further interior damage while waiting for the local citizens to organize, but the projected price tag of renovation was too daunting.

Watt Matthews and Clifton Caldwell, both devoted to historical preservation, figured out how the project could be made affordable if a group got tax-exempt status. In 1990 a diverse group of citizens under Caldwell's leadership gathered to form the Aztec of Albany, Inc., and the owners gave the new group the building.

Then Watt Matthews led off with a generous endowment, and several other families followed. Nancy Birdwell, a native of Albany, living in Austin, contributed her skill at fund raising, and it worked. The Texas Historical Foundation, Jeanne R. Blocker Memorial Preservation Fund, the McDermott Foundation of Dallas, the Meadows Foundation, the King Foundation, Dunnigan Foundation, Mabee Foundation, the Rockwell Fund of both Houston and Albany, and countless small contributors chipped in. And volunteers showed up in droves to do whatever they could to stretch the money.

Since nobody told Albanians little towns didn't hire big city restoration architects, they contacted Bill Booziotis, FAIA from Dallas.

8

Connected to Albany through relatives, he assigned the project to his architectural intern, Amy Wingrove and agreed to supervise.

What it was going to take was too much to accomplish all at once, so they did it in two phases. First they removed whatever didn't work and did large structural work like increasing the stage space and restoring the exterior. By 1992 Phase II began, involving a complete remodeling of the 288-seat interior. Also they extended the lobby onto a vacant lot so they could add a kitchen, restroom facilities, and a meeting room. This provides space for organization meetings, reunions, and receptions. As civic leader Robert Echols said, "It's Albany's answer to a convention center."

Once again, the little town lucked into the services of a professional who had been an Albany native. Fort Worth interior decorator Ann Law Harwood donated her services, even repainting the "scenes" in those six faux windows with the help of her daughter. By the end of the project, Albany Aztec, Inc. had spent less than a third of the projected estimates,

Clifton Caldwell photographer

and the Aztec won the Main Street Association award for Best Community Restoration.

In 1999 Echols organized the Albany Mainstreet Playhouse (AMP), an arm of the Chamber of Commerce. Echols' volunteer accomplishments have been recognized all the way to Washington, D.C. where he went to receive an award for volunteerism in 2001. All that and his day job too, as general manager of the "Best of the West" motels!

The AMP performs comedy and drama plays mainly at the Aztec, but sometimes they have done dinner theater at another theater in town, the Whitney. At Christmas the *Nativity* is performed on even years and another kind of holiday production on uneven years. Other productions held at the Aztec are performed by traveling college groups, dance and musical groups, church revivals and gospel choirs, and the annual cancer drive, "Albany City Limits," a musical jubilee.

It is impossible to talk about Albany's performing arts without mentioning the *Fandangle*, which is held the last two weekends in June. This musical play dramatizes Albany's history as a frontier town and is staged in an acre-sized prairie amphitheater. The thirty acres of Gourd Ranch is *Fandangle's* permanent home for $1 a year, thanks to the J. A. Matthews family. According to a special visitors' guide published by the *Albany News*, "Watt Matthews commented . . . that the theater would be situated on the most worthless piece of pasture on the ranch, but the site seemed perfect for the envisioned theater."

Robert Nail, Albany native and Princeton graduate, wrote the scripts for not only the *Fandangle* but also the *Nativity*. Many of the same theatrical volunteers, such as Robert Echols, participate in both the *Fandangle* and Aztec performances. The *Fandangle* began in 1938 as a high school senior play on the football field. It took a hiatus during World War II when Nail and all the other young men went to war. After that it ran sporadically—until the grand opening of the Palo Duro Canyon amphitheater, out of Canyon and Amarillo.

It is well known that the pageant *Texas*, written by Paul Green, is now produced at that amphitheater by a professional company all summer every year. Not so well known is that for the amphitheater's grand opening, the Albany cast and crew were asked to perform the *Fandangle*. This production has even performed at the LBJ Ranch.

In 1997 Watt Matthews died at the age of ninety-eight, but the institutions he preserved have made him a legend. Before his death, Albany began holding an annual "Watt Matthews Cowboy Day" each October. The day's festivities culminate in the evening at the Aztec when the AMP presents a melodrama, and the Spanish Gourd Award is given to a person who epitomizes Matthews' spirit of western preservation. This award, a replica of the ranch brand, which Matthews often wore embroidered on his shirt cuffs, is not limited to the local area. For example, two of the recipients have been Governor Dolph Briscoe and Helen Kleberg Groves of King Ranch fame.

Much of what makes Albany big for its size is the heritage Matthews left behind. An article in *Southern Living* once stated, "Albany, Texas, is by no means a big city, or even a large town. But nobody ever told its people." And Albany native, Shirley Caldwell, vice-chairman of the Texas Historical Commission, wrote an article about the Aztec in the publication *Heritage*, saying, "The restored Aztec Theater is a brick and mortar monument to what can be accomplished by even the smallest community—especially one that is not content to part with its past." *—Joan Upton Hall*

For information:

Aztec website:
www.albanytexas.com/attractions/aztec.html

Other attractions:

Old MKT depot (now visitor center)
Fort Griffin State Park
Georgia Monument
Historical Ledbetter Picket House
Old Jail Art Center
Lakes, seasonal events, hunting

Annual events:

Watt Matthews Cowboy Day
Fort Griffin Fandangle

For details and accommodations:

Chamber of Commerce
P.O. Box 185
Albany, TX 76430-0185
(915) 762-2525
chamber@albanytexas.com
www.albanytexas.com/

3

Alpine: Rangra (1927)

Stacey Hasbrook photographer

Finding a theatre in Alpine turned out to be quite an Easter egg hunt. Theatres seem to be a well-kept secret in this town since even a young woman at the Chamber said she didn't think Alpine had one. Other sources kept insisting that there was one though, so eventually we called in the police to search for the missing entity. Sure enough, Donna Breeding, the deputy sheriff, and Ron Breeding, the assistant chief of police, confirmed the existence of one Rangra Theatre owned and operated by Dr. Avanesh Rangra, a professor at Sul Ross University. I must confess it helped that Donna is Joan's niece and Ron is Donna's husband.

But actually knowing there was a theatre didn't make the chase any easier when we got there. Everywhere we turned was conflicting information. Everyone we talked to seemed to believe the Granada Theatre, which is closed down, was older than the Rangra, and many others thought there was no theatre other than the Granada. Melita Bell, archivist for the Sul Ross University library helped clear up that confusion.

She showed us the Sanborn Insurance Company maps of the city blocks from 1927. These records showed a building constructed by Dr. Benjamin Berkeley, a physician, bank president, first mayor of Alpine, and state senator. In this building is a section labeled "movies" where the Rangra is, and on down the street, an empty lot where the Granada should be. Subsequently, the 1933 maps show the Rangra as "not in use" while the Granada shows up in its correct position. The Granada was actually built in 1928, but the original building which houses the Rangra has brass letters in the concrete slab just outside the door that read "Berkeley Building, 1921."

The Rangra was originally named the Tivoli and ran Spanish movies, which may explain why so many English-speaking people didn't remember it from their youth. Wally Davis, long-time manager of most of the theatres in town, was quite the businessman it seems. An old ad proclaimed, "When they make better movies, we will run them." In addition to the numerous theatres he managed, he also ran multiple liquor stores. One he had for about fifteen years was in the front left side of the Rangra, which now serves as the box office and snack bar area.

As many theatre managers did during WW II, Davis got involved with bond drives. According to an archive interview by Jim Cullen in the eighties, Davis remembers, "I left so quick; they just come by and said 'we're goin'' and you're goin' with us!' And—that started on War Bond Drive #5." He left his sister, Mrs. Anita Powers, his secretary, in control. It cost Davis though. "I lost a ton of money! When I got back here, my business had gone to pot. And they did the best they could to run 'em, but they just wasn't experienced and they just couldn't do it. And, the theatre business had dropped off because there wasn't any push to it."

Except for those times, business was very good, but eventually television finished Davis' involvement with the theatres. "It didn't bother the fella that bought me out at the time because he said you couldn't get television in here because you couldn't bend it. 'Cause you couldn't get it over these mountains. And I happened to have inside information that you could. And he made me an offer for these theatres, and we sold" (in the late fifties).

Earliest known image, photo courtesy of Archive of the Big Bend

Today the Rangra is a plain two-screen theatre that caters mostly to the college students. Renovations include splitting the area for a double screen, putting in new seating and adjusting for handicap access, and upgrading the equipment. David Busey, the Main Street Program director for Alpine, has proposed to include the theatre as part of the downtown renewal plan. His architectural drawing reveals that the front of the redesigned theatre would include a medallion at the top, a rendition of an old thirties picture of a warrior and sunburst. It is an image of a heroic Spanish figure, "El Flechador del Sol," which would glorify that part of history, the Spanish tradition that according to Busey is "really longer than that of ranching, which has only been here about the last 100 years." This would also honor the original purpose of the theatre, the showing of Spanish films.

But for now, Dr. Rangra seems to want to leave it as it is and has a very good reason for doing so. When I asked Dr. Rangra why he bought a movie house in the first place, he smiled and paused. "I like movies." Growing up in India, he found movies a treasured pastime, and now he gets to pass the pleasure on to others.

He has his patrons in mind always. Not spending a great deal of money on the theatre allows him to keep prices very low. Many of the people who come to his theatre have large families and cannot afford expensive tickets. They also need to come to the small community theatre rather than drive many miles to another town. With this in mind, Dr. Rangra also pointed out that he never sells out the house completely; he holds some fifty seats in reserve each night. The reason? "Many people drive eighty miles or more to come here to see a show. I want to make sure they have a seat when they get here."

Up until just recently, Alpine's only claim to theatrical fame was Dan Blocker of *Bonanza*. Now there are rumors of a "Julia sighting." What does that mean? This summer, Julia Roberts has been making a film in the Big Bend area, and according to *The Big Bend Sentinel*, reporters have been chasing her around Marfa trying to get a picture or interview. Someone thought they saw her peering into the darkened windows of the Rangra, but I guess we'll never really know for sure.

The character of the man who now owns the Rangra Theatre shows mostly in our favorite story he shared. The scheduling of shows usually depends on the college holidays, meaning that during Christmas break, the theatre closes down. One holiday evening Dr. Rangra came to the theatre to check on things and found a woman and her grandchild sitting on the sidewalk outside the doors to the theatre. When he asked why she was there, she replied she had traveled quite a distance to bring the child to see a movie. Without hesitation, he opened the doors and ran the movie for an audience of two.

Although there is a grant in the works to purchase and renovate the Granada as a permanent playhouse, the inside has been totally gutted, and there is nothing original left. It will be a good project for other reasons. The Rangra, however, is pretty much what it was, and probably will be for years to come—a place for people to simply come enjoy the pleasure of watching a movie. To our delight, the movie house wasn't really MIA; it simply wasn't wasting money on advertising its presence. —*Stacey Hasbrook*

For information:

Rangra Theatre
109 E. Holland Ave.
Alpine, TX 79830
(915) 837-5111

Other attractions:

Apache Trading Post
Last Frontier Museum
Museum of the Big Bend
Theatre of the Big Bend
Woodward Agate Ranch
Alpine Golf Course

Annual events:

Texas Cowboy Poetry
Gathering

For details and accommodations:

Chamber of Commerce
Big Bend Area Travel
Association
P.O. Box 401
Alpine, TX 79831
(915) 837-2326

4

Anson Opera House (1907)

Don Hall photographer

Talk about theaters that won't quit! Anson Opera House, built in 1907, was once touted as the "fanciest showplace between Fort Worth and El Paso." For about thirty years it presented musical and dramatic productions as well as public events. It also hosted wrestling and bare-fist boxing and, ironically, a dance studio, even when there was a city ordinance against public dancing.

These days the Opera House is hanging onto survival by the fingernails despite a listing in the League of Historical Theatres and a Texas Historic Landmark earned in 1963.

Buildings on either side of this massive brick structure are empty, as are several others around the square. Down the block is a ruined movie theater, its marquee no longer readable. What an entrepreneur's dream! I can imagine shops, loft living space, restaurants, and bed & breakfasts in these solid old masonry buildings. I *can't* imagine why it hasn't already happened. Anson sits a mere twenty-three miles from Abilene at a cross-roads of major highways.

Almost a century has shaped the fate of the Opera House.

The town itself is the namesake of Dr. Anson Jones, last president of the Republic of Texas. Founded in 1881 with only a handful of residents, it served as the hub for the outlying agricultural community. Evidence of this was the fact that M. G. Rhodes built the Morning Star Hotel, which in 1885 began hosting a three-day celebration and grand Christmas ball for these cowhand patrons and families.

But ranchers and travelers needed entertainment the rest of the year too. To accommodate that need, Albert W. Johnson built the Anson Opera House near the hotel. The courthouse wasn't built until 1910, so the Opera had three years of being the tallest building in town. The first floor of the Opera provided room for stores, and while offices shared part of the second floor, the tall-ceilinged auditorium occupied the lion's share.

One ninety-four-year-old lady (name withheld on request) remembers standing room only and air choked with gunpowder smoke when actors fired blanks. For a showing of *The Perils of Pauline*, tickets were bought weeks in advance, and a long line of people with horses and buggies camped around the square waiting to get in.

The front door still opens directly onto one wide stairway, which divides and leads theatergoers right and left into the 225-seat auditorium (originally more). The offices have given way to concessions and restrooms. The balcony is not yet available to the public.

In the early years New York and Philadelphia sent Chautauqua pro-grams. Vaudeville troupes and minstrels came from all over the country. For one drama, *The Klansman*, Sheriff Tom Hudson volunteered his horse for a part, but getting it to the second floor presented a problem. They cut a hole in the back wall and tried to hoist the animal up with a block and tackle. When that didn't work, they finally led the animal up the staircase. Our eyewitness said the operation drew as many spectators as the play itself did.

Interest fell off about the end of World War I (1917-18), traveling troupes fizzled out, and audiences were lured to the new "picture shows"

Two vaudeville posters, courtesy of Mrs. Clifford Thorn and the Anson Opera House

in Abilene and one even in Anson. One account states that the Opera House tried silent and talking movies as "a last-ditch effort before it closed in the thirties." But although events were to threaten the theater further during the next few years, this proved far from the "last ditch" for the Anson Opera House.

A man named Falkner bought the building for an auto parts and craft store while also living in the building. After accumulating so much "stuff" he couldn't keep up with it, he stopped letting anyone come in and became a recluse. He rejected a TV journalist once who tried to do a story on the place. Bats shared the habitation, and he finally moved out. When Falkner died in 1985 leaving no heirs, the building was to be auctioned off.

Enter Diane Dubose, then editor of the *Western Observer.* She wrote the immortal headline "Save the Opera House for Us." In the article she explained that even the building's Texas Historic Landmark designation couldn't protect it if a new owner chose to auction off the very bricks for

19

salvage. Her message got the attention of the original builder's family, whereupon the Johnsons bought and donated it to the city of Anson. Diane Dubose and Mike Herndon became co-chairs of the Opera House board of directors.

A salvage operation sold Falkner's accumulation, but time and nature had taken their toll. Worse, George Dubose said, "By then, the auditorium was completely empty. Even the seats were gone." The pressed tin ceiling was so water-damaged little of it could be saved, but it has since been restored to its original look. At least the "schoolhouse" light fixtures still hung there, and they discovered one great find:

"Though damaged," quotes a Chamber of Commerce's booklet, "the stage's painted drop curtain, an outdoor scene surrounded by local advertisements, is believed to be one of four such curtains surviving from the 'opera house era.' This curtain has been restored by the same company that made it years ago and a copy was made for present day use on stage."

A substantial grant from the Meadows Foundation of Dallas, the continued generosity of the Johnson family, and numerous individual donations gave the volunteer effort hope, but first they had to face the overwhelming task of cleaning it up.

One of four such curtains surviving from the opera house era, Ernest Upton photographer

Impressed with the building and history, the League of Historical Theatres listed the Opera House on its yearly tour. A group arrived by charter busses about three months before the November 1998 reopening when their first play, *Scrooged*, was scheduled. Diane Dubose says volunteers were still shoveling out bat guano. The guests exhibited doubts the theater would be finished, but the show did go on as scheduled—and in a clean building!

But the operation had to contend with more than bat guano. Among the volunteers was a group of elementary school children, and their teacher reported an eerie experience. She had gone upstairs into the auditorium to get something when she saw a man walk across the stage. Since there wasn't supposed to be anyone else there, she called a man working downstairs to come up and investigate. He could find no one at all, though the only exit was through the doors that the teacher had been watching.

Diane Dubose, frequently working at the theater alone, reported other weird occurrences. Once she heard loud hammering inside the building she knew to be empty. Each time she unlocked the door and called out, the sound stopped. When she relocked the door, it resumed.

"What do you make of that?" I asked.

"Most likely?" she replied, "Falkner." I checked my notes, verifying that Falkner had passed on in 1985. I leave the conclusion to each reader.

Although the highly successful Cowboys' Christmas Ball has no official connection with the Opera House, the two entities work in cooperation. The Morning Star Hotel no longer exists, but the annual celebration continues as a popular event to this day.

In 1890 New Jersey poet Larry Chittenden, staying at the Morning Star, attended the ball. He was so affected by it he moved to Anson and wrote the poem "The Cowboys' Christmas Ball," honoring Texas ranchers. More recently, Michael Martin Murphey popularized it in song and has sung at the Opera House.

Native Ansonite Jeannie C. Riley (best known for "Harper Valley PTA") has also sung there. Today the Opera House hosts a country-western music show once a month and other stage productions. A historical play, *Lone Star*, co-authored by Diane and George Dubose, is slated for performance. The bottom floor of the building is available for various occasions.

At this point the Anson Opera House is producing enough revenue for maintenance but must still rely on volunteer services. Also, they have to take restoration one step at a time. They eventually hope to upgrade lighting, sound, and stage equipment as well as completely remodel the bottom floor to be a fitting complement to the theater instead of looking like the plain business space it was designed to be.

With a little help, that "fanciest showplace" just might shine again.
—*Joan Upton Hall*

For information:

Anson Opera House
P.O. Box 449
Anson, TX 79501
(915) 823-3542
goarb@aol.com

Other attractions:

Jones County Courthouse
U.S. Post Office mural
"Cowboy Dance"
Mays Botanical Memorial
Garden Gazebo
Anson Jones Museum
Lakes, parks, golf course

Annual events:

Cowboys' Christmas Ball
Larry Chittenden Cowboy
Celebration
Blue Grass Festival & Jam
Sessions
Jones County Fair

For details and accommodations:

Chamber of Commerce
1132 West Court Plaza
Anson, TX 79501
Phone: (915) 823-3259
Fax: (915) 823-4326

Archer City: Royal (1926)

Ernest Upton photographer

Everybody knows it as "The Last Picture Show"—the Royal in Archer City. Native son Larry McMurtry made it famous in his book by that name and the movie that followed. Well, if it's to be the last, the others have nothing to fear. It's survived hard times, numerous reworkings, two fires, and the Hollywood myth of being gone, but phoenix that it is, it keeps rising from its ashes, and to this day, tourists stop to take each other's pictures in front of it.

Earlier incarnations predated 1926. The Dixie Theater had operated in that building and a hotel/boarding house before that. The second fire that gutted the Royal might have driven the last nail in its coffin, but in truth it hadn't thrived since the first burning in 1947. Closed for a while in the fifties, it was restored by new owner Ben Adams, but public interest in picture shows was suffering before the fire "closed it for good" in 1965.

About a year later Larry McMurtry published his novel *The Last Picture Show*, portraying the demise of the theater, not from fire, but from the end of an era. Movie houses all over the country were experiencing the same downturn. He focused the nation's attention on the phenomenon, and the movie version (filmed by RCA Columbia Pictures in Archer City and released in 1971) added weight to McMurtry's vision in a paradoxical way. This movie about the decline of movies earned eight Academy Award nominations and two Oscars. It virtually launched the careers of young actors Cybill Shepherd, Jeff Bridges, and Timothy Bottoms, and added another layer for those of veterans Cloris Leachman, Ellen Burstyn, and Ben Johnson.

The movie version of McMurtry's sequel *Texasville* (released in 1990) was also filmed in Archer City, but to understand these filmings, let's fast-forward to the time of this writing in 2001.

Gary Beesinger, of Royal Theater Productions (RTP), and Carrie Bloom, administrative assistant for both Archer County Chamber of Commerce and RTP, showed us around. The façade, across from the stately old courthouse, looks pretty much the way it did in 1926—ticket booth, sign, and all. But step around the corner and you'll find it's roofless and the rock wall is mostly gone. "What you see today," Beesinger said, "is a little bit original, a little bit new, and a little bit Hollywood."

The current Royal occupies the space once taken by stores adjoining the old site, and patrons still enter past the original ticket booth. All that's

By 1996 not much left but the sign, photo courtesy of Abby Abernathy

left are the pier and beam supports, the first ten feet of the rock wall, and miraculously the old Royal sign.

Too narrow for a modern theater, the old space has been left open for tourists to see and for special outdoor events. Shaded from the harsh western sun, landscaped with native plants, and paved with $100 bricks on which the donors' names are engraved, the area serves as a fitting testament to the numerous individuals who have contributed. Texas-shaped tiles, also engraved, make up the Applause Wall.

For the filming of *The Last Picture Show*, MGM Studio had to rebuild enough of the theater for a set. "For the filming of *Texasville*, which picked up the story years later," Beesinger said, "Hollywood actually had to put some of it back together to make it look like ruins."

The new inside facility spans the width of two former businesses with exposed steel beams, and it seats 250 concert style or 150 for dinner theatre. Abby Abernathy is credited for most of this construction, supervising the volunteers and a few hirees. Character exudes from the rough-cut stone walls. Restroom walls and stairs to the balcony are made from old ceiling and floor joists. So far the balcony is used only for lighting and sound operation.

Rows of new comfortable chairs faced the stage on the day we were there, just after the first production of "Texasville Opry," a country-western music review that played to a packed house. The emcee, Danny Kirk, had performed the same function in Wichita Falls' "Texas Gold" when it first started, and he pulled in several of those performers. Others came in from area towns, Denton and Dallas.

This is a multiuse building. The chairs can be moved and the stage cut to half size to make a theater-in-the-round, a dinner theater, or a dance space. For example, the Lazy Boy Supper Club has a monthly catered dinner and entertainment by artists singing original songs. RTP might present a murder mystery dinner show or a more serious drama.

Ernest Upton photographer

From 1993 to '98, the Picture Show Players led the way for fund raising to eventually restore the Royal. Performing at the high school auditorium, they put together musical comedies and melodramas using local volunteers and united the town behind the effort. RTP followed. Every year Picture Show Players join with the community choir and local churches to present religious pageants. Until the Royal reopened, all was done wherever space could be found.

I remembered something Carol Hendrix of the Dalhart theater group told me. "When you apply for grants from patrons of the arts, what you're

'gonna-do' doesn't count. You have to show you've already been performing your heart out in every open space you could find." Foundations look
for evidence of your passion for the project in other ways too: being able to
demonstrate the backing of local individuals and organizations and showing efforts to educate and involve youth. Well, it appears Archer City has
made all the right moves.

For the fifth year, RTP hosted a weeklong Summer Action workshop
for twenty to twenty-five area students to let them see what is available in
the arts. Beesinger said, "We bring in professional drama instructors like
Mary Kunicki from New York City and Jana Brockman from Austin."
This year they added Gary Kingcade from Wichita Falls to teach visual
arts.

"We want to work with students." He added with a grin, "Besides, I'm
a born ham." He must have been bitten by the acting bug when he was in
high school, playing a bit part in *The Last Picture Show*. He was one of the
athletes the coach called "You bunch of piss ants!" Gary promises not to
yell any such thing at the students he works with.

The yearly aim of Royal Theater Productions is to do about four serious drama productions, a youth-oriented summer musical (*Li'l Abner* in
2001), and to continue giving local groups a place to hold their events.
Eventually, they may be able to buy the equipment to show movies.

Grants have been earned from the Meadows Foundation and Thomas
and Bridwell Foundations. They have applied for a grant from the Texas
Commission on the Arts for eight shows. TCA grants 50 percent of the fee
for an artist registered with them. If funded, RTP would, for instance bring
in Amarillo Little Theatre's *Always Patsy Cline* at a cost of $5,000. Even at
50 percent they could only present one night.

You get an idea of how McMurtry-centered the town is when you see a
bed & breakfast named Lonesome Dove Inn, but why shouldn't it be? How
many towns, large or small, can boast a Pulitzer Prize winner like the
well-deserving *Lonesome Dove*? One reason Archer City is so loyal to the
writer is that he's still an integral part of the town. His bookstore, Booked
Up, Inc., shares the block with the Royal. It houses 400,000 rare and used
books, the largest antiquarian collection in the U.S. McMurtry works there
for a while almost every day and of course supports the Royal.

The fate of the theater in *The Last Picture Show* is symbolic of what
was happening all over the country, but by calling attention to it, perhaps

McMurtry was instrumental in the salvation of not only the Royal, but many others. The *Archer County News* quoted McMurtry: "My family lived sixteen miles out of town, and we would come in once a week and see a movie together.... We'd talk about those movies in the school yard, the barber shop, and the feed store. Now in the age of TV and multiplexes, you seldom have movies as a community experience." —*Joan Upton Hall*

For information:

The Royal Theater
P.O. Box 1070
Archer City, TX 76351
1-877-729-ROYAL
acchamber2@aol.com
www.archercity.org/royal/rebuild.html

Other attractions:

Booked Up, Inc. (owned and operated by Larry McMurtry)
Archer County Historical Museum (in former jail)
Lakes, golf, city park, hunting

For details and accommodations:

Archer County Chamber of Commerce
P.O. Box 877
Archer City, TX 76351
(940) 574-2489
acchamber2@aol.com
www.archercity.org
Phone: (915) 823-3259
Fax: (915) 823-4326

6

Austin: Paramount (1915)

courtesy of Austin Theatre Alliance

In 1970 the Paramount Theatre in downtown Austin needed an angel. Operating as a "B" movie house and slated for demolition, the once glamorous stage was far removed from the well-respected design of nationally revered theatre architect John Eberson. Popular opinion went against resuscitation. The downtown area had a bad reputation, little or no parking was available, and the building was too far gone. Three saviors refused to accept the death sentence: John M. Bernardoni, Charles Eckerman, and Steven L. Scott formed a corporation in 1973 in order to get a lease on the building. Their efforts served as the bridge between the glamorous past and the elegant future of what is now known as the Paramount Theatre of the Performing Arts.

Built in 1915 and originally named the Majestic Theatre, the Paramount has experienced the gamut of performance venues. Over the eighty-five years, audiences have enjoyed vaudeville, silent movies, "talkies," music and dance performances, local live theatre, and Broadway shows. The part classical-revival, part baroque-classical theatre was built by John Eberson of Chicago in eight months at a cost of $150,000. Although Eberson built over 1,200 theatres during his career, the Paramount is one of less than twenty-five that remain today. On opening night Austin Mayor A. P. Wooldridge introduced *When Knights Were Born* to an audience who had paid twenty-five cents a ticket to attend.

1915, courtesy of Austin Theatre Alliance

During the Roaring Twenties vaudeville commanded Austin's attention followed by silent film and "talkies." By 1930 the Interstate Theatre Circuit, owned by Karl Hoblitzelle, decided to engage in major remodeling plans. The wooden seats were replaced with upholstered chairs, carpet was added, and the best sound system at that time was installed. The cost of such improvement was almost as much as the original building. With the inclusion of Art Deco ornamentation throughout, the Majestic became the Paramount. The rest of the decade saw a variety of performances including the Christmas Revue of Miss Camille Long's School of Dance, afternoon serial mysteries, and live entertainment such as Helen Hayes in *Mary of Scotland* (1935).

Then came the war, but production at the Paramount in the 1940s did not falter. The theatre actively supported the American cause by promoting war bonds and showing army training and recruiting films. From 1942 to 1945 management sold 8.4 million dollars' worth of bonds for which they were recognized with citations and awards from the Treasury's War Finance Committee. The theatre slogan during the war years was "dedicated to community service," and Manager Louis Novy received a war finance silver medal for his efforts. It was also during this time Katherine Hepburn appeared in the stage production of *The Philadelphia Story*. But after that the glamour faded.

In the 1950s the Paramount was almost entirely a movie house, and as with other theatres around the country, in danger of closing due to the popularity of not only television, but the small community movie theatres developing in the sixties. By 1970, with the demolition crew on its way, the trio of John M. Bernardoni, Charles Eckerman, and Steven L. Scott began their efforts to save the building. They started showing classic films for fifty cents per ticket. The first live show in many years was staged on February 2, 1975. And in June of that same year, "legitimate theatre" returned with *Carnival* produced by Center Stage and the Austin Theatre Company. Unfortunately, they were losing money and had to find another way to protect the building.

The corporation decided to apply for funding as a nonprofit organization and for Texas Landmark status. They discovered they would have to raise 2.2 million dollars to restore the theatre to its original style. The extensive restoration began slowly. The name of the theatre was changed to its current title on April 22, 1975. Then on May 6, 1977, it was dedicated with a state historical marker. This did not, however, make the journey any easier.

Raising funds and making the necessary changes came slowly. The Actors Equity Association threatened to blacklist the Paramount unless repairs were made immediately. The dressing rooms were still not up to standard, and the union threatened to cancel a touring company performance of *Guys and Dolls*. Bernardoni managed to get seven motor homes donated at the last minute so the show could continue, proving that Austin could support national performances. Finally on July 8 the theatre was placed in the National Register of Historical Places and qualified for federal restoration money.

By September of that year, the restoration plans had developed into two phases, and Bell, Kline, & Hoffman were hired to plan the changes. One of the architects had a personal interest. David Hoffman's father, Maurice, had played in the house band in the 1930s. With careful planning, performances could continue throughout the renovation process, but keeping the theatre open when at all possible caused problems, specifically with the air conditioning. There must have been a lot of sweet talk going on between management and performers to convince them that the show must go on. Finally, in October of 1980, to the tune of over 2.5 million dollars, the fully restored Paramount Theatre of the Performing Arts reopened with a full season including national touring companies.

Commitment to the theatre is evident in many ways. At a recent event planned by Frank Campbell for Barnes and Noble, Paul Beutel, the director of programming for the Paramount, recalled an incredible story about long-time projectionist Walter Norris. For nearly twenty years Walter had happily worked the projector for the Paramount and commented that it was where he would like to go out. In the summer of 2000, during the classic series run of *Casablanca*, Walter was preparing the second reel when he died of a heart attack doing what he loved so much. The first reel simply ran out and the house manager announced that the film was cancelled for the evening. A memorial for Walter was held in the theatre, and he is greatly missed.

Today the Paramount serves over a million patrons with national touring companies, dance companies, comedians, and musical groups. It has hosted glamorous Hollywood premieres and still manages to show movies. In June 1992 the theatre was chosen to rerun *Casablanca* on its

Stacey Hasbrook photographer

fifty-year anniversary. Those guardian angels have finally earned their wings for working overtime on a good cause, the preservation of a glorious moment in theatre history. They continue to spread those wings with the recent development of the Austin Theatre Alliance, which includes the newly renovated State Theatre and Company next door. From children's favorites to adult entertainment, including the production of its own shows, the Paramount Theatre of the Performing Arts is alive and well in Austin, Texas.

 For information:

Paramount Theatre
P.O. Box 1566
Austin, TX 78767
(512) 472-2901
www.theparamount.org

Other Austin Oldies

The 2001-2002 season fliers have just come out in Austin, and it welcomes the newly formed Austin Theatre Alliance, which pairs the Paramount Theatre and the "new" State Theatre Company located right next door with its own acting company. With this alliance, Austin can offer many more choices in entertainment. The theatres will present local and national productions as well as film in four downtown spaces: the historic Paramount

Theatre (1,300 seats), the State Theater (350), the new Horton Foote Theater (100), and a cabaret theater to be constructed in the basement of the State Theater.

The Alliance web site points out that "It is about people who nurture and celebrate artistic expression by uniting audiences and artists who believe that the performing arts in its many forms add to the lives of Austin's citizens," not to mention the entire central Texas area. One important program is Skinny's Gallery, named after local theater owner Skinny Pryor, who often let children in for "a glass of water and a smile." With this program, the Alliance will bring children in who cannot afford admission so that all children have the opportunity to experience the performing arts.

A more funky opportunity can be found in the Alamo Drafthouse Cinema owned and operated by Tim and Karrie League near Sixth Street. Showings include classic and quirky films that can't be seen elsewhere. Patrons sit in seats with row-length food and drink tables in front of them. Along with the viewing, patrons can order dinner and snacks and drink beer while they watch. In February 2001 the Village Cinema Art closed, and the Leagues decided to jump in with the Alamo Drafthouse North, a four-screen first-run house designed the same way, one of the most original anywhere. —*Stacey Hasbrook*

Other attractions:		For details and accommodations:
Museums, art galleries, parks, wildlife preserves	Indoor rock climbing	Austin Chamber of Commerce
Austin Nature & Science Center	Slaughter Leftwich Winery	111 Congress Avenue
Austin Zoo (childrens)	Umlauf Sculpture Garden	P.O. Box 1967
Celis Brewery	Walking tours	Austin, TX 78767
Farmer's Market	Fiesta Gardens on Town Lake	(512) 478-9383
Jourdon-Bachman Pioneer Farm	**Annual events:**	
Lady Bird Johnson Wildflower Center	South by Southwest Music and Media	Austin Visitor Center
Lake cruises	Old Pecan Street Festival	201 E. 2nd St.
O. Henry home	Texas Book Festival	1-800-926-2282/ (512) 478-0098
		www.austintexas.org

7

Bastrop: Opera House (1889)

Stacey Hasbrook photographer

Close your eyes and listen closely and you can almost hear horses' hooves and buggy wheels crunching on the back driveway. Imagine well-dressed men and women entering the hall for the night's show. The 1889 frontier Opera House was not as fancy as many others, but it provided a stage for local artists to present dance, music, and poetry recitals as well as touring company performances for twenty years. Most of the shows were horse operas (westerns), melodramas, or vaudeville. As Chester Eitze, the theatre's current executive director states, "They weren't classical."

At first the theatre was successful with many legitimate shows coming in from the East. First built as a performance stage, the 1890s version showed good attendance, but as it became a silent movie theatre and vaudeville died out, the audience waned, and the theater suffered a period of financial losses. In 1910 the live performance hall was transformed into a movie theatre.

The proscenium had to be moved and a deep cut made in the ceiling to allow films to be shown. The horseshoe-shaped balcony was truncated off to put in a projection room, which at some time had minor fire damage but not to the structure. The slanted floor in the balcony was left. Moviegoers would come in at ground level and up a few steps into the lobby. It was built as a flat floor theatre, never raked (slanted), and was left that way. At the turn of the nineteenth century, patrons had used outhouses, but moviegoers required the major improvements of installing electricity and building restrooms inside.

Originally another building used for storage, dressing rooms, and stables was connected on back so the entire block belonged to the theatre. In the twenties it lay dormant so other businesses started using the horse lane as a designated alley. The back became an access between roads even though it was not supposed to be.

Financial instability resulted because the facility was quite large for the size of the community so they tried many different uses. The local Sayers Rifle Club held masked balls there, and at one time the theatre served as a pistol range. During WW II nearby Camp Swift became militarily active, so Bastrop became the activity area of the county with the theatre as the focus. Its worst function came in the late fifties and sixties when it served as a teen recreation center. The building took a lot of abuse and then sat empty for at least ten years in the late sixties and seventies when it began to seriously deteriorate. First the roof went then the tin ceiling began to rust. As a result the floor was also damaged. The 1970s brought on the threat of the wrecking ball.

From 1979 to 1982 a group of citizens came together to save the Opera House from demolition but couldn't decide how to use it. They formed the Bastrop Opera House Association and brought Chester on board in 1984 with a summer theatre program, mostly performing melodrama. They ran nine straight weeks the first year and assisted several other theatre projects in the area. The success encouraged Bastropians to get busy restoring the "antique horse-opera house." They desired to preserve it and began raising money to provide a facility that would serve the community as it did at the turn of the century, including use as a meeting hall.

Chester points out, "We have done the best we could with what we inherited from the movie industry." The new curtain is again an "ad drop" with picture advertisements of local businesses. Since the theatre was saved with the intention of being another performance area, they have tried to use the mechanisms of the Victorian theatre. They moved the pressed tin proscenium arch back, and it matches the ceiling pattern. The front is a pressed tin picture frame painted in burgundy with a gold arch. Inside the show portal are columns with painted drapes and gold tassels and an act curtain that rolls up by hand. For historically correct shows, "wing and grooves" slide at least four pieces of scenery to develop the illusion of diminished perspective. "Travelers," scenery on curtains that go back and forth, were added, and painted drops can go up and down. The stage floor is high and sloped, as it was originally, about eight feet back. It includes trap doors with plenty of room underneath to stand, about a seven-foot clearance, as the basement area is thirty inches below ground level.

Some changes cannot be like the original. The stage today is not correct compared to the much deeper one at the turn of the century. A forestage or apron had to be added, which is illogical for Victorian times. They never had a stage that couldn't be accessed from the wings, which this one can't be. The only way on stage is a door to the left from outside or through the house up the front stairs. The Victorians would never have entered through the audience. Their backstage had three arched doorways from the back building for entrances. What was a thirty-foot area now is only ten plus the apron. Some interior changes came while it was still a legitimate movie theatre. The front of the building had been raised and plastered, which was detrimental to the brick so they can't go back to the original.

Many upcoming changes will return the Opera House closer to the original plan. The color of the front will once again be more traditional although the outdoor color scheme will be typical of indoor colors of the time, something like mauve, cream, and perhaps dark green trim. Historically the theatre had a center balcony or porch on the front as a smoker's gallery supported by posts, and a preservation architect is helping with replacement plans. The front doors will need to be changed, but in some way that allows retaining the cut glass sections. Although the lamp posts were added much later and are not native to the area, more than likely they will stay as they have been added to many buildings in the historic area. The side lot will be cleaned up, a memo-

Stacey Hasbrook photographer

rial garden added to the area, and the fire escape refurbished. The Association is also trying to reclaim the property behind the theatre so it is not a drive-through.

Restoration should be done by September, which means a season from fall to fall this year. Normally it is spring to Christmas due to tourism. One of the town's biggest events, Yesterfest, was reinstated as a benefit for the

Opera House on the last Saturday in April in Fisherman's Park on the Colorado River.

During the last eighteen years the community has surprised everyone with very talented individuals. Now Chester is finally getting ready to launch what he intended when he first decided to stay and build a resident company. Although the Bastrop Opera House never was "as opulent as many others, like the Galveston Strand area or even Austin, which had three houses that they have let go," he hopes that "sometime down the road, someone will raise the millions of dollars to return it to the showplace it was." *—Stacey Hasbrook*

 For information:

Bastrop Opera House
P.O. Box 691711 Spring St.
Bastrop, TX 78602
(512) 321-6283

Other attractions:

Golf
Museums
State parks
Nofsinger Home
McKinney Roughs LCRA
Preserve
Cedars on Bergstrom GC

Annual events:

Yesterfest

For details and accommodations:

Chamber of Commerce
927 Main St.
Bastrop, TX 78602
(512) 321-2419
www.bastropchamber.com

Visitor Center
927 Main Street
Bastrop, TX 78602

8

Beaumont: Jefferson (1927)

Jan Johnson Photography, Conrad Schmitt Studios, Jefferson Theatre Preservation Society

Walking through the doors on Fannin St. is like discovering a large unknown cave, like breathing in the cool, earthy dampness of time. Slowly, as
your eyes adjust, the vastness begins to filter in with various shades of almost light. This treasure lies dormant, but only in that total kind of darkness
just before the dawn. With only another $50,000 of a five-million-dollar

fund to go, the Jefferson Theatre is on the cusp of bursting into its original brilliance.

When it was time to tour the theatre, Mike Gillory from the phone company went with us. Gwen Mercer, a volunteer on the project, unlocked the door, and the whiff of age swam over us. In almost total darkness we felt our way down an aisle, and Gwen turned on a single flashlight. "I was here once in middle school," Mike remembers. Gwen took Mike in the direction of the electrical boxes while I stayed back to soak up the energy. "There's no ghost in here, right?" asked Mike. "I've heard rumors." "Scream if you need us, Mike," I teased when Gwen and I left to explore.

There is a rumor of a ghost. Once when Gwen's husband was giving a tour for some young people, they revealed they had heard a story about a little girl in a yellow dress who got lost in the tunnel underneath the theatre. There is no proof, but the tunnel is real and runs from one corner area clear across to another. Unfortunately, Gwen didn't have the key to it. As I looked from the darkened stage at the massive shadows of the seating and balcony, I thought if it isn't haunted, it should be.

Designed by architect Emile Weil, the Jefferson was built by the Jefferson Amusement Company for one million dollars. The *Beaumont Journal* described the theatre. "Of striking Old Spanish architecture, the interior radiates romance and charm in the perfect blending of color, tone, architecture, sculpture, and fabric and breathes an eloquence of grandeur that is felt quite as much as it is seen." It opened on Monday, November 14, 1927, with the Jefferson Grand Orchestra and the movie *Rose of the Golden West*. From the beginning it hosted traveling shows, vaudeville, drama, and motion pictures.

As I looked up the giant side wall close to the stage, I realized I was seeing the organ pipes mirrored with a twin on the other side. The organ is an incredible focus. It is a Robert Morton Wonder Organ with 778 pipes and percussive effects. It has been restored and maintained by the American Theatre Organ Society and is one of only seven disappearing organs in the country that are in the original theatre and actually still working.

Further back on each wall are two niches, which originally had Greek statutes, one female and one male semi-draped. For about a year between when the LBJ Foundation owned the building and when they donated it to the Preservation Society, a preacher held church here. Unfortunately, he

1927, courtesy of Tyrrell Historical Library

decided that they were "an abomination" so he took them out into the parking lot and smashed them to smithereens.

Discovering what this theatre was like in the heyday must have been like a treasure hunt for Conrad Schmidt, who is in charge of the renovation. Gwen showed me his sample treatment way up at the top of the right-hand side of the theatre where they have repainted in great detail. It is breathtaking. As they worked to find the scheme and stenciling, they only had to go down one level to find the original. Another find happened as they searched the top floor. In the corner of a hidden closet, a small section of the ceiling area shows the original colors. A second sample in the balcony shows the brilliant gold trim.

Gwen, who is not from Beaumont, has her own memory of another time and place. Right after high school her parents sent her to visit her sister in Beaumont. As was custom in the fifties, her sister found someone to escort her. "The really special, most wonderful thing a guy could do back then was take a girl to the Jefferson." And when I teasingly said, "And, you fell in love," she responded, "with the theatre." She returned in 1989 when she actually got to perform on the stage and knew she had to help save it.

The theatre closed in 1972, and in 1975 the Beaumont Junior League and Junior Forum formed the Jefferson Theatre Preservation Society (JTPS) with the goal of purchasing and preserving the theatre. Then in 1976 the LBJ Foundation deeded it to JTPS. The Jefferson is listed individually in the Register of National Historic Places and has a Texas state historical marker.

The director of Main Street Project, Carolyn Howard, is proud of the work the community has done. "We started in 1995 the right way, with a business plan and a restoration plan." Planning took about three years. Then the fund-raising campaign began. Long-range goals have been in place from the beginning, and $900,000 dollars of the 5 million has been set aside as reserve for operating. Education is another goal. Children's programming will be essential so they can build their own memories and feel responsible to help maintain it thirty years from now.

The new Jefferson will be a nonprofit theatre and will seat about 1,500. Hopefully the grand opening will happen early in 2003, but the business manager will be on board a year before getting ready for the first season. It will show a classic film festival and possibly special showings, but mostly it will be for live performances of national and regional touring acts with two seasons per year and community shows. The project includes a cultural growth fund for innovative productions, and professionals will lease it for meetings. They are also working

Stacey Hasbrook photographer

on a preservation fund so they don't have to ask the community for funds when things need to be fixed.

At first people wondered if it would be worth it. Now people talk about "when's it gonna open?" The building is a reflection of the people who have worked so hard to raise the money. Gwen pointed out, "Your book title reminds me of these people because over all these years they would not give up on this theatre." Carolyn is serious about its success. "One day, on November 14, 2027, we will celebrate 100 years, and it will have stood the test of time and still be meeting the needs of the community. We will be meeting our commitment in a bricks and mortar sense and in a programming sense because without them together, the building is just an old building."

And the Jefferson means much more than that to this community. As we were leaving, Mike smiled, and I could tell he'd been thinking about his theatre memory the whole time. "By the way, it was not in middle school; it was earlier. I was in Catholic school, and it must have been about second grade. It was cold, probably around Christmas. I can't believe I remember that far back. I sat right over there about the eighth or ninth row. I remember looking at the windows and seeing the bars and knowing it was the organ." He smiled all the way to his truck. —*Stacey Hasbrook*

For information:

Carolyn Howard
595 Orleans, Ste. 1012
Beaumont, TX 77701-3204
(409) 838-2202

Other attractions:

Museums, parks, art galleries, golf
Spindletop/Gladys City Boomtown
Tyrrell Historical Library
McFaddin-Ward House
The Big Thicket
Hardin County Visitor Center
National wildlife refuges, preserves, sanctuaries
Pompeiian Villa

White Haven
High Island Boy Scout Wood and Smith Oaks Nature Sanctuaries

For details and accommodations:

Beaumont Chamber of Commerce
P.O. Box 3150
Beaumont, TX 77704
(409) 838-6581

9

Canadian: Palace (1909)

Ernest Upton photographer

I sensed a touch of mystery and intrigue about the Palace Theatre in Canadian, not the least of which was interviewing the only avowed future ghost I've ever met. "No ghosts yet," said manager Rob Talley, "but when I die, it will be me." It's possible. Living in an apartment above the theatre, he has managed and owned it since 1986. Through the lean years, his tenacity is the reason this little town can have such a classy facility today, "the only THX® approved theatre in the Texas Panhandle."

When I entered the lobby, savory popcorn aroma and neon lights attracted my attention to the concession stand at the left. Just behind that is a sign to "Dungeon Video," and I could see a stone-gray, tunnel-like entrance, with concrete stairs leading downward. I didn't have to ask about it. Talley said, "Every palace needs a dungeon," and renting videos is what he does with his. It's a large concrete lined basement that came with the building. In one place, stairs lead up to a blank wall, making you wonder what's on the other side of it. A couple of Edgar Allan Poe stories came to mind.

In the lobby itself one whole wall is a montage, painted by Tom Gibson of Corpus Christi, depicting old movie stars. John Wayne was probably the latest one. Off to the right is a sitting room, complete with fifties chrome-set kitchen tables. It is decorated with neatly framed vintage posters, pictures, and other memorabilia. One poster read, "March 1909, Deluxe vaudeville road show. Singing, music, and novelty dancing," but the name of the theatre was different. Could it be . . . ?

Again Talley answered my unspoken question. "We didn't have anything but the brick walls and floor left of the original. This theatre burned to the ground twice. I've gone all over several states looking for equipment to outfit this place. The posters aren't original to *here*, but they are originals from *somewhere*." And what a collection he has. A couple of my favorite posters advertise appearances of "the Dionne Quintuplets, world's most famous babies" and a 3-D movie *Ghost Remover* photo with glasses (you couldn't see the ghost without the glasses).

Talley recounted a written account of the earlier fire. The owners had bought brand new equipment when the talkies came in, but a week after they installed it, fire broke out. An explosion blew the projectionist out the door.

For restoration of the exterior of the Palace, Talley said they went by a 1920s photo. For the interior, they went with the fifties decade Art Deco as it had been completely rebuilt following the second fire, only much better. No lean-years budget could have afforded this!

Talley had started out leasing the Palace from a man who didn't want to invest in fixing it up. When he bought it in '86 he was working full time and managing the Palace at night. Unfortunately, the economy was down in Canadian (once a thriving railroad town, then a thriving oil field town, then hard times). He couldn't make any money at the theatre, and it was in sad need of repair.

photo courtesy of Rob Talley

"Once when we were showing *Twister*," Talley said. "Rain poured between the screen and the audience, and people complimented me afterward for my special effects. I was fixing to close it down when Salem Abraham approached me."

The Abraham family is well known for their preservation efforts in the Panhandle. Salem Abraham and his wife had grown up in Canadian and liked the movies. They wanted to restore the Palace for their own pleasure and as a legacy to their children and the community. Abraham had no desire to run the theatre but said he would buy it and fund the restoration if Talley would agree to lease it back when it was finished.

"If you'll let me keep living upstairs," Talley said. Abraham agreed, the "checkbook flew open," and he hired Killis Almond, noted restoration architect.

Instead of getting new furnishings, they wanted the real things, so Talley and a friend started searching and going to auctions. Some efforts

47

worked out better than others. They drove almost as far as Wyoming to buy theatre seats only to have the owner back out, but in a little mining town of Arizona, they found just what they wanted. They bought a set of late 1940s push-back seats, loaded them on trucks, and brought them back to Canadian. A local auto body shop stripped and painted the metal work. The upholstery work was done in South Texas. When installing the seats, Talley said he wanted plenty of legroom. The spaciousness reflects his needs for more legroom than the average person would need.

The sound system and air conditioning are artfully concealed in the décor. Almond had found nooks and crannies where paint hadn't faded so he was able to match the pinks and reds to the original. Between painted. designs on the side walls are beautiful wall sconces. I asked Talley where he got them, and he grinned. "We basically stole them." The owner in Deming, New Mexico, had asked only $600 for the whole bunch, some painted black and some white. Talley said they paid the price, loaded them up, and left that night before the guy could change his mind. Stripped down to chrome and polished, they look elegant.

Talley said Salem Abraham restored the City Drug Soda Fountain up the street from the Palace utilizing the same kind of arrangement as with the theatre. He bought the building, remodeled it, and now leases it back to the former owner. I don't know who was doing the old hotel on the next cross street, but it looked promising when we were there. The Cattle Exchange Restaurant occupies a good-sized portion of the bottom floor. As we traveled through other towns, we heard people say they often drive over to Canadian for dinner and a movie. So I guess that solves one mystery: how this theatre can fill up in such a small town. "If you build it *right*, they will come!"

One of the most intriguing mysteries is yet to be solved, and Talley welcomes any information readers might have about it. It's a concrete square about the width of an ordinary door, which he found out back with grass growing all around it. The artifact bears the rather small prints of a lady's and a man's shoes. The signatures inscribed in the concrete read, "Fred Astaire" and "Joan Fontaine." Are they authentic or not?

Talley said he pursued it pretty hard at first. He asked about it from the son of a former owner. The son told him, "All I know is that it was there when I was a little kid." He sent a picture to Fontaine, asking if she had ever been there. She answered that, with all the traveling she had done, she didn't know and that the writing could be hers, but she couldn't confirm it.

Who knows, maybe somebody out there will remember watching this pair dance at the Palace in Canadian. Hopefully, Talley will have his question answered before he becomes the Palace ghost he promises to be, and he looks like he's got plenty of years left.

I should probably prepare you for one more surprise. Don't expect the predominant flat grassland of the caprock. Canadian is nestled in a tree-filled valley, carved out by the Canadian River. —*Joan Upton Hall*

 For information:

The Palace Theatre
210 Main
Canadian, TX 79014
Dungeon Video:
(806) 323-8810
dungeon@yft.net

Other attractions:
Black Kettle National Grasslands
1916 wagon bridge/hike & bike trail
Lakes, parks
River Valley Pioneer Museum

Annual events:
Seasonal events
4th of July Rodeo

For details and accommodations:
Chamber of Commerce
216 S. 2nd St.
Canadian, TX 79014
(806) 323-6234
www.canadiantx.com

10

Claude: Gem (1915)

photo courtesy of Armstrong County Museum

At first sight, you might think nothing much is happening in the small town of Claude. Guess again! It's a town of individualists whose diverse efforts somehow fit together like puzzle pieces. Take the way they've supported the 1915 theatre now called the Gem, for example. Way before there was a shelter for it, Walter Weaver showed "flickers" in a vacant lot. By 1915 he was able to open an indoor vaudeville/picture show as the "Claudia," a name selected from a public contest. He opened with a five-reel silent movie and presented the first stage show a week later.

The building was part of a complex of buildings built that year, a block from the courthouse square. The theatre was successful under Weaver's management. Before the showing of a silent film, he even had the script printed in the paper for the convenience of patrons.

When my photographer brother Ernest Upton and I came to see the theatre as it is today, Milton Bagwell gave us the tour. J. O. Watson and T. S. Cavins had built this complex out of steel and concrete having learned to think "fireproof" after an earlier fire had destroyed much of the town. Bagwell pointed out that such construction was unusual "for anything but government buildings in those days." I was soon to find out Claude citizens achieved many of their accomplishments in unexpected ways.

Famous rancher of the area and the first white settler, Colonel Charles Goodnight, made a silent movie, *Old Texas*, about cowboy life using his massive JA Ranch as the set. As a tribute to his Kiowa Indian friends, he invited them to come and stage a buffalo hunt, which he filmed. The Claudia hosted the world premiere in 1918.

Through the years, three other movies were filmed entirely in Armstrong County. *Hud* premiered at the Gem (Paul Newman, Melvin Douglas, Patricia Neal, and Brandon de Wilde). The other two, while not premiering, did show there: *The Sundowners* and *Christmas Sunshine*.

photo courtesy of Armstrong County Museum

Other movies partially made in the county were *Leap of Faith* and *Indiana Jones*.

During the 1920s the theatre was renamed "Rialto" according to a theatre chain name. For the same reason in the mid-thirties it became the "Gem," at which time the Butlers ran it.

Roy Rutherford and his wife, Marianne, a descendent of builder T. S. Cavins, met us for the tour. Marianne said she came to Claude as a young schoolteacher. Kids sat upstairs, but adults never did. Once someone threw a live, squawking chicken from the balcony into the crowd. What a shock that must have been! Other people in town told their personal memories of the Gem too, and the same chicken story came up. Several people mentioned how the strict disciplinarian owner, Mrs. Butler, patrolled the theatre during performances to quell any misbehavior. Some say the chicken incident was meant to tease her.

Bagwell, who grew up about ten miles from town, said his large family only came to town a couple of times a year. He was ten or twelve years old before he ever went to the movie and remembers watching Will Rogers and Marjorie Main. "I was nearly grown before I had to pay more than a dime for a ticket."

The theatre closed in the late sixties but became a church in the seventies. After the church closed, the building deteriorated until a determined group of citizens decided to do something about it. One of these citizens, Roy Rutherford, has made the Gem Theatre his major project for the past eight years, and he wrote all its grant applications. A master of efficiency, he handed me a CD full of pictures and a written history to take with me. That's when I found out the unusual but brilliant arrangement of ownership.

In 1990 the Armstrong County Museum (ACM) was incorporated under the Texas Nonprofit Act. Simply put, its mission as a cultural center caused the organization to be given a complex of three 1915 buildings to renovate. By 1994 the ACM had purchased not only the Gem Theatre, but the buildings on either side of it as well. This complex makes up a cultural heritage center that includes an art gallery, museum, and theatre.

The Texas Commission on the Arts has helped fund numerous entertainers from their Touring Artists list to perform at the Gem. Again innovation came in. "We're proud," Rutherford said, "to have been the catalyst for at least five performing groups now listed in the prestigious Texas

Touring Artists Roster." TCA allowed the organization to receive funding for these artists while at the same time applying for them to be listed. They are (in the order of appearance on the Gem stage): The New Musical Grays' Stock Company from Floydada, Kent Watson as Joplin & Co. from Claude, Blue Prairie from Lubbock, the Ottwell Twins with Starjazz from Amarillo, and The String Technicians from Amarillo.

The impressive list of performers is longer than space allows, but an overview reveals a wide array of productions. They are both historically relevant and highly entertaining, such as a dramatic depiction of the lives of Colonel and Mrs. Charles Goodnight. The Rimstone Revue presents musical variety shows that promote and market Texas talent as diverse as western swing and jazz. The Gem even boasts the performance of an original opera written by Gene Murray, who played the lead role for about eighteen years in Palo Duro Canyon's musical drama *Texas*. The Community Heritage Theatre presents plays, including children's shows and youth productions.

I thought I'd heard all Claude's surprises, but there was yet another. In cooperation with the Claude school system, Dr. Carale Manning-Hill, artistic director, is employed to work half time with the school and half time with the Gem Theatre. TCA supports the project through the County

Ernest Upton photographer

Extension Program as do other area foundations. Each July, Manning-Hill stages a Playwrights Festival featuring at least three original plays presented by the playwrights.

Milton Bagwell told of the theatre's renovation process. Attractive light fixtures now replace three naked 100-watt bulbs that hung by wires. All the seats were gone and their grant money used up, but the high school at Spearman was replacing their seats and let the ACM have them just for hauling them off. ACM refurbished the seats and to allow plenty of foot room, installed only 192 of them.

Most impressive to me was the fine woodwork of ceiling and trim. According to Bagwell, it had started out as plain plaster until contractor Tom Walters volunteered to do the work if ACM would pay for the materials. By the time it was done, about $1,200 of the ACM's money and $1,200 of Walters' money made it a job to be proud of. Rutherford added, "Walters' contribution was as significant as our Meadows Foundation grant."

I came away from Claude feeling I had been welcomed to join the fun this community seems to share. I rather hated to leave wondering what they'd think up next. —*Joan Upton Hall*

 For information:

The Gem Theatre
P.O. Box 450
Claude, TX 79019
(806) 226-5409 or
(806) 226-2187
armgem@amaonline.com
www.searchtexas.com/gem-theatre

Other attractions:

Armstrong County Museum, art gallery, & gift shop
Scenic Drives: Palo Duro Canyon and Tule Canyon
Cowboy Morning (chuck-wagon breakfast & supper)
Country Contessa - dinner by reservation on theatre nights
Claude Pharmacy (1890s soda fountain)
At nearby Goodnight: old home place & cemetery, "Hud" House

Annual events:

The Best Christmas Pageant Ever children's show
Playwrights' Festival
Caprock Roundup

For details and accommodations:

Chamber of Commerce
120 Trice
Claude, TX 79019
(806) 226-2187 or
(806) 226-2203 or
(806) 226-7503 (ask for Jere Eisenhour)
katskre@amaonline.com

11
Clifton: Cliftex (1916)

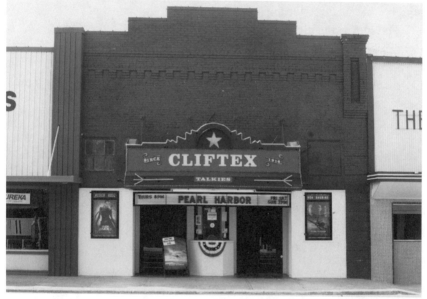

If organization and efficiency are the keys to success, then I have no doubt the Cliftex Theatre will be successful for years to come. When I sat down at the desk of W. Leon Smith, current owner of the Cliftex, he handed me a gold mine: a CD with all the relevant pictures of the theatre, a hard copy of the pictures I would be seeing on the disk, and a handout of a brief history of the theatre. This man wastes no time. Notebook closed. Interview over.

But not really. Leon's a newspaperman too. As editor and publisher of *The Clifton Record*, he knows how to get to the point because it's business. He not only runs the paper and the theatre, but he is also the newly elected mayor. When we entered the theatre for a tour, however, everything slowed down and pride took over.

Over the years the theatre has changed owners and locations several times. Originally opening on September 15, 1916, it was known as The Queen Theatre located across the street and around the corner from today's site in the old Carpenter Building on North Avenue D. It was owned and operated by D. C. and J. J. Caraway whose motto was "High Class Productions." Movies were shown on Wednesday through Saturday nights, often with double features for ten and fifteen cents.

The movie business was so successful that in 1918 they had to move the theatre to a larger site on the west corner of West 5th Street next door to the current newspaper office. Here business continued to grow along with the owner's radio repair shop until 1927. Then again more space was needed and a modern theatre building was built next door on the other side of the *Record* office. At this time the theatre was renamed the Cliftex. In 1929 sound was becoming the new trend so the Caraways, already experimenting in radio sound, invented their own system for the movies and added "Talkies" to the marquee.

In the thirties and forties the theatre opened seven days a week, with double features and a different movie almost every night. Afternoon matinees were added on Saturday and Sunday with prices going up to ten and twenty-five cents. The audiences continued growing to the point that a

1930, photo courtesy of W. Leon Smith

second theatre location was needed. Instead of building another new theatre, the previous location on the corner was used again under the name Gem Theatre. To make this system work, the times of the movies were staggered. The first reel of a movie would start at the Cliftex and when it was finished, it was "bicycled" to the Gem to start there, each reel following until the movie was over. In 1936 another renovation added a starburst marquee, neon lighting, a lobby, and Art Deco house lights to add atmosphere.

Sometime in 1940 E. W. Capps bought the theatre and ran it until 1948 when he sold it to Joe Enochs. The Enochs' thriving business, including construction of Lake Whitney, brought in multitudes of workers who needed entertainment. The name of the Gem was changed to the Cub Theatre, in honor of the local school mascot. This two-theatre system worked for a couple years and then the building was sold to the newspaper and became the circulation department.

The Cliftex has stayed in continual operation as a movie theatre since its opening and has run as a family business featuring first-time films. Although it was not intended as a stage for performing arts, behind the screen is a five-foot-deep stage bordered with light bulbs, with floodlights

photo courtesy of W. Leon Smith

and a curtain mechanism for live performances. It has actually been used for smaller presentations such as Meet the Candidates.

Here and there are impressive details. The light fixtures are pressed-tin, and the side lights are original. The clock over the back door dates to some time in the thirties, and behind the screen area is an original fire extinguisher that looks something like a round red balloon. The two-projector system from the forties and fifties is still used. Leon thinks movies were possibly projected on the wall originally. Outside the projection room is one small balcony that is about four feet wide. The fun part was getting there. Three old windows, the kind that swing open on a center hinge, were waiting. We had to climb through the window to get to the balcony that has one short row of maybe five seats on each side.

Renovations have been constant, but always in keeping with the old-time atmosphere. The changes often reflected the times, such as when the theatre was the local hangout for rock-and-rollers in the fifties. The outside has recently been renovated to resemble the original. And in the total 200 seats, the age varies, but the ones in the back are original.

Extensive remodeling under Scott and Luanne Sandahl's ownership (1995-1999) mainly refurbished some historical features and upgraded the sound system. Under Leon's leadership since December 1999, the marquee has been relit, electrical work upgraded, neon arrows added to the lights, new lobby flooring put in, and the color scheme of the Art Deco lights returned to the soft multicolor rather than white to be more like the original. One major, more modern change is the addition of surround sound.

Although Leon says there's a ghost in the building across the street, there is no ghost in the theatre. However, there has been a shooting. Sometime during the long reign when Capp's father had the theatre, a man from Travis Gap was waiting to see a show. The line was a long one that went all the way around the corner. He had a pistol with him and was drunk. When he starting causing a ruckus, a constable who had been watching him decided to take his gun. In the struggle the gun went off, hit someone in the leg, and went into the wall. My guess is that scattered the line pretty fast.

Keeping the theatre is important to Leon. He points out that a town like Clifton needs activities, and that most of the people "have memories there." Sometimes there is a profit, sometimes not. The theatre lost money last year, but they chalk it up to being a novice in the business. One great smile comes on Leon's face when he talks of certain successes. The big one is when they decided to try an old black and white western, *Who Shot Liberty Valance*. They couldn't get the poster to advertise because of a price tag of about $20,000 so they created their own. Then they searched for a copy of the film for which prints are very hard to come by. They got the last one. Although they lost money on the two-week run, at the end of the first showing, the audience got up and applauded. A standing ovation for a classic, and Leon was hooked.

Today the Cliftex shows first-run movies on weekends. Thursday night is for adults only, not because of rating, but for those with no children in tow. There is one show a day Friday through Sunday at a ticket price of $4.00. And occasionally the Cliftex will show a matinee on Fridays for daycare.

An old movie house is often like going into another world, and I felt a slight shift of perspective when, as I was taking photos, I heard the click of another camera from my left. After all, Leon's other interest is a newspaper so logic says why not get a story while giving one? —*Stacey Hasbrook*

 For information:

W. Leon Smith
306 W. 5th St.
Clifton, TX 76634
(254) 675-1229
record@htcomp.net

Other attractions:

Parks
Golf and tennis
Bosque County
Conservatory of Fine Arts
Bosque Memorial Museum
Juniper Cove Marina & Campground
Soldiers Bluff
Norse Settlement - "Norwegian Capital of Texas"

Annual events:

"Syttende Mai"
(Norwegian Constitution Day) - May
Smorgasbord - November
Norwegian Country Christmas/Lutefisk Dinner - December

For details and accommodations:

Chamber of Commerce
115 North Avenue D
Clifton, TX 76634
(254) 675-3720
www.clifton.centraltx.com

12

Columbus: Stafford Opera House (1886)

Stacey Hasbrook photographer

Although the Stafford Opera House was an elegant place for society to gather in the late nineteenth century, not all her patrons lived a genteel life. Robert (Bob) Earl Stafford, the wealthy cattleman who developed the ICU cattle brand, built the theatre at the urging of his wife and other people in the community. As with many wealthy and powerful men of the time, Stafford was part of a fifteen-year feud between two influential families, the Staffords and the Townsends. On July 9, 1890, Stafford and his brother John were shot to death by Townsend relatives within sight of the theatre and in front of witnesses. Although Stafford did not live long enough to fully enjoy the entertainment hall he built, the Stafford Opera House has lived to see a full century and is looking toward a second.

In December 1885, two years after the Bond's Hotel burned to the ground, Bob Stafford purchased the lot intending to build two commercial buildings. With the news report of the purchase, he was petitioned to build the citizens something large enough for theatricals and local social events. Stafford rethought his plans into one longer building and hired architect Nicholas J. Clayton of Galveston—Texas's premier designer of buildings and residences. The end of 1886 saw the completion of the first floor of the Stafford Bank and Opera House, but work on the theatre continued into 1887. Its grand opening occurred on October 28, 1887, and it is the largest surviving flat-floored nineteenth-century opera house in Texas.

The first floor included Stafford's private bank and a large dry goods store owned by Adolph Senftenberg. Next door, he built the family residence, a large frame house of cypress and pine, and it was rumored he could watch the performances from his bedroom on the second floor. The theatre originally used 800 seats but had room for about 1,000—600 on the main floor and 400 in the balcony. The lower level seats were moveable to provide space for dances. In old photos they appear to be laminated curved-back theatre seats in rows attached to a frame.

Stafford spared no expense for his first-class project. Although the use of kerosene lamps was the most common type of lighting, the large wagon-wheel-shaped chandelier, which hung over the center of the floor, was fed by bottled gas, a luxury at the time. The front façade was composed of cast iron and the fourteen-foot doors of cypress and glass. The theatre originally measured 90 by 66 feet with a 30 by 30 stage that had 18-foot wings. The stage curtain was hand-painted in oils. The entire project cost $50,000, $10,000 of which was for the curtain. The stage set design included painted "shutters in grooves" of a few common scenes that could be stored in the wings. The exterior is composed of four colors of brick, and the unique marble cornerstone shows a steer's head with a lasso looped over the horns and the words "R. E. Stafford's Building" carved in it.

The theatre—always live performances never movies—continued to operate the same after Stafford's death until the early twentieth century, even though the remaining family had moved to San Antonio. Some productions used special effects such as explosions, gunfire, and the staging of a helpless victim tied to railroad tracks. Some controversial topics were attempted but not accepted, and biblical stories were generally not allowed on any stage in the country. The most talked about show of the first season was one with Chinese students in February 1886 sponsored by the Methodist church ladies. The audience booed and hissed, and at the train station the next day, they threw eggs at the performers.

The theatre was sold in 1916, and the downstairs became the Ford Motor Company dealership with cars displayed on the inside floor. The upstairs became an arena for boxing, basketball games, and even a roller skating rink. During WW II the stage was torn out and eight apartments were built to help alleviate local housing shortage. The large theatre area became a storage place for tires.

Finally in 1972 the Magnolia Homes Tour, Incorporated purchased the huge building for $30,000 and struggled for years to raise funds for renovation. They began the restoration in 1975 going through a three-phase plan. The first part involved the exterior and was timed for presentation with the Bicentennial celebration. Next, the more difficult and expensive interior structural work including air conditioning, staging, and dressing rooms was completed. Finally, the auditorium and third floor balcony were restored. Part of the last phase included the $1,000 balcony seats which have name plates honoring the donors who bought a seat for the installation.

The project was completed in 1990 at a cost of $1,300,000 including two major grants and several large gifts. The gala reopening in October 1990 was a showcase. The town square was covered in tiny white Christmas lights, and searchlights flashed in the sky. Clayton's daughter Mary presented the building with a hand-colored portrait of her father, and the

Stacey Hasbrook photographer

leaders of the project received an award from the League of Historic American Theatres.

Today the Opera House seats 600 and is the property of the Columbus Historical Preservation Trust, Incorporated. It is listed on the National Register of Historic Places. The first floor, originally a commercial space, rents offices and houses the Chamber of Commerce, the Magnolia Homes Tour, Incorporated, the Preservation Trust, Incorporated, and the Convention and Visitors Bureau. The theatre hosts a variety of professional and amateur performances from September through May and is used for community events including banquets and weddings. The seats downstairs are stacking chairs and tables for dinner theatre but easily converts into traditional seating.

The planning and restoration of the Stafford Opera House has taken nineteen years and a lot of effort, but it is finally restored as "authentically as possible." There is a Stafford Museum Room that covers the 104-year history located in the corner of what was once the private bank of one of Columbus' most memorable characters. Although I heard hints of strong feelings that still exist in the community, the family feud is nowhere in sight. *—Stacey Hasbrook*

For information:

Stafford Opera House
425 Spring St.
Columbus, TX 78934
(409) 732-8385

Other attractions:

Museums, golf, recreation centers
Alley Log Cabin
Bed and Breakfast Registry
Colorado County Courthouse
Columbus Opry
Live Oak Art Center
Texas Pioneer Trail
Attwater Prairie Chicken Refuge
Walking/driving tour
Eagle Lake
Fayette Lake
Splashway Family Water Park

For details and accommodations:

Chamber of Commerce
Columbus Convention & Visitors Bureau
P.O. Box 98
Columbus, TX 78934
(409) 732-8385
www.intertex.net/users/

13

Dalhart: La Rita (1920s)

Ernest Upton photographer

Ere these portals ye open
Let not your memories falter
For those whose toil and vision
And dreams and tears and laughter
Were diligently poured into this cauldron
Where brews the magic—called theatre.
(Carol Hendrix)

This verse is etched in the concrete at the threshold of Dalhart's La Rita
Theatre. It took on more meaning when I entered and began hearing the

65

tales of how La Rita was brought back into being by a tireless crew of volunteers.

Carol Hendrix, president of the organization until 1998, said, "The last cowboy rode across La Rita's silver screen in 1957." After the theatre closed, the front part was partitioned off into offices, stores, and upstairs apartments. In what was left of the auditorium, all the seats had been taken out. By the time La Rita Performing Arts Theatre, Inc. (LRPAT), under the name of "Dalhart Community Theatre," bought it in 1988, the place was in a terrible state of disrepair.

photo courtesy of La Rita Performing Arts Theatre, Inc.

Hendrix described the volunteer effort as people doing whatever they were good at. "Picture a seventy-year-old woman swinging a sledge hammer to knock down walls; an elderly man going around grinding off bolts that stuck out of the concrete so people wouldn't trip over them; and truckers hauling off twenty-two dump truck loads of debris."

But vision had to come before all that toil. The group had a ten-year history of putting on performances in whatever space they could find. Once it was a bull-barn. Another time it was K-Bob's Steak House where every night they put up and took down their stage. "You have to prove yourself," Hendrix said, "before you ask for grants and donations."

The theatre they rebuilt is more beautiful than its predecessor had ever been. Not much of the original remains except a beautiful tile drinking fountain. For the sake of efficiency and eye-appeal, they completely rear-ranged the lobby, concession stands, and restrooms. Small details added to

Ernest Upton photographer

the impact, such as the signs on the restroom doors fashioned from antique cigar labels. Once a woman tried to buy the picture of "La Rita" because that was her own name. Instead of restoring what little bit of 1930s Art Deco that still showed, LRPAT decided to go with an elegant Victorian style.

"The seats were scattered all over town," past president Bob Langhorne said, "but we got all 230 of them back." Prison labor refur-bished them. Every other row contains an extra wide "love seat" that assures no seat is directly behind the one on the next row, hampering your view.

Food and drink are not allowed in the auditorium proper, though there's a level area just inside where a couple of times a year they present dinner theatre. This area (accessible for wheelchairs) and the box seats can accommodate ninety.

Dressing rooms were added at the back of the building, but actors had no "rat run" for moving from the front of the building to the backstage area. To remedy this, they built a concealed passageway behind the box seats that were added along both side walls. Actors no longer have to run through the rain to get where they need to go, and the box seats are popular with patrons. Exquisite, curved wooden railings on these match the rest of the fine furniture look that is so prevalent. How could they afford such woodwork? They commissioned specific parts so volunteer craftsmen didn't have to leave their shops. Later the parts were assembled on site.

One man who came in to see what he could do commented, "Looks to me like the easy end of this deal is writing a check," and he handed one over for $5,000 "to pay for a box." After that, Hendrix persuaded others to do the same. When she announced, "We've sold all the boxes," somebody said, "Well, hell, let's build some more!" So they created more of the curved rail seating on the raised level area just behind the regular seats.

Asked about a ghost, my tour guides didn't hesitate. They all admitted having had eerie feelings when only two or three people are working on sets late at night. One of them asked the others, "How would you describe that noise 'La Rita' makes?" They came to the consensus that the sound was a cross between percussion and creaking.

Asked about the worst setback they've ever had, Hendrix said, "That would have to be our plumbing problem in 'Hell.'" Ah! A familiar term from Shakespeare. In the bard's day, the under stage space called "Hell" was used for storage and for "ghosts" to appear and disappear through a trapdoor. For this theatre, the term was especially apt for a while, Hendrix said. Foul water periodically surged through their Hell. They had to go to all the neighboring businesses and have them flush their commodes to find which one was tapped into the theatre's line (unbeknownst to any parties involved). Once found, the matter was remedied.

The shows went on even before construction was finished, and the group won the Amarillo Chamber of Commerce's coveted "Golden Nail" award for their summer season. Later they won the award again for the building itself.

When I visited the theatre, an elaborate stage setting for *Beauty and the Beast* was on display (traditional rather than Disney version). Dale Palmer, who was introduced to me as "Mr. Everything," constructed much of it (according to Hendrix's design). Palmer's name appears on numerous playbills, not only on technical and set crews but also on the board of directors. LRPAT plans to enter this set in next year's Texas Nonprofit Theatre drama and design competition.

Ernest Upton photographer

Texas Commission on the Arts has given grants to bring in popular entertainers such as Red Steagall, cowboy poet; Don Edwards, cowboy balladeer; the Starjazz Trio; Tammy Hysmith; and the Otwell Twins (from the Lawrence Welk Show).

For many years a three-day gathering has been held every August in honor of the XIT ranch, "world's largest ranch under fence in the 1880s, 3 million acres." As explained in *Texas State Travel Guide*, the state "... far richer in land than cash, granted [this land] in 1882 to a Chicago corporation for construction of a state capitol. An English company, the Capitol Freehold Land & Investment Company of London, operated the immense spread that covered parts of ten present counties." To this day, an estimated 25,000-30,000 people attend this celebration.

LRPAT's theatrical contribution, in the form of a musical "mellerdrammer," packs the house. La Rita's regular patrons come from not only the Texas Panhandle where it is located (the northernmost theatre named in this book), but also from Colorado, Kansas, Oklahoma, and New Mexico.

A graceful portrait hangs in the stair landing. It was given as a tribute to the subject, Carol Hendrix, but she says modestly, "It should be a group picture." While I thought the individual portrait was fitting, I understood what she meant because of all the effort this group has put into the project. But it's not just about a building. This group would perform on the desert if they had to.

Moliére, the French actor and playwright, said that for theatre, all you need is a platform and a passion or two. Or as the inscription out front suggests, perhaps *anywhere* can be "the cauldron where brews the magic—called theatre." —*Joan Upton Hall*

 For information:

La Rita Theatre
311 Denrock
Dalhart, TX 79022
(806) 244-6222 or
(806) 244-5646
larita@xit.net

Other attractions:

Dallam-Hartley Counties
XIT Museum
Empty Saddle Monument
Lake Rita Blanca Wildlife
Management Area
Lakes, hunting

Annual events:

XIT Rodeo, reunion &
world's largest free
barbecue

For details and accommodations:

Chamber of Commerce
P.O. Box 967
Dalhart, TX 79022
(806) 244-5646
chamber@dalhart.org
www.dalhart.org/

14

Dallas Theatres

Pamela Robison photographer

The Majestic (1921)

"Restoration where feasible; renovation where necessary," was the guiding principle behind saving the Majestic according to a Dallas Management Group brochure. In Big D, a city with no room for deadwood, perhaps this practical guideline is what saved the grand old structure. And beneath its opulence, perhaps this practicality has always been its greatest strength: whatever flexibility it took to suit its patrons.

One sign of its hold on both its past and present is executive director John Wilborn's attitude. When I had to leave a message for him to return my call, he responded quickly and courteously—no nonsense, no time wasted—clearly a businessman. Yet along with giving me all the data I needed, his pride in the old theatre was unmistakable. He'd had a good model to follow.

Karl Hoblitzelle's Interstate Theatres were the first in the Southwest to have air conditioning, earphones for the hearing impaired, "crying rooms," "kiddie seats," and eventually wiring for sound. Hoblitzelle also set the tone for clean family entertainment.

Before he set out to build the Majestic in 1921 as an Interstate flagship theatre, an even earlier Majestic (in a different location), dating back to 1905, had burned to the ground. He engaged Romanian-born John Eberson to design it. Eberson, having tired of conventional theatre designs, had already begun experimenting with atmospheric style, in which details such as gardens, fountains, and statuary reflected his European heritage. The Dallas Majestic's five-story, five-bay Renaissance Baroque exterior prepares you to expect this style. At the entrance to the theatre area, it sets the Roman gardens theme with an overhead trellis and auditorium space that accommodates 1,648. Elaborate balconies and Corinthian columns flanking the proscenium arch heighten the illusion of being outdoors. Imagine further that there were once real stuffed peacocks sitting above the arch and boxes.

Although the decorating style has remained constant, the Majestic's personality changed through the years to suit the clientele. Troubled by vaudeville's risqué side, Hoblitzelle first billed the 1921 Majestic for "seven clean acts of vaudeville twice daily." Short films later supplemented live acts, and going to the theater had an entirely different meaning than it does today.

"Majesticland," in the basement provided free baby-sitting, offering milk and crackers, a playland that had a merry-go-round, fanciful playscapes, and a petting zoo—even Treasure Island. Also the "Land of Nod" nursery was staffed with trained nurses.

By 1932, while movies grew in popularity, vaudeville was discontinued entirely. It was cheaper to transport film than a troupe of actors. For part of this period during the Depression, the RKO theatre chain owned the Majestic. When it fell on hard times, Hoblitzelle came out of retirement to repossess the organization and save the jobs of many associates and employees. People could pay for tickets with canned food or up to four IOUs. Out on the street, carnival barkers tried to lure customers in.

Hoblitzelle always attuned himself to what other attractions might draw customers away. Besides Majesticland, the basement area also offered adults a chance to listen to favorite radio shows and then return to the movie upstairs. With all this, no wonder people scraped up their pennies to go to a movie.

The array of stars who performed or made appearances on the Majestic stage was impressive, beginning with ballerina Olga Petrova. Later entertainers were Jack Benny, Burns and Allen, Bob Hope, Milton Berle, Mae West, and Houdini. Ginger Rogers began her career there (by winning a Charleston contest). James Stewart, John Wayne, and Joan Crawford made appearances as did the bands of Duke Ellington and Cab Calloway.

But in postwar times, for all the reasons cited in this book's introduction, movies simply could not draw the crowd needed to make the large downtown theatre profitable. Similar to Hoblitzelle's radio offering of earlier days, in '48 he experimented with large screen television wrestling matches or ball games shown before the movie started. It didn't help much. Then in 1949 an attempt to revive vaudeville failed too. By July of 1973 the Majestic had to close down. Ironically, the last movie shown was the James Bond film *Live and Let Die*.

Karl Hoblitzelle died in 1967, but his words on the Majestic cornerstone still serve as a reminder of purpose: "Dedicated to art, music, and wholesome entertainment in grateful recognition of the support given me by the people of Dallas."

The Hoblitzelle Foundation stepped forward. In 1976 it presented the Majestic as a gift to the city of Dallas on the understanding that the theatre would continue the founder's vision as a center for the performing arts. Four million dollars in bonds for renovations were approved in 1979, and a "Light up the Majestic!" group donated a million dollars in private funds. The huge task of remodeling began.

Remember that guideline, "Restoration where feasible; renovation where necessary"? The main lobby has retained much of its baroque detailing, and 23K gold leaf was reapplied to interior decorative accents and molding. The foyer's black and white Italian marble floor has been carpeted, and where an original chandelier once hung, there is a stunning replacement from the Crystal Ballroom of the demolished Baker Hotel.

Concessions were not available to patrons until the 1940s, but the marble fountain, which Eberson had copied from one in the Vatican gardens in Rome, has given way to a concession stand. Classical architecture and detailing still prevail.

Pamela Robison photographer

Pamela Robison photographer

Rededication of the remodeled theatre took place in January of 1983. Since that time the Majestic, home of Dallas Summer Musicals (DSM), has provided a stage for most of the theatre, dance, and music organizations in Dallas. It has also hosted national pageants, corporate conventions, dinners and banquets, lecture series, and Broadway touring productions. The city of Dallas rents the building to groups, and as one brochure states, "Because after 75 years, the Majestic Theatre still stands to serve the people, its use is available to those who wish to continue its heritage."

At the head of the grand staircase overlooking the main lobby is the Terrace Room, which accommodates weddings and other types of receptions, parties, and book review presentations. It is a perfect place for dinner parties, offering "package" options in catering, etc.

The lower floor, once occupied by Majesticland, continues to serve youth. Dallas Summer Musicals' "School of Musical Theatre" provides for students (ages fourteen and up) to study music and dance. These students also have opportunities for auditions and critical review by nationally known producers and theatrical companies. A future goal is to complete a "Black Box Theatre" (seating up to 180 people) for small theatrical productions and experimental theatre.

Another innovation is that the Bistro bar opens into the Majestic's main lobby or through a separate entry on Elm Street. Many theatre patrons gather there to enjoy music and beverages before or after the production. The Majestic is close to the Morton H. Meyerson Symphony Center and Dallas Museum of Art as well as historic districts: eastward the thirties blues area known as "Deep Ellum"; westward, the "West End" warehouse district; and just south of the theatre entrance, the original Neiman-Marcus and Dallas Convention Center.

The Majestic Theatre today holds a City of Dallas Historic Landmark, a Texas Historic Landmark, and a listing in the National Register of Historic Places. Any metroplex that incorporates its history into its progress deserves commendation. Past and present are delightfully interwoven in Dallas as is cooperation between public and private sectors. Together the citizens have restored, renovated, and given new life to historical institutions like the Majestic and other vintage theatres that remain an important part of the bustling city.

For Information:

The Box Office at Preston Center
6013 Berkshire Lane
Dallas, TX 75225-5705
(214) 691-7200

or

DSM Management Group
The Majestic Theatre
1925 Elm St.
Dallas, TX 75201
www.dallassummermusicals
.org/majestic_des.htm

or

P.O. Box 510188
Dallas, TX
75315-0188
(214) 880-0137

Who says antique neighborhood theatres can't survive in a metropolis? Big D has two: the 1938 Lakewood on Abrams Parkway and the 1935 Village at Highland Park; or three if you count the younger Inwood at Inwood and Lovers Lane. And these aren't *about* to go the way of the dinosaurs.

Village (1935)

photo courtesy of Henry S. Miller Interests, Inc.

The Regent Highland Park Theatre started off as the Village in 1935. It was an integral part of the "town square" approach envisioned by the entrepreneurs and embraced by the area citizens, who have managed to keep the integrity of beautiful Highland Park even while Dallas surrounded it.

To understand the theatre's history and character, it is necessary to understand Highland Park itself. In 1906 entrepreneur John S. Armstrong bought 1,326 acres of land and with his two sons-in-law, Hugh Prather and Edgar Flippen, hired architect Wilbur David Cook, the designer of Beverly Hills. Cook was assigned the task of planning a high-class community with fine homes. Because the elevation was 130 feet higher than Dallas and 20 percent of the land was to be dedicated to parks, they named the town "Highland Park," which opened a year later. By 1912 Flippen and Prather lured a country club to open there and attract wealthy citizens of Dallas. It worked, and the Dallas Country Club is the oldest country club in Texas.

Next Flippen and Prather decided Highland Park needed a shopping center, intended to function as a town square, but bankers and merchants were reluctant to accept the idea. After all, business had always been conducted downtown. Undeterred, the developers traveled to Barcelona and Seville to Mexico and California, studying the architecture for their retail center. They hired architects Marion Booshee and James Cheek to design the Mediterranean Spanish masterpiece, which has became "downtown Highland Park."

Highland Park Village, which opened in 1931, started the trend for neighborhood shopping centers. The Urban Land Institute called the operation "the first planned shopping center in the United States with a unified architectural style and stores facing in toward an interior parking area, all built and managed under a single ownership."

Long-time residents remember the grand opening as a community carnival. It had a Ferris wheel in the middle around which were booths and games. The prizes were a little different from those of the average carnival, however, a pony for the grand prize winner. Annual Village fiestas for several years afterward continued to raffle off a pony.

The center began with a sales office in the middle, the first retail section in the southwest corner, and a filling station on Preston Road. This road originally followed an ancient Indian trace that had bisected the

Armstrong-purchased property. In the early years patrons sometimes rode horseback on one of the area bridle paths to do their shopping or dining.

Today the Highland Park area boasts more million-dollar homes than any other comparable-sized area in Texas. Like everyone else, however, the Village suffered a downturn during the Depression, and it took about twenty years to complete. It began to thrive again in 1935 with the opening of several new stores, including later a sporting goods store owned by hometown football hero Doak Walker.

Also opening that year was the Village Theatre, the first luxury suburban theatre in Texas. It was built at a cost of $100,000 with a seating capacity of 1,350.

Ownership of the shopping center changed from time to time. After Hugh Prather Sr. died in 1959, his sons John and Hugh Jr. ran it until 1966, when it was acquired by the Howard Corporation. For about ten years attention to detail and upkeep went downhill: inattention to the optimum tenant mix, deterioration of landscaping, allowance of overhead wires, and "inappropriate" signs. Worst of all, tenants were allowed to alter the facades and cover up the classical architecture.

When the Howard Corporation decided to sell, it enlisted the help of the Henry S. Miller Company. After several prominent investors turned it down, Henry Miller Jr. himself stepped in. His father had been an associate of the Flippen-Prather Realty Company from 1917 to 1919 as well as a close personal friend of both partners. Besides this sentimental attachment, Miller was able to see the unrealized potential of the property.

He and his partners purchased the Village for $5 million and began at once to renovate and refurbish the infrastructure and to re-tenant the center. In 1986 this nationally recognized landmark development received a bronze plaque from the Park Cities Historical Society in recognition of its historical and architectural significance. Vision and hard work of the founders and Miller combined to make the Village a unique development.

Today the Spanish Plaza design centers around a fountain and ten acres of brick paths with plenty of benches. These paths wend through lush landscaping that attracts birds and butterflies. The rows of buildings have arched doors and windows, imported red tile roofs, overhanging balconies, ornate tile work, and finely crafted embellishments. Nowhere are these details more evident than in the Village Theatre as shown in the photographs.

Pamela Robison photographer

Pamela Robison photographer

The restructuring and renovation of this theatre was one of Miller's proudest accomplishments. Although the cost was greater than it would have been to build a new four-screen theatre, he respected the historic one as a landmark and recognized that it would attract patrons and help other tenants.

Within the ten largest cities in the U.S., the Village Theatre was the last independently operated theatre to show first-run films in 1987. At that time, American Multi Cinema (AMC) leased it and divided the space to accommodate four screens. In January of 2001 the growing theatre circuit called Regent Entertainment Company acquired the lease. This company also owns the Regent Showcase in

Hollywood and is "selectively pursuing exhibition venues, providing an automatic network of distribution for its own theatrical releases." The theatre has managed to maintain the high-toned character of the Highland Park area while making the changes necessary to succeed in competition with the sprawling multiplexes we know today.

Highland Park Village has been designated a National Historic Landmark. Surrounded by Dallas, this "town-square" approach has truly anchored the community. The center caters to the retail, dining, and entertainment needs of the patrons. It also hosts horse-drawn carriage rides, an annual Christmas Tree Lighting event, and other celebrations you would expect to find only in small communities, and it does so in its own inimitable style.

 For Information:

Regent Highland Park Village
32 Highland Park Village
Dallas, TX 75205
(214) 526-9668
ctw2021@aol.com

Lakewood (1938)

How has the Lakewood managed not only to survive but thrive? "Creativity and versatility," operations director and president Keith McKeague answered the question of the Lakewood's success.

I would add that it's also marketing skill and an inviting attitude. One look at Lakewood's web site gives you an idea of this. For one thing, it lists seven possible e-mail contacts. I went straight to the top to explain our book project and—will wonders never cease—McKeague responded! McKeague's cooperation surprised me even more when I realized the only week I had left to talk to him was the week he was preparing for a huge gala.

The Lakewood has regularly hosted fund-raising events for hundreds of local and national nonprofit organizations. Now it was their turn. Some of their sixty-two-year-old systems needed upgrading. Designated as a

photo courtesy of Keith McKeague

Dallas Landmark, the theater had every right to ask for help. McKeague commented if he had a dime for every time he'd heard something like, "What a wonderful place. I hope it never goes away," "Thank God they haven't torn this one down too," or "It's like nothing else in Dallas," he wouldn't need to have a fund raiser.

In his patron newsletter, he said, "Put your money where your mouth is. The Lakewood was built by a community, for a community, in a community, and it will take the community to keep it going."

The fund raiser, a 1940s style U.S.O. Show and Swing Dance, promised to be worth the price. Patrons could simply buy tickets to the gala or buy a membership, which included tickets. Donated merchandise was sold in a silent auction, and he gave merchants plenty of ideas about how their gift could pay off in sales.

Built by Interstate Theaters, it was the first theater in Dallas to have air conditioning. Starting in 1938 the Lakewood showed movies only. In '84 new management bought it and made improvements, but before McKeague took it over in about '95, it had been closed down a couple of years. He made still more improvements until it became literally the "showplace" you see today.

The cylindrical tower bearing the name of the theater reaches into the sky. Opening the doors into the lobby, rich with maroon and gold, promises something special. Porthole windows split into hemispheres as you swing open the doors. Graceful Art Deco curves lead your eye upward where recessed lights accent whimsical figures on the upper landing. Inside the auditorium, maroon seats are offset with green walls and Art Deco designs.

The Lakewood can seat 1,000 regularly. For cabaret seating, tables with snowy tablecloths are placed across every other row of seats. McKeague said this works well, but he's building the prototype for an improved table of this kind. The concession area offers a full bar and gourmet fare, but full dinners are catered in. The theater presents movies, concerts, and plays and has also been the scene of independent film and music festivals and premieres. People rent the place for corporate and private special events such as weddings.

Graduates of the local high school hold class reunions there. Janet Hershman of the Class of '51 recently attended her fiftieth. She lived in the area all through school—grade school, junior high, and then Woodrow Wilson High School. "And almost every Saturday," she said, "I went to the Lakewood to see the serials and all the Roy Rogers and Dale Evans and the Gene Autry picture shows." When she was older her attention turned more to the "love seats" at the ends of alternate rows. She and her friends usually stopped in at Doc Harrell's Soda Fountain a block away. The drugstore is gone now, but she remembers Mr. Harrell not putting up with any misbehavior from the kids.

She said she couldn't imagine a better place for their class reunions because of the nostalgia. Many classmates won't miss a reunion if they can help it. For those who hadn't been back since graduation, "it was a dèja vu experience." The marquee welcomes the class and then they come in for good food, music, and fellowship. They enjoy the cabaret seating and have a band that plays music from the forties and fifties. For payment the last band asked the group to write a check payable to their favorite charity.

Much of what the Lakewood does is for private parties, so McKeague started looking for a way to welcome the public with more movies. They're equipped to show films by DVD, laser, 35-millimeter, or even the old 16-millimeter. The trouble with first-run movies is having to commit a screen for two weeks, though he recently showed the newly released *Pearl Harbor*. On the other hand, he didn't want to go to $1 movies either.

One thing he decided to do is a classic night the second Tuesday of each month. A patron can buy a ticket for fifteen cents and popcorn for twenty-five. "In other words," he said, "Forty people can attend for the price it would cost one person in a modern movie house, and people seem to like the nostalgia."

People sometimes stop in to see the old place, pleased to find it so well kept. One day an older couple came in, the original ticket taker and an usher. This was where they had met and fallen in love. They told stories of theater memories. One was of the popcorn machine having to be placed outside for venting purposes. They recalled a man sitting in the parking lot watching to see that every sale was accounted for.

Being an antique hasn't stopped the Lakewood from trying new approaches and listening to what its patrons want. What will it offer next? McKeague is open to suggestions. As the web site says, "Your imagination is our only limit!"

photo courtesy of Keith McKeague

 **For information:**

Lakewood Theater
1825 Abrams Parkway
P.O. Box 720147
Dallas, TX 75372
(214) 821-9084
general@lakewoodtheater.com
www.lakewoodtheater.com

Other Dallas Oldies

Dallas's Texas Theater (1931) is slated for renovation due to the efforts of many Oak Cliffs residents and Preservation Dallas. It may be in operation by late 2002. This is the theater where Lee Harvey Oswald was captured.

Dallas's Inwood Theater (1947), also a Dallas Landmark, is going strong. Its web site includes great ghost stories. www.landmarktheaters .com/Market/Dallas/InwoodTheaterB.htm.

We hope there are more. To find web sites, try keying in the names of the above theaters. —*Joan Upton Hall*

Dallas's other attractions:	Aquarium, Zoo	For details and accommodations:
Museums & art galleries	McKinney Ave. Trolley	
Arboretum & Botanical Garden	Fair Park	Dallas Convention & Visitors Bureau
Professional sports events & complexes	Medieval Times	1201 Elm Street, Suite 2000
Dallas Symphony Orchestra in Morton H. Meyerson Symphony Center	Palace of Wax/Ripley's Believe it or Not!	Dallas, TX 75270
Key districts on DART routes (Dallas Area Rapid Transit)	Six Flags over Texas	(214) 571-1000 or (214) 571-1300 or 1-800-232-5527
Theater Center (Frank Lloyd Wright)	Zero Gravity Amusement Park	Events Hotline: (214) 571-1301
	Lakes, parks, shopping	info@dallascvb.com
	Annual events:	www.dallascvb.com
	State Fair	
	Seasonal events	

15

Denison: Rialto (1920)

Don Hall photographer

Denison, which once had thirty theatres, probably portrayed theatre history better than any other town we visited. Following the Rialto's ups and downs gives you an idea of what was happening nationwide. As Billy Holcomb notes in his book *Theater Row: Movie Palaces of Denison, Texas*, the very name "Rialto" is symbolic. William Shakespeare uses the Rialto Bridge of Venice at various times as a meeting place for all classes of people. Theatres do this too.

The Rialto had to wait for a few forerunners to pave the way for it. The town was settled by tough railroad men and cowboys, for whom saloons were diversion enough. Opera houses came later to provide entertainment for respectable ladies and families, from classic opera and Shakespearean plays to top comedy vaudeville acts.

Denison contributed to the success of one of these acts that went on to become one of the most famous groups ever. Three brothers traveling with their aunt and a young woman were booked to sing for two performances. The act was so bad the manager demanded they give a comedy routine for the second performance. The group came up with "Fun in Hi Skule," playing to a delighted audience. After that, with the help of their two other siblings, they stuck to comedy and became the Marx Brothers.

Just after the turn of the twentieth century, "flickers" brought a new technology to Denison, usually held in a store using whatever makeshift seating that could be pulled up. By 1906 movies were recognized as more than a passing fad, and movie houses were built, sometimes one beside the other, as happened in Denison. In 1920 L. M. Rideout, who already owned another nice theatre, opened "the pinnacle of luxury," the two-story Mediterranean Revival-style Rialto. Comfort and refinement had become important, and one old ad bragged, "Rest Rooms for Ladies and Gentlemen...no feature has been omitted." According to an article in the *Denison Herald* (October 4, 1992), the Rialto cooled its auditorium with fans blowing across up to 300 pounds of block ice from its own water tower.

Interviewed in the same article, long-time manager Harry Gaines told of a momentous day in film history. On October 6, 1927, Al Jolson came on the screen in *The Jazz Singer* and said, "You ain't heard nothin' yet, folks!" Talkies were born to the rapid retirement of silent films, mechanical pianos, pipe organs, and the vaudeville acts that often accompanied them.

The Rialto was the first theatre in Denison to convert to sound. It used the Vitaphone System, something like a large phonograph record to produce the dialogue and sound effects. Synchronizing the film and the sound had to be very tricky business.

Another tricky business was controlling the danger of fire in projection booths. In the old days, the combination of carbon arc projectors and nitrates in film made fire highly likely. Also the projectionist had to watch closely and be ready to switch between two projectors every twenty minutes when a reel ran out.

The only movie house better than the Rialto was Interstate's flagship theatre, the Majestic of Dallas. Indeed Interstate bought the Rialto in 1932. Though the Depression and expense of converting to sound had closed many theatres, surviving theatres became the haven for people to momentarily escape reality. Theatres helped in other ways too, offering the fun of game nights with practical prizes like dishes, money, and even bags of groceries. When it was remodeled in 1939, a photo of the grand reopening shows how they displayed framed advertising signs dating back to 1920 around the stage.

photo courtesy of Donna Hunt

Again and again during our research, we ran across the name Karl Hoblitzelle. He and his brother George had founded the Interstate Amusement Company. They believed theatres' motives should not be only for profit, but should reflect community values and offer citizens the best entertainment in town. Karl repeatedly stepped in to hold the Interstate chain together until his death in 1967, and even since then, the Hoblitzelle Foundation has aided many a theatre.

During WW II and after, the Rialto thrived, hosting a huge 1948 premiere of *Red River*, starring John Wayne. The movie industry expected the boom to continue, but it dwindled instead in the fifties due to several factors. Harry Gaines largely blamed anti-trust laws for breaking up the control of chains like Interstate that provided quality movies.

Donna Hunt, former park manager for the Eisenhower birthplace, remembers the theatres as an important part of her growing up. Her mother went to morning events like cooking school at the Rialto, which filled every seat. Donna and her friends passed for twelve-year-olds as long as they could because the price went up to a quarter after you turned thirteen. During her high school years, they often went to the midnight show at the Rialto, "which always had first-run movies," she said. Harry Gaines was her favorite manager, but once when she tried to enter a movie, he told her it wasn't suitable for a young girl and wouldn't let her in.

As an adult, Donna worked for the *Denison Herald*, writing promotional pieces for the theatre page. She even got to interview some of the actors either by phone or when they were visiting. She especially liked Dale Evans and Roy Rogers, James Garner, and Vincent Price.

Preceded by other Denison theatres, the Rialto failed in 1975. Several attempts were made to revitalize and reopen it after that, but it finally shut down as a movie theatre in 1986, the last one out of thirty.

Today interest has swung back to the abandoned downtown areas that were once shunned. Main Street Programs are uniting people to revitalize all kinds of run-down buildings, historic theatres among them if still standing. For the Rialto it was the Main Street Country Showcase that opened it back up in 1998. Renovations of the balcony were still in progress while we were writing this book. This project will increase seating from the present 362 to a total of 662, and if popularity is any indication, the space will be filled.

Every Saturday night it plays to a packed house, coming to Branson-style productions of country-western, gospel, and fifties music. Well-known entertainers come mostly from the four neighboring states, but it has its seasoned regulars who got tired of doing road shows. Also local talent is encouraged to audition. Kelly and Shawnda Rains of Durant, Oklahoma, just across the border, first leased then bought the Rialto for the show. Shawnda brought with her the experience of nineteen years as a regular performer. She had been named Female Vocalist of the Year for '95 and '96 at the Johnnie High Country Music Review in Arlington.

photo courtesy of Main Street Country Showcase

To read the history of Denison's theatres is to understand what happened across the nation. The survival of one wonderful old theatre out of thirty epitomizes both the loss and the rebirth of theatre business as an institution. What a fortunate choice to name this theatre "Rialto" to symbolize a meeting place for all people. —*Joan Upton Hall*

 For information:

Main Street Country Showcase
Rialto Theatre
424 W. Main St.
Denison, TX 75021
(903) 463-1690
skrains@simplynet.net
www.mainstrreetshowcase.com

Other attractions:

Old Katy Depot
Historical walking & driving
tours
Denison Dam (tours, exhibits)
Eisenhower birthplace & state
park
Grayson County Frontier Village
Hagerman National Wildlife
Refuge
Lakes, parks, golf, & specialty
shopping

Annual events:

Seasonal events almost every
month
U.S. Aerobatics Competition
American Bass Anglers National
Tournament
Art & Wine Fest & Fine Art Tour
Texoma Lakefest Regatta

**For details and
accommodations:**

Chamber of Commerce
313 West Woodard
P.O. Box 325
Denison, TX 75021
(903) 465-1551
denisoncoc@texoma.net

16
Eastland: Majestic (1920)

photo courtesy of Ed. Allcorn

Citizens of Eastland can tell you "small" doesn't mean "insignificant." Take two of the town's best-known features, the Majestic Theatre (originally the Connellee) and Old Rip, the mascot whose likeness you'll see stamped on signs and brochures.

Regarding the theatre, a 1947 article in the *Eastland County Record* stated that Karl Hoblitzelle, president of Interstate Amusement Company, "took such personal pride in the Eastland enterprise as to decree that it should be the equal in every way, except perhaps in size, of the very best shows in the larger cities of the state... [and he called] it the Majestic, a name dear to his heart."

The other case in point, Old Rip, was a horned frog that exemplified the theatre and town's spirit of survival. The story is that somehow the poor little creature stayed dormant but alive from 1897 to 1928 in the courthouse cornerstone. When the building was torn down, he was discovered. He died of pneumonia a year later, but during that one glory year he went on tour, even visiting President Calvin Coolidge in the White House. Old Rip now lies in state inside a glass-front coffin in the new courthouse.

Eastland sprang up with the oil boom of the teens and twenties. Six silent movie theatres and two air domes (open-air theatres) flourished there. One theatre was right beside the Connellee. It was the Princess, which shared a building with the Stanley Hotel. The space is now a B&B, but the wall shows evidence of stairs that went up to the projection booth.

The Connellee, named after the town's founder, Charles U. Connellee, had opened as an opera house in 1920 to provide both live performances and silent movies. Every Saturday night a live radio broadcast was made from there, and once Gene Autry and Champion (his horse) visited.

Then, with the oil "bust," Eastland, like Old Rip, suffered virtual dormancy. The Connellee was the only theatre that stayed open, under the management of various theatre chains including Interstate Theatres, which bought it in 1936.

The company closed it briefly for renovation ten years later. It reopened in 1947 as the "Majestic" (not to be confused with another Majestic that had operated nearby during boom times). According to the souvenir program of 1987, Interstate had spared no expense to decorate it in the popular mode of the day, "futuristic Art Deco style, featuring sweeping curves and rounded corners, which may still be observed in the scalloped proscenium arch that frames the stage, the curving walls and recessed lighting in the lobby and mezzanine."

However, the same loss of public interest plaguing the whole theatre business about that time led to the Majestic's demise too. By the seventies and eighties it had fallen into such a state of disrepair springs poked through the seats. It ran B-grade movies, and the saying was, "If you're thinking of seeing a movie at the Majestic, it might be a good idea to do it right away." Sure enough, despite heroic efforts of various civic organizations, it closed its doors in 1986.

Heirs of the Connellee family sold the theatre to the city of Eastland, and the Eastland Fine Arts Association was set up to govern it in January 1987. With the assistance of a grant from the Hoblitzelle Foundation, they set to work.

Needing a consultant to do a proper restoration, they called in Ed. Allcorn, then manager of both the Abilene Paramount and the Abilene Philharmonic Orchestra. He has been a consultant for not only the Paramount, but also such theatres as the National in Graham, the Aztec in Albany, and the Texan in Hamilton. Under his direction, a crew of volunteers brought the old girl back to the forties look. They restored the painted designs, replaced the carpet, reupholstered seats, and refurbished the neon marquee. They also installed air conditioning and technical equip- ment (all of which has since been updated).

In only nine months, the theatre had its grand reopening and featured Woody Herman and The Young Thundering Herd. Other grants and awards have followed: a Texas State Historical Marker (1990) and financial contributions from the Meadows Foundation and numerous local organizations and individuals. In 1989 Allcorn became manager of the Majestic as the only paid staff member.

When I came to tour the building under his guidance, for once my dilemma wasn't to *find* a suitable historical photo, but to choose from many. Thanks to Allcorn's expertise and attention to historical detail, I enjoyed a trip back in time.

Graceful floral designs adorn the ceiling, and silhouettes of cowboys on horseback march across the walls in soft colors of mauve and aqua, as fresh as they must have looked in 1947. In 1920 the theatre had accommodated 1,000 to 1,200. It now seats 850, having sacrificed numbers for comfort. Unusual "Exit" lights date from 1947. The fifties popcorn machine still serves up an irresistible aroma and taste of the old days. Plastic marquee letters won't do for the Majestic. Allcorn proudly showed the cast aluminum Adler letters still in use.

Allcorn said the theatre had also possessed the original brass horns, used to amplify the actors' voices, but these relics were too valuable not to sell to a museum. They had of course already been replaced by magnetic speakers for "talkies," one cost that priced many theatres out of business. Today the Majestic's first-run movies require surround sound, but the speakers occupy the same places earlier speakers did.

On the way up to the balcony, we stopped off at the mezzanine floor, created from space once occupied by the

photo courtesy of Ed. A*

"Mary Louise," Eastland's first gift and beauty shop. The large open area is used as a meeting room and display for historical objects and vintage posters. One poster showed Errol Flynn in *Robin Hood*; another promised "Frankenstein in person" at *Asylum of Horrors*. I saw antique showbills and congratulatory telegrams from Hollywood stars, a veritable museum.

Like other early theatres, the balcony used to be where minorities were segregated. Beautiful original stenciling is still visible in a part of the balcony now occupied by a closet. Today only adults are allowed to sit in the balcony for safety reasons as children have a tendency to hang over the railing. Much of the seating space has had to yield to technical equipment.

The theatre has hosted its share of famous people. George W. Bush spoke from the stage when he was campaigning for the office of governor.

Connellee/Majestic and Princess Theatres, 1923 Parade Day. photo courtesy of Ed. Allcorn

A John Philip Sousa performance was scheduled there. In the early fifties the Trapp Family Singers performed at the Majestic.

Eastland's own Virginia Weaver Russell got her start at the Connellee in the thirties. She and other high school students had the opportunity to act alongside professionals. Later as a graduate of Yale Drama School, she wrote the play *A Drama for Boredom* (1939) under the name of George Spelvin and had it performed there.

Today high school students use the Majestic for graduation ceremonies and to perform University Interscholastic League plays, and the city uses it as a civic center. Movies are the latest releases, and like the rest of Eastland, there is an over-all sense of pride. Unlike the glass-casketed Old Rip, the Majestic is more alive than ever. —*Joan Upton Hall*

 For information:

The Majestic Theatre
P.O. Box 705
Eastland, TX 76448-0705
(254) 629-2102
majestic@txol.net
(The Chamber of Commerce web site has both a Majestic and a Chamber link.)

Other attractions:

"Old Rip" in Eastland
County Courthouse
Kendrick Religious Museum
$5 million post office mural
Great Race (vintage cars)
Walking and driving tours
Lakes, hunting, fishing, camping, golf, shopping/trade days

Annual events:

"Old Ripfest"

For details and accommodations:

Chamber of Commerce
102 S. Seaman
Eastland, TX 76448
(254) 629-2332 or
1-877-2OLD RIP
ecofc@eastland.net
www.eastland.net/eastland/

17

El Paso: Plaza (1930)

photo courtesy of Plaza Theater Restoration Project—El Paso Community Foundation

How long would it take to gather one million dollars by putting pennies in a fish bowl? Only two months if you are in El Paso and the passion for theatre motivates you. That's the time and money amount the El Paso Community Foundation (EPCF) was given to save the Plaza from becoming a parking garage. And they did it!

Once "the Showcase of the Southwest," the Plaza, which opened September 12, 1930, was built for vaudeville with 2,410 seats, but during construction, plans were modified so movies could also be shown. El Paso Street was the theatre district during the twenties, and the phone directory reveals about seventeen theatres in this one small area. All have been demolished or completely changed except the last one created, the Plaza.

Referred to as an "oasis in the middle of the Great Depression," it was the first theatre in the U.S. to boast refrigerated air. As with all atmospheric theatres, H. T. Ponsford and Sons spared no expense, including a twenty-ton pipe organ reverently referred to as the "Mighty Wurlitzer." Gordon Johnson remembers that time. "Watching the organ rise from the depths was always a great plus. . . . It became obvious to me that right here in a little old West Texas town, during a depression, that we had one of the most modern and beautiful theaters in existence at that time."

photo courtesy of Plaza Theater Restoration Project—El Paso Community Foundation

From the balcony there is an overwhelming view, but it doesn't feel like the stage is far away. You do not feel disconnected from what is happening. Dana Shelton has fond memories of the grandness. "For a little girl... the Plaza Theatre became a 'palace for a young princess.' What could have been more like a palace than beautiful red carpeting, gilded chairs with red velvet upholstery, ushers (my private pages) in red uniforms with gold trim? And there was the elegant 'powder room'... for a private boudoir."

Early theatre had a burlesque feel about it substantiated at the Plaza by an unusual circumstance. During the forties a group of dancers were performing in December, but there were not enough dressing rooms so they had to go outside to change costumes. It was snowing so the police department formed a semicircle barricade around the freezing dancers to keep gawkers from staring. I wondered who kept the policemen's eyes covered?

Another favorite risqué story centers on Sally Rand, the famous fan dancer. One night her performance involved large, clear balls that looked like bubbles. The lighting tech knew to avoid the clear slot on the wheel because she was "au natural" and that would make the bubbles transparent. Accidentally, he put on the clear light, and everyone saw what she didn't intend to reveal. She got red in the face but went on with the show. Afterwards, she threw on a robe and read him the riot act in front of everyone.

The most famous actors from this area are Gilbert Roland (*El Paso*) and F. Murray Abraham (*Amadeus*). The most famous movie stars to come to the Plaza include John Wayne, Rita Moreno, Ethyl Barrymore, and Mae West who had a special request before she would perform in the 1930s. Her dressing room had to be painted light pink, and it is still the same color today. The room is very small compared to today's dressing rooms, and truthfully, I can't imagine her being able to turn around in it, much less change clothes.

The *Gone with the Wind* premiere occurred simultaneously at the Majestic in San Antonio and the Plaza, so the cast was split with Clark Gable and Leslie Howard coming to the Plaza. One of the ushers here that night remembers being sixteen years old and standing in the corner selling programs for a dollar. The best part was that he sold out before the show started and that allowed him to go meet the stars, shake Gable's hand, and then go home early.

Due to anti-trust legislation, the Plaza closed in the early seventies. Down came the marquee, and the entrance was barricaded as homeless people began to create a fire hazard. Interstate recalled all the artwork, and the furniture was thrown in the garbage. The head artist begged and was permitted to take some of the furniture home, but most was just scrapped, lost forever. His daughter, a local pharmacist, has kept what remains and will allow the EPCF to study it for reproduction.

Throughout the seventies, countless efforts to determine how to save the theatre failed. Finally, Golden Chain Investments reopened it in the late seventies to show Spanish movies out of Mexico and Latin America until 1985. In 1987 a downtown revitalization study revealed the most productive way to use the property was to demolish it and turn it into a parking garage. The El Paso Community Foundation started negotiations immediately. They launched an aggressive campaign to meet the deadline. The culminating show brought Rita Moreno on stage the night before the deadline, and that night they finally went over the amount needed.

However, the EPCF didn't know what to do next. Fixing the roof for $100,000 was the first priority so the building wouldn't erode further. In 1990 they donated the building to the city and in '92 proposed how to restore it using dual funding from the city. It passed the city council, but the mayor vetoed it.

The next move? The EPCF secured a thirty-year lease on September 14, 1999, so they wouldn't have to worry about political change and other priorities. On April 18, 2000, the theatre was designated as an official project of "Save America's Treasures," and it is listed in the National Register of Historic Places, which opened up the opportunities for future grants and special benefits.

When asked about ghosts, Roman Herrington, program officer for the EPCF, hesitantly admitted there were a couple of stories. In one, a GI who wasn't feeling well got up to get a drink and smoke a cigarette. Supposedly he dropped dead on the site, and people up in that balcony have reported seeing a small amber glow or smelling smoke where neither could be. Then Roman said, "As far as anything actually happening, I don't know that ... well now, I take that back. There is ... uh ... two people that I know that have seen ... *something* in the theatre."

There's the young eighteen-year-old artist from the forties. Behind the stage area was the artists' room where they would make the marquees and decorations. The artists used ramps out the back to move the art around to the lobby so as not to chance getting paint on anything. When walking up the ramp, he looked up and saw some sort of apparition just from the waist up that was "just kind of hovering there looking at him." After a while it floated up in the air and disappeared. "It's only been in the last five years that he's kind of talked about it."

Then there is a lady who ran some sort of children's theatre company back in the eighties in the basement underneath the stage. They never really saw anything, but there is a light bulb that hangs down on a cord with a string at the end of it to turn it on. "Every once in a while the string would sway back and forth and sometimes it would look as if somebody

sign advertising Rita Moreno benefit show; Stacey Hasbrook photographer

had just tapped it. They said it wasn't like a malicious kind of a feeling, but kind of just odd...playful." The woman, Jan Wolf, who is a life insurance agent now, jokes that you can't complain about a ghost because it's a theatre buff. That's a good ghost.

When I asked if the EPCF would take the theatre back to original form, Roman smiled. "Charm is in the historic feel. People remember their first dates, their first kiss, going to a premier and seeing the Hollywood movie stars. To alter the theatre in some ways beyond what it was doesn't do it service. The question is how can we preserve the historical integrity of it but also make sure it is adequate for today's patrons."

The organ, which took more than a year to restore, is the only part completed so far. It has 1,071 pipes and was once described as "part one-man band, part symphony orchestra, and part sound-effects department." Its appeal is the way it produces sound. Like an original sound system, everything works together to produce music that can be felt as well as heard. Today it is on grand display at the Sunland Park Mall until its former home is ready to reclaim it.

The Junior League has adopted the theatre as a project and will develop a curriculum for education and conduct tours to give the students cultural opportunity.

The EPCF has bought the building next door to help develop a downtown cultural arts district with the museum to the other side and to allow more space for marquee development. Activities are planned using the symphony, Kids and Co., and other fund raising not only to bring in money but to get people used to coming into the theatre. The El Paso Community College is interested in managing it when it opens.

photo courtesy of Plaza Theater Restoration Project—El Paso Community Foundation

Of all the theaters in town, the Plaza is the most viable for renovation. It is the only theater in its original state. Although this giant "now hibernates—quiet and dark—surrounded by the din of dinner dates, jackhammers, and cement mixers in a downtown rife with reconstruction," an architectural firm is on board to evaluate what to do, how it can be used, and what it will cost. Then the EPCF must rally the community one more time.

It all goes back to the philosophy of some of the early builders of theatres. One of the large movie magnates, Marcus Lowes, is credited as saying, "I sell tickets to theatres, not to movies." If they fell in love with the theatre, they would always come back. Now it's up to the El Paso community to decide if that holds true for the twenty-first century Plaza as well. My bet is they'll say "yes." —*Stacey Hasbrook*

 For information:

Roman Herrington
P.O. Box 272
310 North Mesa
El Paso, TX 79943-0272
(915) 533-4020
rherrington@epcf.org
www.plazatheater.org

Other activities:

Museums, parks, golf
Mission tour
Western Playland
Chamizal National Memorial
El Paso/Juarez tours
Insights - El Paso Science Center
Tigua Indian Reservation:
Ysleta del Sur Pueblo
VIVA! El Paso
El Paso Zoo
Fort Bliss
Fray Garcia Monument
Magoffin Home State Historic Structure
San Jacinto Plaza

San Elizario Presidio Chapel
Buffalo Soldier Monument
Nuestra Señora del Carmen

Annual events:

Wells Fargo Sun Bowl
Music Under the Stars
Tigua St. Anthony's Day

For details and accommodations:

El Paso Convention and Visitors Bureau
10 Civic Center Plaza
El Paso, TX 79901
(915) 534-0500

Fort Worth: Casa Mañana (1936)

The sight of the futuristic looking Casa Mañana and the meaning of its name, "House of Tomorrow," might lead you to think it's a science fiction movie set. As one child said, "It looks like it's made of diamonds." It's hard to believe it originated as an open-air theatre in 1936. Even though the silvery sixty-six-foot-high geodesic dome didn't appear until the theatre was rebuilt in 1958, the original version was a marvel of ingenuity.

Amon G. Carter, publisher of the *Fort Worth Star-Telegram*, hired top Broadway producer Billy Rose to design a showplace and production befitting the Texas Centennial Celebration. What came out of this vision was the world's largest revolving stage and the nation's first permanent theatre for musical productions in the round. A 600,000-gallon moat, complete with singing gondoliers to entertain patrons until the show began, surrounded the stage. Instead of a conventional curtain, fountains shot water high in the air, creating an illuminated wall of water. On the floor level, 1,000 people could enjoy dinner while balcony tiers accommodated non-dining patrons, and for the first hundred days, Carter paid Rose $1,000 a day to dazzle the patrons.

President Franklin D. Roosevelt opened the extravaganza by remote control from a fishing boat in Maine. During that centennial year, one of the entertainers who attracted the most attention was stripper Sally Rand, who always managed to stay barely covered in her famous fan dance. Even after the centennial, the theatre thrived, hosting nationally renowned stars such as Wayne King, Eddie Cantor, Martha Ray, Ray Bolger, and Edgar Bergen and Charlie McCarthy.

Because the shows were so successful, Carter continued to operate the open-air theatre for four years, June through September. But alas the threat of World War II halted the operation in 1940, and the old theatre never reopened. The cost of producing such a grand show was too much, and the structure was mostly dismantled to provide metal and other material for the war effort. Even though a citizens committee organized a bond drive,

photo courtesy of Casa Mañana

wartime halted the progress, and the funds that had been raised lay untouched for several more years. What was left of the old building was eventually razed.

Hope reared its head again in 1956 when Melvin O. Dacus, general manager of the Fort Worth Opera, and oil magnate James H. Snowden, president of the Opera Association, approached the city council requesting the funds to build and operate a theatre primarily for the production of Broadway musicals. The council approved but stipulated that the summer musicals would be separate from the opera, so Dacus and Snowden traded their former positions with the Opera Association for similar positions in the not-for-profit Musicals, Inc., which could lease the building from the city of Fort Worth.

Construction began in January 1958, just east of the original site. The idea was to introduce "musicals-in-the-round" to the southwestern United States. Improvements were made from the old theatre venue. Considering Texas heat, open-air (even under a tent top) would not have been desirable, and a geodesic dome (a design pioneered by architect Buckminster Fuller) made air conditioning economically feasible. The stressed aluminum skin roof covers diamond-shaped panels joined by gold struts, providing comfort for 1,805 patrons who surround the oval, 30 x 34-foot, non-revolving

photo courtesy of Casa Mañana

stage. A ring housing lights and microphones is suspended above the stage, and it can be raised and lowered. Technicians in the booth control sound and lights. Wings off the auditorium hold dressing rooms, wardrobes, and storage. Gene Almy, director of sales and marketing, said that rehearsals are held in a small studio behind the theatre, and that room is also dedicated for theatre school classes, storage, etc.

In record construction time, Casa Mañana opened in July 1958, presenting five Broadway musicals in its very first season. Since then it has continued to show productions year round. It has brought in such notables as Jerry Seinfeld, Bill Cosby, Tony Bennett, Sinbad, the Neville Brothers, and Johnny Mathis.

A long-time aficionado of Casa Mañana nostalgized to me about actress Ruta Lee returning every year to perform at her "second home." However, Gene Almy clarified that she had not been back since 1997 when she performed in the musical *Grossingers*.

After the old Worth Theatre was demolished in 1972, the F. Howard Walsh family rescued its six-ton gold and white antique pipe organ and found a home for it in Casa Mañana. Some of Casa Mañana's productions are presented at the larger Nancy Lee and Perry R. Bass Performance Hall.

One of Casa Mañana's greatest accomplishments is the Children's Playhouse, one of the largest and most successful children's theatre operations in the country. It has been recognized not only by Fort Worth I.S.D. but also by the National Endowment for the Arts and the Texas Commission on the Arts for its outstanding work. Casa educates youth about live theatre to provide a future audience and supplement arts education that schools simply haven't the means to provide. It offers internships for children in a theatre school. Casa Kids Outreach Program draws a performance troupe from this theatre school. Casa Kids tour schools, nursing homes, hospitals, and arts festivals to take theatre to people unable to go there. They have also represented Fort Worth in Japan through a Sister Cities program.

Casa Mañana is also a founding member of the National Alliance for Musical Theatre, which encourages new American musical works.

This unique theatre has proven itself to be not only a "house of tomorrow" with its innovative design and education of future generations, but also of the past for the rich history it recalls and for present pleasures it provides for audiences.

 **For information:**

Casa Mañana Theatre
3101 West Lancaster Ave.
Fort Worth, TX 76107
(817) 332-272 or 467-2087 or 631-2087
www.casamanana.org

Other Fort Worth Oldies

I am indebted to certain individuals for their help in searching out Fort Worth's qualifying theaters. Fort Worth native Bob Thompson worked at several of them and was able to set me on the right trail. As he told me about them, he showed me books of their glory days. In one of these books, several of the Casa Mañana photos were credited to the "Quentin McGown Postcard Collection," so I looked this up on the Internet. I had the good fortune of actually contacting Mr. McGown, general counsel at Texas Wesleyan University. He loaned me some of his collection to try scanning (yes, actual picture postcards that once went through the mail—for a penny!). Unfortunately, the scans were not clear enough to use. Nevertheless I felt richer for having had the opportunity of seeing them.

Bob Thompson's information, including news clippings, provided a starting point for me to ask the Fort Worth Library if there were any other theaters we had missed. The librarians verified Thompson's information about two that were slated for restoration as part of the Mercado project in the cultural district.

The Rose Theater on North Main Street was rebuilt in 1920 (original date unknown) as the Roseland. It became the Rose in 1929 and then the Marine in 1945. It is currently undergoing renovation.

The 7th Street Theater, built by Boyd Milligan in 1946, has been in the family all these years but has been closed since the death of Michael Milligan, who ran it with his father. According to the *Fort Worth Star-Telegram*, the FPA Foundation, a Texas nonprofit organization, bought it in April of 2001, "projectors, popcorn machine, and all." The theater is on a block "that would be affected by...a six-point intersection of Camp

Bowie Boulevard, University Drive, West Seventh St., and Bailey Ave," but apparently the theater is to remain a theater.

On a sadder note, I found, on a web site forum, questions from a home-owner regarding the materials used to build his/her house and the neighboring one, which had been built about 1967. Were these really salvaged from the demolished Majestic of Fort Worth? These materials included bricks, ceiling beams, and "a gorgeous arched glass front door" (possibly it had been the door to the ladies' lounge). The answers that came in seemed to support that claim as the theater was demolished in the early sixties to make room for the Convention Center. At least parts of it are scattered around, appreciated by individuals.

The architects supposedly had wanted to preserve the Majestic, one respondent said, "because it was more beautiful and ornate than the Dallas Majestic, but it was the cheapest property available at that time."

Need I state the moral to this story? —*Joan Upton Hall*

Other attractions:	Stockyards National Historic District	For details and accommodations:
Amusement parks/sites	Motor Speedway	
Six Flags over Texas	Zoo	Chamber of Commerce
Will Rogers Auditorium in	Lakes, parks, shopping, walking & driving tours	777 Taylor St., Suite 900
Cultural District at Amon Carter Square		Fort Worth, TX 76102-4997
Nancy Lee and Perry R. Bass Performance Hall	**Annual events:**	(817) 336-491
Museums & art galleries	Livestock Show & Rodeo	jcashman@fortworth-chamber.com
Botanical & water gardens, other nature centers	Seasonal festivals	Also visitors centers for various historic districts
	Chief Quanah Parker Comanche Powwow	

Gainesville: State (1919)

photo courtesy of the Cooke County Heritage Society

The old vaudeville line goes, "You're so talented you oughta be on the stage. There's one leaving in ten minutes!" Well, in the case of the Butterfield Stage Players (BSP), it's no joke. They'll be glad to carry you along with them, figuratively speaking, for any show they perform. Maybe that's why Gainesville's energetic theater group took its name from the stagecoach stop that used to be there.

Most of the time we found that theaters and their "keepers" reflected the city's history, and a look at Gainesville's history bears this out. The settlement began in 1850 near the military outpost of Fort Fitzhugh. The stage line set up a station in '58, and the Chisholm Trail and California Trail also went through at this location. Butterfield closed the stage stop in 1861, perhaps, as the *Texas State Travel Guide* said, because the town was "too convenient to hostile Indian attack." The cattle barons and cotton brokers who founded Gainesville didn't let that scare them off. They built fine Victorian homes, attaching watchtowers as lookouts for bandits and Indians.

photo courtesy of the State Theater of Gainesville

Apparently Gainesville citizens continue to stick together and face hardships without looking for help.

The Majestic Theater (as originally named) may have been built on the site before 1919, but that's the earliest provable date. It was the city's major playhouse until a fire destroyed the building in 1932. The "Greater Majestic" was reconstructed later the same year, and it showed both movies and live performances. Again it was gutted by fire, leaving only the exterior walls. In 1938, as if a name change might bring better luck, they tried again with the "State" to show motion pictures. Its Art Deco style remains today.

With an Army training facility, Camp Howze, located there, Gainesville boomed during World War II, and a half dozen theaters sprang up. Then, in '44-'45, the base became "home" to 3,000 German POWs, which brought in an estimated 30,000 soldiers.

Cooke County had a high proportion of German-Americans who could speak the POWs' language, and the prison labor force was a great help. Shana Powell, curator of the Morton Museum, said they came in especially handy after a devastating ice storm in '45 left Gainesville in need of major carpentry repairs. When the war ended and the population suddenly dipped, however, many businesses failed. As for all those theaters, only the State stayed in business, and then only by splitting it in two and calling it the "State Twin." By 1997 even that business dried up, and the building was in danger of being torn down.

Local businessman David Jones said, "I had seen an old opera house torn down, and I didn't want to see that happen to the State." So he bought it to use the back of the building for a drive-through for his adjoining business, Parker Electric. At first he had no interest in operating the theater. In the evenings for the next two years, he sorted through all that was left, hauling off a great deal of trash and selling or donating a few usable properties. "But when I started messing with the marquee and all that, it got to me," he said. He began renovation slowly at first then picked up speed when he hired carpenters and other workers. BPS gave him some advice on what was needed to outfit a modern theater. In 2000 the State finished the year with a grand opening at which BSP produced the play *Sanders Family Christmas*.

The original appearance was restored, neon marquee and all, but Jones had rebuilt it with the future in mind. They have installed state-of-the-art sound and lighting. The back wall of the stage has been specially prepared for lighting effects and movie projection. New areas were added for dressing rooms and storage for props and equipment. Jones heard about a church fund raiser in which a college had donated ninety-six theater seats with foldout tables suitable for seminars. He bought them on the spot and installed them in the front and center section. He's ready to host business meetings.

The facility is available to rent for all kinds of private and public functions. Full movie projection capability is planned in the near future as well as opportunities for organizations to present concerts, plays, festivals, ballet, and orchestra performances. Current projects include cooperation with BSP to produce plays and once a month, the increasingly popular Texas country gospel show hosted by "1 A-chord" and the Jones Family Singers (no relation to David). This group has had a regular national TV program every Saturday evening for years, and a couple of times it has been filmed at the State.

photo courtesy of the State Theater of Gainesville

113

David Jones also purchased the building next to the State. He is proud of the original wood floors they've revitalized. It's almost finished as the Backstage Café, which opens through French doors into the theater lobby. Cathy Lloyd, manager of the State, also plans to manage the café. She said they patterned the soup and salad tearoom after the highly popular Coffee & Pie, Oh My! in Whitewright. She was looking for a front end person and chef at the time I talked to her. "Right now I'm it—janitor, usher, concession operator, promoter, booking agent, you name it," she said while painting baseboards at the café.

When they began to refurbish the theater, there was an abundance of thick paint, which the crew called "free blue." Lloyd explained, "It had to have been free, it was so ugly and there was so much of it. Even the frame of a massive mirror was covered with it. When the frame was stripped to repaint some tamer color, they got a nice surprise. It was brass, and a local company polished it to its original luster.

They were able to save other originals too: handsome moss green tile in the restrooms and a drinking fountain that was a relic of segregation days. "To remind everybody the terrible way people were treated," Jones said, they use it as a planter today.

The seats were so dirty Lloyd said they unbolted them from the floor and took them to a car wash. An upholstery cleaner came in to finish the job. The seats were back in place in time for a special showing to people who had taken an interest. The seats felt dry, but by intermission the whole audience had wet bottoms. For the next act they passed out trash bags to sit on.

"We kept the number of regular seats to 399 because the royalty for producing a stage play goes up at the 400 mark," Lloyd explained. They can, however, bring in extra chairs and wheelchairs so that for other kinds of shows, they can "pack in" 420 to 430.

Gainesville was recently accepted for a four-year grant from the Main Street Program. Lloyd commented that sometimes the BSP group feels like an underdog for lacking "not for profit" status, but they aren't sure they want that. It's a self-reliant group, and now that they no longer have to watch out for bandits and hostile Indians, the Butterfield Stage Players are ready to use their energies to carry you away to the fantasy world of entertainment. —*Joan Upton Hall*

For information:

State Theater
200 E. California St.
P.O. Box 797
Gainesville, TX 76240
(940) 612-2000
statetheater@cooke.net
www.statetheatergainesville.com

Other attractions:

Historical District walking and driving tours
Museums: Morton and Santa Fe Depot
Frank Buck Zoo (Buck was a native son)
Antique & specialty shopping, outlet stores
Brewer Miniature Horse Farm
Lakes, parks, golf, Bulcher ATV & motorcycle trails

Annual events:

Depot Days
Germanfest
Fun Run & Bike Rally
Chamber of Commerce Rodeo

For details and accommodations:

Chamber of Commerce
101 South Culberson
P.O. Box 518
Gainesville, TX 76240-0518
(940) 665-2831 or
1-888-585-4468
info@gainesvillecofc.com
www.gainesville.tx.us

Galveston: Grand Opera House (1894)

photo courtesy of Grand 1894 Opera House

When Will the electrician gave me a backstage tour of the Grand Opera House, he had me stand on the front section of the stage, the part on hydraulics, and sent me to the bottom of the orchestra pit and back. It was the slowest thrill ride of my life. Then when he gave me a display of the incredible lighting system, I could not resist having him take my picture on *that* stage, not just once, but several times. To stand on the same boards that Sarah Bernhardt, Anna Pavlova, Al Jolson, John Philip Sousa, William Jennings Bryan, and countless others had. To stare into the same blinding lights. It stirred awe in my heart for the history I was feeling, and I began to sense the enormity of performing in the grand style.

What is grand? It is not exclusively grand opera. "Grand" refers to the building itself and the scope of the facilities it offers to any type of performance. The Grand started and continues today as a performing arts hall for a variety of venues including motion pictures. On the morning of January 4, 1895, *The Galveston Daily News* raved, "The most important dramatic event in the history of the city took place last evening when the new and magnificent Thespian temple, the Grand Opera House, was formally thrown open to the public."

Galveston as a major immigration port was the cultural center of Texas for several decades. It had outgrown the Tremont Opera House so Henry Greenwall, one of the outstanding theatrical magnates of the country, became the driving force behind construction of a new theatre. Greenwald raised the funds in one day. It only took seven months and $100,000 to build and open the Grand Opera House the first time, but eight million and thirteen years to restore it. It is the only Greenwall theatre still using the original building.

The house was designed with four floors that included the theatre, a hotel, and shops. As a "hemp house," an old sandbag and rope system of pulleys was used for the curtains. It still has some of the original hemp ropes. It had a different type of seating called "parquette" arranged in a curve and steeply stepped downwards towards the stage, giving everyone a clear view. No seat in the house is more than seventy feet from the stage. This theatre was designed to be comfortable with a large ventilator in the ceiling, many windows, and two hot-air furnaces in the basement. The lighting was gas and electricity with electric lights exclusively on stage to reduce the risk of fire.

The most striking feature was the drop curtain, a copy of *Sappho and Her Companions* surrounded by plush draperies. It was among the first theatres to provide running water indoors for the dressing rooms. The trains would come down the alley and unload directly in the back. It had the largest stage in Texas and the Southwest at the time and was one of the first auditoriums to use modern theories of acoustics. Breaking tradition of older theatres, they eliminated corners and flat walls, using curved surfaces and rounded walls to enhance the sound. It housed over 1,600 seats originally with bleachers in the top balcony, a section with a separate entrance for blacks.

Then came "The Storm" in 1900 with over 6,000 deaths in one weekend. The theatre suffered major damage as the entire east stage wall and roof collapsed and the north wall partially collapsed. The west cupola and part of the hotel roof was also gone. Maureen Patton, theatre director, points out that, "It really could have been torn down, but it got restored very quickly. It was up and running the following September 1901. The community realized there needed to be a place the people could meet together. That's the role the public assembly places filled. These folks needed to come together and join hands and get it together again."

In 1924 Atillio Martini, who owned some thirty-eight theatres, bought and renamed it the Martini Theatre. He remodeled the building into a movie house, showing the first full-length movies at that time. But motion pictures did not replace the desire for live performance. In 1937 one of Martini's new Art Deco theatres was named Martini, and the Opera House became the State Theatre until the family divested it to the Interstate Company. By the sixties its popularity gave way to the convenience of shopping mall theatres.

In 1974 the Grand finally closed but only for a few months until Betty Hilton stumbled on it and discovered the quality of its incredible acoustics. Hilton, director of community theatre, and Marc Ligon were looking for a place for live productions and went into the State Theatre. They separated inside and Hilton asked, "Where are you?" Ligon answered, "back here" in a normal voice from the very back of the theatre. She, however, was in the balcony and heard him clearly. Realizing it was a real theatre, not a movie house, she took the project to the arts council. Since major restoration was being done on The Strand, the Galveston County Cultural Arts Council purchased the theatre in the same year it had closed.

The goal was to stop further deterioration with minimum construction to allow it to be used until more money could be raised. The first phase was completed in 1979 with restoration of the stage only. The first performance in 1981 was a centennial revival of Anna Pavlova's choreography. Then money was raised from 1979 to 1986 and restoration began in earnest. The major part was completed by Killis Almond Jr. and was based on information and photos from 1900 to 1920. It involved demolition of all modifications since the early part of the century and returned basically to the post-Storm era. The final phase started in May 1985, when at the end of the Performing Arts Season, it closed for construction.

Stacey Hasbrook photographer

It was a challenge. The woodwork had about eight layers of paint, the seats were aluminum with orange leatherette and corduroy, the walls an institutional green, and there was an overwhelming smell of mold. Now the finished theatre seats a total of 1,008 with an additional 32 that can be added in the orchestra pit. It is completely handicapped accessible. The top two floors of the hotel are apartments, and the second floor is office space. The first floor, the Grand Tier, and the third floor used part of the original hotel for lobby space. They created ramping and restrooms and put in an elevator and fire stair without taking seating. Earl Staley from Houston was commissioned to re-create the painted canvas curtain by using photographs and descriptions of the original. The cupola, however, has never been replaced.

The Grand reopened in January 1986 and has followed the same history, always a roadhouse, not a production house. Eclectic scheduling includes ten to twelve dance troupes, a banjo band, and the world premiere of *Red, White, and Tuna*. Named by the 73rd Legislature as "Texas's Official Opera House" the grand reopening benefit was held ninety-one years after the original, with Steve Lawrence and Edyie Gorme in concert and dancing to the big band sounds of Count Basie afterwards. When it reopened, it was like "the shining star" for the city and continues to be a major tourist attraction.

So the "grand style" continues. As Maureen says, "The people who have come in the last twenty years, who know the history, gather additional inspiration and strength from walking those same boards." A favorite story from the early days tells of the time a circus came, complete with camels. The only problem was they left their fleas, and the theatre had to close for fumigation. This season the theatre comes full circle with Doug Balm and the Texas Camel Corps coming in for storytelling. Maureen, however, made them promise to leave the fleas at home. *—Stacey Hasbrook*

For information:

Maureen M. Patton
2020 Post Office St.
Galveston, TX 77550
(409) 763-7173
mpatton@thegrand.com
www.thegrand.com

Other attractions:

Museums, parks
Historic homes, churches, and buildings tours
Beaches, fishing, golf
Moody Gardens
The Strand
Garten Verein
Rosenberg Library
Texas Heroes Monument
Treasure Island Tour Train
Trolley cars
Bosque County
Conservatory of Fine Arts
Fort Crockett
Norse Settlement

Annual events:

Dickens on the Strand
4th Monday Trade Days

For details and accommodations:

Chamber of Commerce
8419 Emmett F. Lowry Expwy
Texas City-LaMarque, TX
77592-1717

Galveston County Visitors
Center
13001 Delany Road
Texas City-LaMarque, TX
77592-1717
(409) 938-0772

Georgetown: Palace (1925)

photo courtesy of Georgetown Palace Theatre, Inc.

Because we live near Georgetown, the Palace restoration project was the proverbial "wake up call" that prompted the writing of this book. Fortunately, local attorney Gene Taylor heard the alarm years earlier. Like an old friend having surgery, the Palace is fully recovered now, but I was shocked to learn two other theatres on the square had been obliterated beyond archeological detection. Where else had this happened? That's when Stacey Hasbrook and I started our search.

The Palace began as a silent movie theatre in 1925, soon going to "talking pictures." In 1936 the management remodeled it in Art Deco style. The theatre weathered the loss of popularity suffered by "old-fashioned" theatres better than most through the sixties to eighties. It was the longest continuously operating movie theatre in Williamson County. When the multiplexes were built closer, however, the Palace closed its doors in 1989.

Near the end of 1990 its existence as a theatre was threatened. Gene Taylor led a group to form Georgetown Palace Theatre, Inc. (GPT) and purchased it as a nonprofit facility for performing arts. In one week the community, far and near, raised $10,000 for the down payment. Countless

circa 1936, photo courtesy of Georgetown Palace Theatre, Inc.

Opening night 2001, photo courtesy of the *Williamson County Sun*, photo by Deja Elder

hours of volunteer work went into the cleaning and repair work, as well as donations and grants, but only occasional shows and events took place there. In 1997 the Palace was able to hire Tom Swift part time as an artistic director and began playing full seasons.

The following year GPT launched an aggressive campaign to fund a complete restoration and expand its functionality. It was hailed as the community's millennium gift to itself and to future generations, and they targeted the 1936 heyday as the style to restore, only better—much better.

They hired a historic preservation firm from Austin, Gregory Free & Associates, to design a state-of-the-art multipurpose performing arts and meeting facility, with A.T.C. Services of Georgetown as the general contractor. They moved their base of operations nearby into a former dentist's offices. According to an article in the *Austin American-Statesman*, "Financial negotiations and inexperience slowed the project, and construction didn't start until April 2000."

"The hardest part," said general manager Jerry Potter, "is not doing what we do best." Performances have had to take place with simple sets and small casts in mind, using sites such as Sun City's ballroom. But their one annual presentation, *You Can't Do that, Dan Moody*, hasn't missed a year since 1988, the 75th anniversary of the local court case it commemorates. They perform it in the actual courtroom of the historic Williamson County Courthouse where the groundbreaking case was tried. Tom Swift collaborated with district attorney Ken Anderson to turn Anderson's book by that title into the stage play. The subject, Dan Moody, was then a young district attorney from Taylor, Texas, and the story dramatizes how he fought and won against the Ku Klux Klan at a time and place no one believed he could. (This is the same Moody who went on to become state attorney general and then governor of Texas.) The play has become a tradition and brings sell-out crowds.

Another regular user of the Palace is the Georgetown Opry, owned by board member Jimmy Sims. Displaced but not discontinued, the group was looking forward to getting back on the Palace stage, according to an article in the *Williamson County Sun*. Sims regularly showcases local and regional talent but has brought in such big names as Hank Thompson of the Country Music Hall of Fame.

Swift's experience in New York theatre has been an asset. His acting included off-Broadway parts. The prospect of a family brought him and his wife back to Georgetown. His very first job was selling popcorn at the Palace, and he hopes Palace artistic director will be his last.

As a light and sound technician, Jerry Potter has worked for stars such as Willie Nelson, Dolly Parton, Mickey Gilley, and Rotel and the Hot Tomatoes. Looking for a "sabbatical" from 340-days-on-the-road years, he considered the Georgetown Palace at the urging of Jimmy Sims. He used his sound system on an as-needed basis and was voted onto the board of directors. Later, given a choice of working full time with the Palace and a "bigger" job in Austin, he decided, "At the Palace, I can make a difference," and he has.

He referred me to Swift for stories about their resident spirit, "Cecil B. DeGhost." For some people it's just things being moved when they're sure where they put them and have witnesses. For an anonymous observer working alone at the theatre, it was seeing a figure in the balcony run from the stairs to the projection room. He called and immediately went to see about it, noting that the doors were indeed locked. With no exit possible, he could find no one.

Another time while rehearsing for *I Never Sang for My Father*, the light board was on stage for rehearsal purposes. Tom and the co-author of this book, Stacey, who was playing a role, were pointing to where a spotlight would illuminate a scene, saying, "And an area here..." The spotlight came on at that exact spot, no one at the controls. Stacey said that after a moment of silence somebody said, "smoke break," and they all went, whether they had the habit or not.

Whether Cecil B. DeGhost will rejoin them after the theatre is back in operation remains to be seen.

Early stages of construction were held up when they found a sinkhole under the old floor and had to pump the water away. It turned out to be one of the natural springs in the area. The water tested out with no fluoride, petrochemicals, or sewer contaminants. Some have suggested that the Palace bottle their own "Palatial Spring Water" for sale as the old Driskill Hotel in Austin does its spring water, but with all the other delays, most of the board members don't want to talk about it.

Another mystery is that while excavating, they discovered the rock wall of a cistern built to contain the water. It was full of old bottles and other artifacts that will go on display at some time. Makes you wonder why someone would purposely cover a good cistern and lay a concrete slab over it, doesn't it?

Potter showed me other items to go in a display: a bit of molding signed by the trim man and a ceiling board signed by the contractor, tinner, and helper—all in dim pencil. "Now what are the chances we'd find these in all the rubble that was hauled off?" he pondered. It seemed to me the men who built the place knew pride of workmanship would outlast their own lives.

As Potter toured me through the construction zone of the Palace, I visualized the Art Deco designs, barreled ceilings, and dark red leatherette doors. The tiered seating will accommodate 296. Already in place were the enlarged restrooms, concession area, expanded stage, storage space, and dressing areas, not to mention the creation of a much-needed fly-loft.

They took an undamaged carpet scrap to a manufacturer who wove a replica. It will now be shown in the company's samples as something like "Georgetown Palace" pattern.

Before closing, the theatre was in use only about 70 nights a year. Potter expects it, as a multipurpose facility, to be in use 180 nights a year, which will draw more people to the Square, or as the brochure says, "a reason to be, stay, and spend in Georgetown at all hours." Besides a place to hold meeting events and to perform local talent, the facility will be able to attract touring performing artists. It will even go back to showing movies part of the time. During the summers, GPT shows outdoor "Movies on the Square."

The challenge will be for the Palace Theatre Guild to find rehearsal space while the stage is being used by other groups. Luckily, they still have the dentist's office leased for another year.

Renovations were completed in October 2001; it has already hosted "Gershwin Galore" and a cellist/piano concert. The first play will be *Fiddler on the Roof.* All of us who have been saying, "I'll be glad when the Palace opens again," will be in for a treat. We'll not only have our old friend back, but she'll be restored to health and good looks. Hopefully we will all remember that good friends don't thrive on neglect. May she live on into the next century as well, a legacy for future generations. —*Joan Upton Hall*

For information:

Palace Theatre
P.O. Box 1516
Georgetown, TX 78627
(512) 869-SHOW
georgetownpalace@aol.com
www.thegeorgetownpalace.org/

Other attractions:

Historic district walking & driving tours
Family Playscape
Inner Space Cavern
San Gabriel Park
Candle Factory tours
Exhibits at Southwestern University & County Museum
Lakes, specialty shopping, golf

Annual events:

Poppy Festival
Christmas Home Tour & Stroll
Sheriff's Posse Rodeo

For details and accommodations:

Chamber of Commerce
100 Stadium Drive
P.O. Box 346
Georgetown, TX 78627-0346
(512) 930-3535
info@georgetownchamber.org
www.georgetownchamber.org
or
Georgetown Convention & Visitors Bureau
P.O. Box 409
Georgetown, TX 78627-0409
(512) 930-558 or
1-800-436-8696
~ dac@georgetowntx.org

22

Graham: National (1920)

photo courtesy of Don Hall photographer

I could tell I might expect more than just a movie when we parked in front of the National Theatre. Right and left of the movie house are signs: "The Big Chill" ice cream parlor; "The Last Action Hero" delicatessen, and "The Last Pizza Show." What's more, there are three choices of screens behind the simple façade: the National itself, the Staircase, and the Northstar, and they're showing first-run movies. The original owner, "Pic," a master of showmanship, would have approved.

But in 1989 after sitting closed for years, the theatre must have looked more like "The Grapes of Wrath." When David Scott suggested to his wife, Pam, that they restore it, she told me all she could think of was the trash, dilapidation, and smell of mildew. Nevertheless, they bought it, and she didn't warm to the project until they were well into cleaning it up. They found priceless movie memorabilia such as a 1930s movie projector, display cards, congratulatory telegrams from celebrities on the forties reopening, and cans of film. Now the theatre is her love. "It gets in your blood," she said.

Mentored by Ed. Allcorn, who had just left the Paramount in Abilene and taken over management of the Majestic in nearby Eastland, the Scotts began to learn the ropes. Through the Texas Historical Commission, they matched paint, refurbished seats (hand-painting details on the ends), and restored the color scheme of red, tan, and dark blue used in 1940. It had been rebuilt in Art Deco Moderne style following a fire.

In 1920 M. W. "Pic" Larmour opened the National to show silent movies and vaudeville acts. To understand the theatre's history, you need to know the kind of man this first owner was. His son Jim remembers practically growing up in the National, and he began to help his parents at an early age. "[My father] had big shoulders and his arms were as big as my legs are now," Jim said, "and he'd been a first sergeant in an artillery battalion after lying about his age to get in the Army." He started into the theatre business as a troubleshooter, booking vaudeville acts out of Waco. Instead of money, he carried diamonds in a pouch when he traveled.

As owner of the National, he did elaborate promotions for his featured films. Jim pointed out one photo in the lobby of a typical display in which Pic used a costumed mannequin. He made his own posters, copied from box office magazines and press books. Though lettered freehand, the surviving examples look very professional. "But we washed and reused these wooden boards over and over." Jim said.

He remembers celebrities appearing there who included Wild Bill Elliott, Madame Petticlair, a soprano from the Metropolitan Opera, and a man claiming to be Jesse James who scared Jim to death, pulling out his pistol and firing as he talked.

They had game nights, playing "Show Ball," a game Pic had invented. The game was enough like Bingo® to make a company representative come and tell him he had to quit infringing on their patent. When Pic demanded to see the patent, the representative told him it was filed at the home office. Pic pulled out his copyright, saying, "Well, mine's right here," and they had to let him go ahead.

The prizes were usually movie tickets, sometimes money (as much as five dollars), and once it was a free puppy. Today the Scotts display this game and other relics in a game room where they can have kid parties or people can sit at tables.

Ernest Upton photographer

Of all the items left at the National by patrons, the most unusual was a baby. The mother apparently got all the way home before realizing her baby wasn't with her. She called Larmour's house, and he came back and unlocked the theatre to find the tot sleeping in the seat where she had left him.

Pam showed me Pic's printing press where he ran his own handbills for the movies. Being big on civil defense and the Rotary Club, he also printed a newsletter, and after his death, money was found stashed all around in his office where people had sent in for subscriptions and donations, many of their envelopes never opened. The office has been left much as it was.

Jim remembers the lobby floor having to be repainted periodically with a design of squares. He was still a small boy when his father had a terrazzo floor installed by the same people who did the floor in the state capitol. Extending outside around the ticket booth, this floor looks good as new since the Scotts had it revitalized.

Jim Larmour, like his father, Pic, had fun in the theatre business and agrees with Pam Scott that "it gets in your blood," but he finally closed it and retired. "Your blood gets thin after forty-eight years," he quipped.

The Scotts have done an exemplary job of keeping the theatre's original character. The League of Historic American Theatres has honored it, and it's listed with the National Register of Historic Places. In 1995 American Movie Classics screened *Oklahoma* there, and in 2000 the National hosted a special screening of *Fluffy* even though they had to locate a 16-mm film projector to do it. Director Earl Bellamy attended along with his friend Cliff Robertson.

The theatre, however, is definitely in tune with its modern audience too. By taking in adjoining buildings, the Scotts can operate three separate theatres, one of them upstairs. "The Last Pizza Show" opens into the theatre lobby and serves as an intimate dining area, the walk-in vault of the previous business.

"Kids need a place to hang out," Pam Scott says. "But film companies won't let you split a screen." (You can only show the film on the screen you rented it for.) "After they've seen one movie, they have others to see or things to do. Also, parents can see the movie they want to see while their youngsters go to the kid show."

A roll-up screen, on occasion, makes way for school plays and charity benefits.

Pam Scott said if there was one thing she could tell new owners of motion picture theatres, it would be to remember they aren't only museum curators. The business must sustain itself. There are certain seasons the film industry releases big movies because they have learned when the public is occupied with other pursuits. Theatre owners who stay in business must learn when to expect these slow times too and also stay on top of new developments. In the twenties owners had to convert to sound; since the fifties, it would be such innovations as Cinemascope and larger screens, digital surround sound; and now it's stadium seating with rocking chairs and cup holders.

What's next? Pam talked about that too. The cost of converting to digital "will be astronomical." The Association of Theatre Owners wants the film industry to share the expense since they will save dramatically. "For instance," Pam explained, "instead of having to make prints at $1,500 to $3,000 per film, the industry will be able to make a disk that is almost indestructible. And think of the shipping cost difference between those heavy reels of film and a disk."

The first owner of the National knew it took imaginative promotions to bring in the public, and once he got people in, he made them want to come back. He made going to the movies an event. It appears the Scotts know this too, and it's still working. *—Joan Upton Hall*

For information:

The National Theatre
522 Oak
P.O. Box 83
Graham, TX 76450
(940) 549-5358

Other attractions:

Confederate Air Force - Robert E. Richeson Memorial Museum
Fort Belknap (restored buildings)
Lakes, specialty shopping
Graham Drive-in Theatre
Graham Leader (1876)

Annual events:

Texas Outlaw Corvette Club Rally
Ft. Belknap's Birthday Celebration
Seasonal events

For details and accommodations:

Chamber of Commerce
608 Elm Street
Graham, TX 76450
(940) 549-3355 or
1-800-256-4844
grahamcc@visitgraham.com
www.visitgraham.com or
www.wf.net/~grahamcc

23
Granbury Opera House (1886)

Don Hall photographer

I had heard Granbury Opera House was "good," but when I first went to it in 1998, I was hooked as an aficionado. Inside, period chandeliers and wall sconces lit the auditorium. Exposed stone walls, original doors, molding, white-painted balcony rails, and authentic needlepoint seats evoked the 1886 atmosphere of the theatre's birth.

Charming, yes, but the smallness (only 303 seats) gave me pause. Could the cast pull off such an ambitious undertaking as Lerner & Loewe's *My Fair Lady*? How could the stage possibly accommodate the sweeping scenes of squalor in the streets and opulence at the embassy ball? I was in for a surprise. Beautiful costuming, clever use of sets, choreography, superb talent, and the overall skillful direction of managing director Marty Van Kleek pulled it off admirably.

I should have expected it. The Opera House has been featured in numerous state media venues as well as the national ones, *20/20*, *Southern Living*, and *People Magazine*. It has received several grants from the TCA and earned the Governor's Award, a Daily Point of Light Award (for volunteerism) from President George Bush (the 1st), and the Ruth Lester Award for Meritorious Service for Historic Preservation from the Texas Historical Commission. Along with the whole Historic Granbury Square, the Opera House is listed in the National Register of Historic Places and is a *charter* member of the League of Historic American Theatres.

Starting as a trading post on the Brazos River in 1847, the settlement was later named for General Hiram Brinsom Granbury. It became the county seat of Hood County, created in 1866. Carpetbaggers coming in after the Civil War made a law that a county seat had to sell liquor, and before long Granbury had six saloons and seven bawdy houses. The same year the theatre opened as the Kerr Opera House on the second floor of the building it occupies today. It began as a stage for touring groups.

It is rumored John Wilkes Booth did not die in the barn but came to Granbury as John St. Helen. If so, he performed Shakespeare in the Opera House. A 1900s vintage photo shows it sharing the building with a saloon and, as the web site says, "performed many forms of entertainment." Granbury's very colorful past, however, led to the Opera House's demise.

Carry Nation visited this iniquitous venue to establish a Women's Christian Temperance Union. She stayed at the home of an influential family, the Nutts (before the well-known Nutt House ever opened as a hotel and restaurant). She led the townswomen to force the closing of saloons and other businesses connected with them. The Opera House closed in 1911 and lay abandoned and empty for sixty-four years.

Mary Kate Durham, who was the box office manager from the time of the reopening, has been a resident of Granbury all her seventy-six years. She remembers of all the buildings around the square, the Opera House was the last to be restored. She said, "People were always saying, 'Something ought to be done with it.'" Immediately when the owner put it up for sale, Joe Nutt bought it and began looking for backers to restore it as a theatre. He found plenty, but by the time citizens banded together, the

1905, photo courtesy of Granbury Opera House

stone walls were almost all that was left, and the restoration estimate was too high.

Jo Ann Miller, experienced in theatre business, saw it while visiting a friend she had known in New York. As she told Mrs. Durham later, "I said, 'Somebody ought to do something with that building,' and I never got to go home!" Her leadership was welcomed. She hired a new architect to restore the rustic character of the place, expanding it to both lower and upper floors. Then, as Durham said, "She bought herself a pair of khaki pants, shirt, and boots and went to work personally."

They were blessed with backers who could convince other backers. Cynthia Brants pitched in to help, not only painting backdrops and an advertising drop curtain but also drawing in influential contacts in Dallas and Fort Worth. Chairman of the board Clyde Wells, a graduate of Texas A&M, used to call up all his old friends. "When he asked for funds," Durham said, "It looked like an Aggie Muster."

Miller organized the nonprofit Granbury Opera Association, and restoration was completed at a cost of a half-million dollars, all paid for with private money. At last the curtain rose again in 1975 with the melodrama *Gold in the Hills*. Miller stayed on as managing director for twenty-one years, establishing it so well it has apparently suffered no periods of decline since.

The very first summer, she set a precedent that has continued. They hired a director from Tarleton State, who hired college students to do work in training. Durham said the students only earned a pittance and had to live in a terrible dormitory they called "Opera Hilton." The only commode in the theatre was one behind the curtains on stage, and she recalls a sign above it that read, "Do not flush during performances."

While building sets and making costumes, they presented a new show every two weeks—all for the chance to work with seasoned theatre professionals, brought in from such theatres as Casa Mañana in Fort Worth. Today's summer seasons include internship of college students from all over Texas and even from other states. These interns receive housing, a small stipend, and college credit. Van Kleek said, "Our interns play leading roles in our musicals and work alongside performers with Broadway credits. We are very proud that many of our interns have made a career in theatre."

According to Durham, Van Kleek herself was one of the first students. Having moved around a lot as the daughter of a military father, she once told Durham, "Do you realize I've lived here longer than anywhere else?" And Durham remembers, when Van Kleek's dog "Biscuit" died, it was buried on Opera House grounds.

Today the complex consists of the theatre itself, an improved company dormitory, a structure for housing scenes and props, dressing rooms, and rehearsal space, and a building for costume construction and storage of an extensive costume collection. All are debt-free, and the yearly income of the Opera House is $700,000+.

Communities that want to know how to promote their town as a destination for tourism could "go to school" on what the community of Granbury does and how well each business supports the others. People at the Opera House are apt to say something like, "Don't forget our Brazos Drive-in Theatre (a fifties thing, one of the few still in operation) and Granbury Live ('Branson on the Brazos')." The centerpiece of Granbury's success is the Opera House, one of the state's oldest theatres. Its preservation "just in the nick of time" was perhaps what united the town.

Van Kleek told me (in June 2001) the latest thing going on is that a group is coming to research the resident ghost. "You can hear footsteps pacing in the balcony frequently," she said. "Those who have seen him say he wears a white shirt, dark pants, and tall, heavy boots. He never does anything more than move props and play with the lights and door locks."

I've returned to Granbury Opera House many times. I can't promise not to be amazed if I see the ghost, but the versatility of the resident acting company no longer surprises me. It presents dramas, comedies, and musicals. A new show is offered each month, the season ending with a children's Christmas show. So whenever you come here, don't let the small size fool you. This 303-seat dynamo becomes even more impressive when you learn 75,000 people attend per year. The Texas Tourist Commission estimates the Opera House brings in more than $4.5 million to the small town of Granbury each year. —*Joan Upton Hall*

For information:

Granbury Opera House
P.O. Box 297
Granbury, TX 76048
(817) 573-9191 or (866) 572-0881
granburyoperahouse@hcnews.com
www.granburyoperahouse.org

Other attractions:

Museums
Other entertainment venues
Comanche Peak Nuclear Power Plant (exhibits & tours)
Lakes, parks, golf, and novelty entertainment
Specialty shopping
Walking, driving, & bus tours

Annual events:

Fairs and rodeos
Gen. Granbury's Birthday Party/ Civil War Reenactment

Antique Engine and Tractor Show & Historic Light Plant Tour
Candlelight Tour of Homes
Seasonal events every month

For details and accommodations:

Granbury Convention & Visitors Bureau
100 North Crockett
Granbury, TX 76048
(817) 573-5548 or 1-800-950-2212
www.granbury.org

24

Hallettsville: Cole (1929)

Stacey Hasbrook photographer

Ever since opening in 1929, the Cole Theatre has reflected the impact of a theatre on those who choose it and the community it serves. It is something that gets in the blood and doesn't seem to let go. Art Cole originally owned a chain of thirteen theatres including the Cole and the haunted one in Rosenburg, which is now being renamed the Liberty for its original name. According to Bobbie Drozd, who literally grew up in the Cole Theatre, the impact is still an important one. "It was a good place to grow up. We're lucky we have the theatre."

This main source of entertainment for people in Lavaca County had a Spanish décor with murals painted across both sides in the late forties by local artist Mr. Alfonse Schubert. Today the murals are hidden behind the acoustics drapery but intact. Richard Orsak, theatre manager and son of the current owner Bill Orsak, explained that they left as much of the original theatre as they could. They did have the murals tested for asbestos to make sure they didn't have to scrape it all off. It includes everything from cactus to haciendas, verandas, and flowers. Although Mr. Schubert started painting in 1948, Bobbie remembers watching him up on the scaffold finishing in 1951. She also recalls a giant, concrete sequoia statue at each exit sign, but Bill says they were gone a long time ago. Bobbie says they were so heavy "it would have taken an act of congress to move them." Makes me wonder if as a child she had tried.

The Cole opened with 700 seats, and Saturday was the busiest day. Most everyone would come to town for shopping, banking, and watching a movie. Then many would visit the local saloon and spend the night in town. Tickets were twenty-five cents for adults and nine cents for children. Instead of air conditioning, fans would blow across blocks of ice. Blacks were allowed to sit upstairs, which had maybe 500 seats at one time. The Orsaks were told that the theatre may have had up to 1,100 seats, but I can't figure out how.

Caravan tours with stars like Gary Cooper would come. A platform was built for the star and a reception held at the theatre. During the Depression and WW II there was no television so newsreels informed the public. During the Allied invasion of France, people waited in long lines to view actual film footage of the fighting. As an escape from life, the latest releases and films of the latest entertainers singing current songs of that time would play. The theatre had to be remodeled after the 1940 flood, again in the sixties, and one more time after the flood of 1981.

Louis Schott Jr. was one of the first employees and then managed the theatre for a number of years. As a freelance artist he would build special props for films. For *Gone with the Wind*, he built a cannon to display in front of the theatre. With a musical he would put speakers outside and play the music. Traveling magic acts would come, and at least once a year area

photo courtesy of Bill Orsak

photo courtesy of Bill Orsak

schools would watch specific films. Mr. Schott also ran the projector, worked the concessions, sold tickets, and did repairs.

When Bobbie's dad died, she and her mom moved to Hallettsville in 1951 to manage the Cole. She remembers the time when there "darn near was a riot." One night they scheduled a horror show, and it was packed. She sat through most of it but had to go to the ladies room, which unfortunately was located through the cry room. She never made it as the cry room was jammed packed with ladies and men who couldn't take

139

the horror any more. Then the real trouble started. During the afternoon, one of the showmen had found an old prop, a dummy named Old Red, up in the balcony's lost and found. The show was so dark and scary that when he ran down the balcony steps and threw the dummy over the edge into the aisle below, nobody had a clue it wasn't a body. "The people liked to have killed themselves trying to get out, and those in the top ran right into those coming out from the bottom. It was a mob scene outside."

Once she sneaked into the old opera house across the square and found some old seats, a Cole Theatre banner, and some 1919 silent movie advertisements and knew a movie house had been there. Her mother later confirmed that it was where the movie theatre had started before its present location. They tore that building down, and the memorabilia was destroyed. She wishes she'd had the courage to steal it. Likewise, she lost her collection of standup cutouts of stars like James Dean when her mother cleaned out. It was just stuff they had lived with that didn't seem important.

The theatre closed down for a few years in the eighties and didn't open up again until the nineties when the Orsaks stepped in. Bill Orsak was fifteen when he worked as an usher at the Victoria Theatre, but he never forgot the smell of popcorn, the sound of an audience laughing, or the anticipation of opening night. He and his wife immediately fell in love with the rundown theatre and leased it in 1993. It needed a lot of work, but in a month, he, his wife, and their son repaired and repainted the outside, cleaned and refurbished the 200 seats, and installed state-of-the-art sound. They also installed a new screen, a big one that "almost requires moviegoers to turn their heads to catch all the action." On July 31 they opened the sixty-seven-year-old theatre to rave reviews, and steady business quickly convinced them to buy the Cole.

Today the Cole entertains people "in the grand tradition of yesteryear" with a completely automated digital sound system and current films. It is one of only two theatres in the area with such sound. The presentation is extremely good since the theatre size is almost exactly the same as a sound stage, so the surrounds are right on top of the audience and it is exact.

The old balcony is not used now. In fact, old gum on the floor has worked into the wood and looks like petrified bubbles. The original sound booth was too small so they expanded it, and it looks like a brand new room. People from as far as Columbus, Victoria, even El Campo come. It is once again like the entertainment hub of all the little towns. Bobbie agrees. "When *Titanic* came out, I couldn't believe it. There were people clear around the block. It was nice to see the line like that again, like the old times." Future plans call for installing an even more impressive sound system, Dolby Digital Surround® that will help the Cole maintain its technological edge over competitors. "We cater to our customers, and that's what keeps them coming back again and again."

The National Association of Theatre Operators recognized the Cole in 1996 for its role in preserving the community theatre. It may be all cleaned up and new, but the details are a flashback. The lobby ceiling has been dropped down to make it look older, and in the center is a round seating area covered in red with a pole that supports the balcony. When they first opened, Richard says, "people would come by and just hang out and ask to come in and see the place. They always commented on how clean it was." Victoria radio personality Joseph Friar feels strongly too. "I love that theatre. There's nothing like going to a theatre that's been around for so long; I like the nostalgia. It may be a forty-five-minute drive to Hallettsville, but it's worth it . . . I guess you just get spoiled." —*Stacey Hasbrook*

 For information:

Richard Orsak
608 Perth
Victoria, TX 77904
(361) 572-0930
wtraics@cox-internet.com

Other attractions:

Museums, golf
Lay-Bozka House
Texas Championship
Domino Hall of Fame
Texas Fiddlers Hall of Fame
Painted Churches Tour
Railroad Tower
Spoetzl Brewery
Splashway Family
Waterpark

Annual events:

Czhilispiel
Prazska Pout
Tom-Tom Festival

For details and accommodations:

Hallettsville Chamber of Commerce
Highway 77 N.
Hallettsville, TX 77964
(361) 798-2662

25

Hamilton: Texan (1940)

photo courtesy of Lambert Little, Pete and Marge Jordan

Some individuals have a knack for recognizing intrinsic value when they see it. Steve and Robbie Pettit of Steve Pettit Productions fall into this category. When I arrived in Hamilton I discovered the theatre had been bought just two weeks before and was closed for renovation. I thought, "Uh-oh." I got that sick feeling in my stomach until I caught Steve working at the theatre. Not only have they maintained an old church for their company, but now they are looking to restore this theatre closer to the original. And they

142

are ambitious, intending to reopen, at least the downstairs, in about a month. Whew!

Until 1998 Lambert Little was the last of his kind. He projected films by "doing it the old way—striking carbon arcs, watching for cues at the end of each twenty-minute reel, and performing changeovers from one projector to another."

Harold Stroud, who eventually had three theatres and a drive-in at some point, built the Texan in 1940 as one of the first neighborhood theatres built on the concept of making moviegoing easy and pleasurable. It was one with the unique features of a smoking room up in the balcony for the gentlemen and "cry rooms," sometimes called "monkey rooms." Then it burned down in '49.

It was immediately rebuilt and reopened in 1950, the heyday of movies. In version two they added a balcony by raising the roof, created an apartment upstairs, and advertised fluorescent lighting and soundproofing on the walls. And most importantly, it was air conditioned, which according to Little was really "just swamp coolers." At that time the sweetheart seats were coming back into vogue too, and the theatre now had about 750 seats.

Stroud sold to a man named Haney who was really good at marketing. He brought in double features and some films during the week. The theatre was then sold to the Johnsons from Granbury and then to Lam and Elaine Guthry who had it for fifteen years. At this point the local theatre group needed a place to perform, and board of directors members Lambert Little and Pete and Marge Jordan bought it in May 1992 with the agreement that the theatre would be renovated. They spent three months working on it and then had the grand opening in September.

The theatre became a community project. People would just drive by and volunteer to help. They removed the seats and built terraces for dinner theatre. When the seat standards were sandblasted, the local newspaper took a picture and headlined it "Standing Room Only." The good press coverage throughout helped promote the renovation. A volunteer took charge of reupholstering all the seats. They were very forward thinking in some areas such as building sets that were hinged to lay flat on the floor so movies could be shown right over them.

One of the subtle beauties of the work is easy to miss. On the walls is a two-tone painted molding curving up toward the balcony. When they

Texan Theater Fire
Sunday Afternoon, May 8, 1949
Picture made and unscaled by

photo courtesy of Lambert Little, Pete and Marge Jordan

added the terraces, Lambert made metal railings that matched the shape and colors of the molding exactly. "It was fascinating to find out what kind of skills people have. As a result it was a great team building effort and everyone had a vested interest in it."

What brought the most joy though is the eighteen-foot neon sign. Since it was a civic endeavor, the electric company volunteered to send the line crew the next time they were in town to lower and then replace the huge neon sign that needed repair. Since the sign is so tall, it's quite possible they were really a little nervous that volunteers would take out the entire city's electrical supply otherwise. Ray Hall out of Abilene restored the neon part—the actual vacuum tubes—but in order to do that, Lambert had to draw an outline of the entire sign on paper including the placement of letters and sockets so it could be reconstructed at the shop. Meanwhile, Lambert painted the can and screwed in the glass sockets and got the sign hoisted back up into place. Then he had to put a ladder in the back of his pickup in order to reach the marquee to attach each of the bulbs individually. "We lucked out with the neon and getting it right," he chuckled.

When the sign was finally turned back on, he noticed a guy sitting outside in his truck just staring at it. He was a local businessman, and when asked why he was just sitting there, he asked how much the lights on the sign cost. Hearing that each one costs about $50, he confessed that as a kid he had gotten a new BB gun for Christmas and had shot out one of the lights. After feeling guilty for thirty years, he handed over a $50 bill and paid his longstanding debt to society. As beautiful as the sign is to the community, Lambert doesn't feel it is finished. It used to have travelers, which means one light comes on and then the next so it looks like it's moving, and that has yet to be done.

Although the building was purchased with the civic theatre in mind, they kept movies running every weekend for a year to show the civic theatre that it could be run with volunteers and provide a home to the performers. When the year was up though, the theatre group thought that the three managers had done a great job. It was a time-consuming job, so for convenience, they eventually changed the projection over to the platter system. In the last few years, though, running the theatre had become too much to handle as the Jordans own a drugstore in town, and Lambert had become the city manager of Mexia, too far away to run the theatre by phone.

In stepped the Pettits. The new owners want to take the theatre back to near original form with the focus on movies. The first order of business was to remove all of the costumes and props from the theatre days. That cleared a lot of space including the entire balcony. A lady out of Dallas is coming in to clean the screen and new fire extinguishers are being added. The building could use a new metal roof to take care of leaks. Then there's the upgrading of equipment to hopefully include a silver 3D screen and bringing in a consultant to tweak the surround sound and screen speakers. Luckily they paid cash for the building so there is no rent to cover.

Then promotion must be considered. As a production company, the Pettits already have the experience to excel in this area. They will create a slide show called the "Texas Cavalcade" to show before movies and create a CD collection of orchestral music from films. Later they will sell photos as advertisement and have already done a postcard depicting the theatre in the fifties. They are civic minded and will not include any X-rated films in consideration of the audience they will serve. And Steve wants to figure out something really neat to do with the smoking room above the balcony. Security in the area is not strong enough to bring in his production equipment, which would make sense, so another purpose will be created.

Steve describes the building, a surprising three stories high, as "ephemeral" with soft walls, a very intimate space. If everything goes as planned, the Pettits will develop a Texan that will once again be a place to comfortably watch a good movie and build some family memories.
—*Stacey Hasbrook*

 For information:

Steve Pettit
6880 FM 932
Jonesboro, TX 76538-1132
1-888-559-8418
spproductions@htcomp.net

Other attractions:
Hamilton County Genealogy Society Library and Central Texas Research Center
Hamilton County Museum
Pecan Creek Park
Perry Country Club
Bluebonnet Country Club

For details and accommodations:
Chamber of Commerce
204 E. Main St.
Hamilton, TX 76531-1920
(254) 386-3216

26

Harlingen: Municipal (Lon C. Hill) Auditorium (1936)

photo courtesy of Municipal (Lon C. Hill) Auditorium

I have to admire Harlingen's gutsy attitude. This relatively young town takes a backseat to nobody. Whether this trait came from unhesitating actions of Lon C. Hill, the town's founding father, or the lusty pioneers who settled it, it seems to have carried over to Hill's namesake auditorium, which townspeople call simply the "Municipal Auditorium."

When Hill came to the Rio Grande Valley in 1900, there was no city at all, just brush land and ranches. Immediately seeing the agricultural possibilities in this "most fertile valley on earth," he gave up his law practice and bought 41,000 acres of it for the price of $1 to $2.60 an acre. The temperate climate lends itself to a year-round growing season for one crop or another, so he persuaded farmers to come in and cultivate it.

By 1904 Hill had also used his influence to bring in the railroad that linked St. Louis, Brownsville, and Mexico. This construction called for a town site, which Hill named "Harlingen" (after a city in Holland). He also envisioned the Arroyo Colorado River as a barge canal (which it later became) from the Gulf of Mexico to Port Harlingen. The town wasn't incorporated until 1910 with a population of about 600. As late as 1915, frequent "target practice" around the Weller Saloon earned Harlingen the nickname of "Six-Shooter Junction" from railroad personnel.

Yet it couldn't have been all wild. Only yards from his home, Hill built a 1,700-seat auditorium for performing arts in 1936. Early celebrities who performed there included Jeanette McDonald, Nelson Eddie, and John

Lon C. Hill's home (at far left) was next to the auditorium

photo courtesy of Municipal (Lon C. Hill) Auditorium

Philip Sousa. Chairman of the board Charlie Feldman remembers, "My mother took me by the ear to operas at the community concerts, and now I'm glad she did."

Hill's house was moved twice, the first time to be used as a public building. Today it has been restored and furnished as the Hill family home and is part of the Rio Grande Valley Museum Compound (along with the original hospital and 1850s Stagecoach Inn).

The auditorium was remodeled in 1977-'78 and again in '92-93. The most recent renovation included the 13,000-square-foot hall Casa de Amistad (house of friendship). While building around the old façade, they connected the two facilities. This allowed for wheelchair accessibility, double areas for lobbies, concessions, and box offices as well as dressing rooms, restrooms, and an administrative office. Sound and light systems, fire curtains and alarms, and landscaping were also upgraded. In 2000 new seats and carpet were installed downstairs. The next project will be to replace carpet and the seventies seats upstairs.

Harlingen is the only city in the Rio Grande Valley with a city arts division. To govern the facility, the city established an Auditorium Advisory Board (AAB) and hired Arts and Entertainment (A&E) director Joel Humphries in early 2001. He was formerly the executive/artistic director at Brownsville's Camille Lightner Playhouse (built in 1963). A native Texan, Humphries has been performing since the age of six and at the age of thirty-seven has "already pushed the quarter-century mark in show biz." He has acted in over 5,000 performances on numerous stages from Seattle to Dallas and has been a member of such nationally renowned companies as the Village Theatre and Casa Mañana. He has film credits in HBO, Pro-Cuts, and the award-winning film *The Blue Jean Jacket.* One of his and the organization's strongest interests is education, and he has taught numerous children's workshops across the country.

The list of celebrity guests Charlie Feldman rattled off is too lengthy to name here, but later performers have included Victor Borge, Pete Fountain, Debbie Reynolds, and Ann Sheridan. Feldman said he had a chance to visit with some of the stars, and they gave high praise for the Municipal Auditorium. Two of his favorites were Dorothy Lamour, performing *Hello Dolly*, and Louis Armstrong.

The first season opened in 1994-95. Harlingen A&E presents Broadway shows and children's theatre by national touring companies throughout the year. The Spotlight Series features three performances. The Children's Classics Series features three to five performances and has been made available to all children through the schools and to families through Saturday matinees. The auditorium has a seating capacity of 1,746 and hosts Harlingen Community Concerts, South Texas Chorale, and Harlingen Proud (an annual community production). The complex is also a rental facility, but for school events the school is not charged.

In 1998 A&E started a program that raised over $40,000 with 100 memberships in categories for individuals, couples, and businesses. It also established two arts alliances. The Harlingen Arts Alliance serves the various arts and community entities while the Valley Arts and Cultural Alliance serves those in thirteen surrounding valley cities. This service will encourage free or low-cost programs to educate and bring arts of all kinds to the public in general and to children in particular. Public enthusiasm is evident in financial support, sold-out performances, and public expressions of appreciation. Its 2001-2002 series shows great diversity, ranging from *The Buddy Holly Story* to Gershwin's *Porgy and Bess*.

Humphries said, "Our state's arts scene, specifically theatre, is a great and well-kept secret." But Harlingen A&E is doing its best to reveal that secret for South Texas through education and topnotch entertainment.

The Municipal Auditorium hasn't quit since its opening day except to upgrade and remodel from time to time. —*Joan Upton Hall*

For information:

Harlingen Municipal Auditorium
1204 Fair Park Blvd.
Harlingen, TX 78550
(956) 430-6690 or
(956) 430-6699
harlingenarts@xanadu2.net
www.ci.harlingen.tx.us

Other attractions:	Annual events:
Walking & driving tours	RioFest
Museums and Art Forum	Jackson Street Jubilee
Gallery	10K Rio Run
Valley International Airport	Rio Grande Valley Birding
Laguna Atascosa National	Festival
Wildlife Refuge and birding	
sites	**For details and**
Forever Living Aloe	**accommodations:**
Plantation	Chamber of Commerce
White Wings Baseball minor	311 E. Tyler St.
league	Harlingen, TX 78550
Valley Race Track	(956) 423-5440 or
Parks, hike & bike trails,	1-800-531-7346
golf, specialty shopping	visitorinfo@harlingen.com

27

Hillsboro: Texas (1932)

Stacey Hasbrook photographer

When I first drove up to this theatre and parked across the street, it was obvious that it was somehow a little different from the others I visited recently. The doors were already opened and a matinee was in progress. I dodged traffic to get the outside photos and then walked into the lobby where three men suddenly stopped talking and waited. As I introduced myself and explained the project I was working on, they laughed and pointed to the guy in the middle as the one I should talk to. He blushed a little while the others talked about the theatre and then left. Why they seemed to be joking with him became clear. Mike Murray is the new manager and has been in charge about a month. Yet they identified him as the one who could tell me about the place.

The theatre closed in October 2000 for two or three months due to lack of business. All of the recent managers had been young, and their choice of movies did not serve the majority of the community. They reopened to full strength in June 2001 and have been functioning ever since. Hence the business plan in action. The intention was not to restore, but to make the theatre a viable economic project.

Of all the theatres I've visited, the Texas in Hillsboro is probably the one that most resembles modern theatres. The outside is still pretty much the theatre that opened in 1932, but the inside purposefully does not re-create the times. The theatre now belongs to Showcase Cinemas, a small independent chain of four or five theatres including one in Waxahachie, two in Ft. Worth, and the Eastland Majestic. In fact, Mike explained that one of the men standing with him in the lobby was the owner, and the other was the regional manager. They weren't able to share much about the history either.

One story relates that the theatre was actually built three years earlier, but the guy quit, and it stood empty until 1932. At one time there were four theatres on the square, but by 1975 the Texas was the only one left. The auditorium is not original, and only a couple of reminders can be found of the total renovation that occurred in the forties. There is an orchestra pit behind the screens, and the floor is gray, wooden, and slanted like many old movie houses were.

Judy Trantham, whose husband ran the theatre for a long time starting in the fifties, thinks the building was built as a theatre in the late teens or early twenties. The Tranthams had two theatres and a drive-in at the time, but the second theatre was weekends-only during certain seasons: the fall and cotton-picking time. After a while that theatre closed and the drive-in blew away in a tornado. They leased the Texas for about ten years and then bought it. The community was "very supportive at first and then interest waned" so it was hard to keep the business going.

In the eighties the theatre opened only on weekends, and finally they put a "for sale" sign in front of it. It sold the next day. The young woman who bought it promised to keep it as a theatre but after working very hard on it, brought in country music on weekends instead. Soon, the bank repossessed the building. Then Mrs. Trantham believes it stayed closed for a while until Donald Joe Bennett bought and leased it to Mike Self, who tried to make a go of it from his home in Ennis. History repeated with initial support and then lack of backing, so he had to give it up and find another full-time job.

Remodeling in late 1997 created two screens rather than one large one. They have fairly new equipment, and the DTS® sound system was bought from the best theatre in Waxahachie. The house seats 143 on the left, and 103 on the right. Years ago people would stand in the back in a full house. The original seats are stacked haphazardly behind the screen and will probably be given away. Eventually they will probably hook up an automated system where you flip one switch and everything runs. For now though, there is some interest in the old style as Mike's son is his

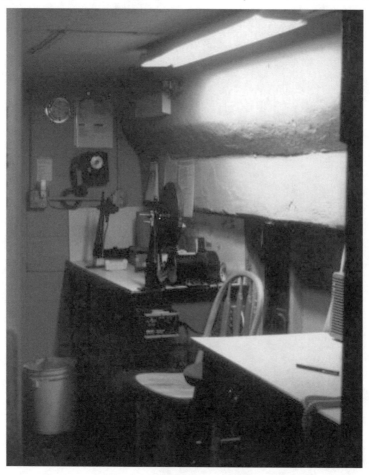

the projection room, Stacey Hasbrook photographer

projectionist and assistant, and he wants to redo the apartment upstairs and live there, as many of the employees of old theatres do. Even Mike's younger son who is fifteen can run the equipment, having learned when he was only nine or ten. There is still some work to do, however. There are no firewalls, and the current walls are deteriorating.

The Texas is open seven days a week with three shows per day during summer. It is a little slower during the school year. Mike is trying to get all first runs "on the break," which means between destinations to larger towns. When they are lucky, some are seen here for the first time anywhere. Once Mike gets a handle on the new job, the theatre should continue to be even more successful and give the patrons the modernized movie viewing that sells. Finally the repetitive cycle of loss may be broken. —*Stacey Hasbrook*

 For information:

The Texas Theatre
Mike Murray
107 S. Waco
Hillsboro, TX 76645
(954) 852-3599

Other attractions:
Museums and lakes, state park
Victorian House driving tour
Over 200 antique dealers
Prime Outlet Mall

For details and accommodations:
Chamber of Commerce
115 N. Covington
P.O. Box 358
Hillsboro, TX 76645
(817) 582-2481
1-800-HILLSBORO
ballard@hillsboro.net
www.hillsboro.net/chamber

28

Jefferson: Ruth Lester Memorial and Playhouse (early 1900s)

Don Hall photographer

The Jessie Allen Wise Garden Club of Jefferson grows a lot more than flowers. It owns and promotes the Excelsior Hotel, railroad magnate Jay Gould's private railroad car, and the Jefferson Playhouse and Ruth Lester Memorial—three of the best-known tourist attractions in a town that calls itself "the B&B Capital of Texas." The Excelsior Hotel now has a "Diamond Bessie Suite" as well as other rooms named for famous guests—two U.S. Presidents and Lady Bird Johnson, who grew up in the area, to name but a few.

When the Playhouse came into existence is not an easy question; it's so interwoven with the building's unusual past. The residence was built in 1860 by Robert W. Nesmith, a contractor of stagecoach lines. Nine years later the Sisters of Charity bought it to be St. Mary's Convent and Hospital. With the number of Catholics living in Jefferson, it seemed feasible to open a parochial school, but only five students enrolled and three of them were Protestants.

In 1876 the Sinai Hebrew congregation bought it for their rabbi to live in and added a synagogue separated from the house by a mere walkway. From the street it appears to be one huge house. The synagogue, which supported dramatic and literary events, closed about 1900, but several Jewish families maintained it.

The garden club president, the late Ruth Lester, had a daughter, Mary Evelyn Martin, who had created a drama about a famous murder trial in Jefferson and was looking for a staging place. Ruth saw the vacant house and synagogue as both a heritage to protect and a place for a small theatre.

The garden club became trustees in 1954 under the leadership of Ruth Graham Lester. It became what it is today: house and/or auditorium available for dramatic and literary events, variety shows, weddings, and other gatherings. Since 1955 its major presentation, *The Diamond Bessie Murder Trial*, has given six performances a year to a full house. It is held in conjunction with the annual spring "Pilgrimage," a commemoration of the town's amazing history. Consider a simplified view of that history.

To look at the map it seems impossible for Jefferson to have ever been an inland shipping port, second only to Galveston. But large steamboats did once travel from New Orleans up the Mississippi River, then the Red River, and finally what is today a cypress creek navigable only by small boats. It was a different story from about 1844 to 1903 though. So many people were coming and going the population was hard to count. In its heyday, various sources reported it at anywhere from 7,300 to 30,000. The bustling town had thirty-two taverns and numerous hotels.

What happened to bring this about and what ended it? In 1811 an earthquake deposited a log jam (or "raft") that effectively dammed the Red River near tiny Shreve's Landing (later Shreveport), Louisiana. Water diverted by this dam found its way around, raising the level at Jefferson. As a Confederate port, it played an important role during the Civil War and then was heavily occupied by Yankees during the Reconstruction.

The U.S. government decided to have the Army Corps of Engineers clear access to the upper Red River for the greater good. By 1873 the invention of nitroglycerine made it possible. Unfortunately for Jefferson, the city fathers had refused a major railroad line, so Jefferson was left literally "high and dry" while Shreveport boomed.

Meanwhile legends grew around the port city. One is documented as the major murder trial that inspired Jefferson Playhouse's *Diamond Bessie Murder Trial.* Here's the story: About 1870 Abe Rothschild, son of a wealthy jeweler family, came upriver from New Orleans on business. Accompanying him was a shady lady, the beautiful Bessie Moore (born Annie Stone). Legend says the couple stayed at the Excelsior Hotel.

Despite frequent arguments, Bessie and Abe went on a picnic. He later came back alone, wearing the diamonds she had been wearing. He claimed they had agreed to split up, and she had boarded a stagecoach to go home to Cincinnati. Then ten days later her body was found with a bullet through the temple. The local sheriff went after Abe in Cincinnati, killed his two bodyguards, and brought him back to jail, which was to become Abe's home (without bond) for the next seven years through a series of trials. He made the best of the situation, however. He persuaded his jailers to remove the bars from adjacent cells for expansion, had the walls paneled in walnut, moved in luxurious furniture, and ordered his meals specially catered.

Just how shady Bessie had been is uncertain, but she wore numerous diamonds given to her by other gentlemen besides Abe Rothschild. Chairperson of the building Carol Randle says the play script refers to her as a "dramatic actress"—a shady enough profession in those days. Vernon Randle says the script used transcripts from the trial, and two of the recent actors have been Texas Supreme Court Judges, William Cornelius and Ben Grant.

This play, written by Mrs. Lawton Riley, takes place the last day of the trial in 1877. In recent years director Margaret Jones says different actors have given a more melodramatic flavor to the performances, but veterans keep it from crossing the line.

Vernon Randle explained that in 1877, one had to be a male landowner to sit on a jury, and there were few enough that the Rothschild family was able to "buy" all who fit that description. Given those conditions, the outcome of the trial isn't hard to guess.

On the day I toured the theatre, I had just missed the play, and there were stage sets at either side of the rich wooden church altar (which makes a surprisingly good court scene). I could see how well it would work for jail, graveyard, and court scenes. Actors such as Bessie's spirit visiting Abe in jail can slip into a curtained area through the same door the rabbi used to enter from his living room. Jurors file through the audience.

Pews, dating from 1876, still seat about 130 people, and the balcony, where the women used to sit, can accommodate 35 more. Original gas wall sconces and a center chandelier are outfitted for electricity these days to make them compatible with air conditioning. Margaret Jones said the chandelier was given to the Playhouse by the Episcopal church after it was found in their attic, and she pointed out that the design matches that of the sconces. "Maybe it was here originally," Carol Randle suggested. A prominent member of the Episcopal church, Ruth Lester might well have stored it there during renovation.

Margaret Jones remembered also an early photo showing a pipe organ on stage, but this instrument now sits in the living room of the house. The garden club has enlarged and modernized the bathrooms and kitchen to make the site viable for other events. Lester's daughter gave a gazebo as a memorial to her father, and it graces the lawn of the Playhouse entrance and back of the house. An ambiance of the Old South permeates the area.

In 1971 the house was entered on the National Register of Historic Places. A Texas historical marker tells that Governor John Connelly appointed Mrs. Dan Lester (Ruth) to serve on the Texas State Historical Survey Committee from 1964 to '68. And in 1966 she was honored by Lyndon B. Johnson at the White House for her important achievements. Her portrait hangs in the house, testament to her fostering a garden club full of women who have a green thumb where it comes to growing ideas.
—*Joan Upton Hall*

 For information:

Excelsior House
211 W. Austin
Jefferson, TX 75657
(903) 665-2513 or Fax: (903) 665-9389
www.excelsior@jeffersontx.com

Don Hall photographer

Other attractions:	Annual events:	For details and accommodations:
Boat rides (Caddo Lake, Cypress Bayou)	The Pilgrimage	Marion County Chamber of Commerce
Historic homes tours	Civil War Reenactment	Jefferson, TX 75657
B&B Capital of East Texas	Marion County Fair	(903) 665-2672
Carriage tours	Seasonal events every month	www.jeffersontx.com
Museums		
Parks, lakes, golf, specialty shopping		

29

Llano: Lantex (1927)

Ernest Upton photographer

My co-author Stacey Hasbrook grew up with San Antonio's Majestic. For me, it was the Llano Lantex, and, for all the Majestic's—well—majesty, I wouldn't trade experiences for the world. As much as going to see a movie, a small town theater is a gathering place to see people you know. There, popcorn is more than popcorn, seeming to trigger a mystical connection between viewer and screen. Movies and live theater have given me some of my greatest pleasures.

People in the theater business are rarely driven by a profit motive. Nina and Chuck Harris, who run the theater, said, "What keeps us going is to see people having a good time." Cheryl and Jerry Crabtree of the Llano

Community Performing Arts group (LCPA) agreed this was the reason the city gave LCPA the money to buy the theater when they reopened it in 1997. The group having been organized under a different name since '89 had established credibility.

For the Saturday Opry Night, a lot of people come who aren't able to drive to another town. One regular patron has to be brought in a wheelchair. Nina Harris said he once kissed her hand and said, "You give me a reason to get out of the nursing home."

A family drove over from Austin so their children could experience going to an old movie. At the snack bar, Nina told the man he owed $13.75, and he insisted she "ring it up" again. Ready for a complaint, she did and came up with the same price. "My-y-y mercy!" he said. "In Austin this would have cost me fifty bucks."

More often, children from a little town don't go to movies at all, so Chuck Harris decided to give them that experience. About three times a year, the Harrises arrange with the school to bring students in groups by the busload. For $1 each they get popcorn, a small drink, and a movie. Cokes and popcorn are lined up to hand to each child going through the door. They can run a group through in an hour and 45 minutes—just time enough to let the next group repeat the process. Nina says you can tell this is the only time many of them get to go to a movie. As one little boy said, "Man! That's the biggest TV screen I've ever seen!"

You might say the original building started out in 1880 as an entertainment venue of sorts as the Parlour Saloon and a barbershop. From about the turn of the twentieth century to the late twenties all kinds of other enterprises took their turns there. In 1927 George Shaw tore the old building down and built the Lantex Theater. Other owners operated it from time to time, Rex Wooten longest of all.

Wooten did various promotionals to get people into the theater. My earliest memories include the Saturday shoot-em-ups complete with cartoons and a short serial. Later on after I was too old for the bargain, I heard kids could buy a ticket for one Gandy's milk bottle top and a quarter.

When the Lantex burned in 1951, I was a freshman in high school, and I remember the whole town being devastated. High school kids drove to Burnet to see a picture show, but Mr. Wooten soon rebuilt a totally modern Lantex. How fancy it was! Grownups thought the soundproof "cry room" was the greatest. The youth were just glad to see the balcony again.

photo courtesy of Martha Gilliland Long and the Llano County Museum

In the mid seventies the Lantex operated under new management, but it closed for good in '82. Working on this book gave me an excuse to pay the restored Lantex a visit. In 1997 Chuck and Nina Harris agreed to manage the theater for LCPA using their own equipment but since then have become the lessees. I was glad to see the building looking great, but getting it that way must have been no easy matter. In the projection room, the Harrises and Crabtrees had found carbon dust an inch thick from the old-style projectors, not to mention rat droppings they could have sold by the pound as fertilizer. They at least got some laughs from the cans of old horror films still there.

Did they find any ghosts as well? Chuck said "no," Cheryl and Nina said "yes," and Jerry wasn't talking. Both Nina and Cheryl have heard someone walking around upstairs when no one could have been there. Back in Rex Wooten's day, if the kids in the balcony were acting up, he'd kick the bottom step with his heel to settle them down. Occasionally the ladies have both heard that sound. I like to think if it's Mr. Wooten, he'd approve of what they've done with the Lantex.

All 400 of the seats in the auditorium, vintage fifties, were still good after cleaning them up, but the forty-six in the balcony, vintage '27, had to be replaced. They have kept the cry room and enlarged the concession stand. Local artist Beth Fry completed the mural on the backstage wall just in time to picture in this book. She will eventually do the walls of the auditorium. Chuck is proud of his equipment. The sound system and screen are new. He got the rebuilt projector in Las Vegas along with platters for winding the film.

art by Beth Fry, Jerry Crabtree photographer

Friday through Monday the Lantex shows currently popular movies in Dolby® surround sound. Once a month comes the highly popular Opry on a night that doesn't conflict with the movie. Area musicians usually furnish the talent, but sometimes more widely known stars have entertained. When the Lantex hosted Kitty Wells, 1,000 people crowded in for two performances.

For the 85th birthday celebration of Floyd Tillman ("It Makes No Difference Now"), they brought in all the chairs they had room for and still had people standing all around the walls. Celebrities showed up unannounced too, Willy Nelson, Johnny Bush, and Johnny Gimble to name but a few—all to honor Mr. Tillman. Cheryl said, "The only way we could have gotten another person in here would have been with Vaseline and a tongue depressor."

The building is available for organizations to use. At least once, a town meeting was held there to discuss a vital bond issue. LCPA has not regularly produced plays there, but it is an option. Certainly there's no shortage of talent: Martha Long for one, the historian who found the old photos for us. She and her husband, Hudson, have both played in TV commercials and bit parts in Hollywood movies.

The Harrises like to get to know the people who cross their threshold. If they haven't met you, they'll introduce themselves. Out-of-towners have been known to come back whether they know what's playing or not. In all these years, show business at the Lantex has been more about giving people pleasure than getting rich. —*Joan Upton Hall*

For information:

Lantex Theater
P.O. Box 102
Llano, TX 98643
(915) 247-2524

Other attractions:

Historic walking & driving tours
Enchanted Rock
Vanishing River Tour at Canyon of the Eagles
Longhorn Cavern
Llano County Museum & art galleries
Fall Creek Vineyards (tours)
Lakes, parks, hunting, golf, & specialty shopping

Annual events:

Seasonal events almost every month
Llano County Rodeo

For details and accommodations:

Llano County Chamber of Commerce
700 Bessemer
Llano, TX 78643
(915) 247-5354
contact@llanochamber.org
www.llanochamber.org or
llanotx.com

30

Lubbock: Cactus (1938)

photo courtesy of Don Caldwell Productions

The Cactus Theater Corporation makes no bones about it. It has no intention of being a nonprofit enterprise. It operates under the premise that artists shouldn't be asked to perform free, and every performer who walks on stage gets paid. For the managerial staff, it's a different story. Because they believe in the project and consider it an entrepreneurial venture, several, such as assistant Linda Ashley, have worked free for two years. President and general manager Don Caldwell and his wife, Terri, have put in countless volunteer hours, and both are musicians themselves (Terri's specialty, "Always Patsy Cline"). Other investors volunteered too, wanting to get the program started. The company has never asked for a single grant.

Can drives collected metal for war effort. Photo courtesy of Don Caldwell Productions

Historical preservation of the building was only part of the goal although they succeeded at that too. It's listed on the National Register of Historic Places. "Lots of buildings are renovated," said Caldwell. "But if nothing's going on, the building goes back downhill. Since 1971, when I was primarily in the recording business, I saw great artists leave West Texas to go wherever they could get careers going because the community wouldn't support them." He realized it wasn't so much the community's refusal to invest in them as not knowing they were there. Artists needed a nurturing environment to showcase their talent.

It turned out nobody could be prouder of its own than Lubbock citizens (and tourists who come to see for themselves what this is all about). At 8th and Avenue Q, you can visit the Walk of Fame honoring West Texas natives who have contributed significantly to the entertainment industry. For instance, according to the *Texas State Travel Guide*, plaques include Mac Davis, Waylon Jennings, Jimmy Dean, Bobby Keys, Ralna English, G.W. Bailey, Barry Corbin, four members of the Crickets, Tanya Tucker, Joe Ely, Roy Orbison, Bob Wills, the Gatlin Brothers, Thomas Leslie "Snuff" Garrett Jr., and members of the Maines Brothers Band. At the center of it all stands a bronze statue of Lubbock's favorite son, Buddy Holly.

You can find the Cactus at the corner of 19th and Buddy Holly Avenue, as shining and new looking as the day it opened in 1938. But it took an enormous effort to bring it back to respectability in 1993 after it had been closed for thirty-five years.

The original Cactus had 720 seats, "with washed-air cooling and a marquee which featured 750 feet of neon lighting." It was Lubbock's seventh theater of the seventeen in town by 1957. Then TV and six new drive-ins closed down the walk-ins, the Cactus included.

The Caldwells had bought the building with the intention of making a recording studio of it. There were no entertainment venues in the entire block and only one in the district, the Depot Restaurant. Owner Ronnie Thompson started the whole concept of turning the Depot District into an area for entertainment, and the Caldwells decided a recording studio seemed detrimental to the idea. The district today has turned several historic buildings into nightclubs and restaurants, featuring a variety of live music and fabulous food. The Caldwells have turned the Cactus into an important part of the concept.

Don Caldwell organized Cactus Theater, Inc., with a group of area investors. Granite blocks pave the front walk, and the names engraved on those blocks all represent contributors. Making it into what it is today, however, required a giant risk. "Every night," Caldwell said, "I woke up thinking, 'Man, you have lost your mind!'"

By 1993 the theater's original appearance was a mystery. The marquee was gone, and the front had no walls although the balcony still stood. It was nothing but a big empty box, and to get historical designation, Cactus Theater, Inc. had put the façade back as it had been (the interior could be changed somewhat with permission). They studied old photographs and figured out the dimensions of the ticket booth by marks on the concrete where walls had been laid out. The original tile had been stuccoed over, but when the restoration workers cleaned it, they were able to match what they needed for replacements. They copied the marquee from photographs, and they kept anything inside they could.

Caldwell said, "I make sure the audience and performers are equally comfortable." Space is limited in the wings, so when they have a large cast, they move unused props and equipment to a garage at the end of the block where they also keep most of their sets.

The renewed theater accommodates fewer patrons, 420, but it does so more comfortably. All the technical equipment was moved downstairs at the rear of the auditorium. The balcony seats had been so cramped Caldwell took out every other row. That has made the balcony a premium place to sit, and gracefully curving staircases lead the way to it.

Viewing the wall murals is especially satisfying from the balcony. It looks as though the seats meld right into the landscape of Caprock Canyon, painted by artist John Russell Tomasson. Soft-hued clouds painted above the mesas and "stars" lighting the ceiling add to the illusion that night is about to fall, and when the performance begins, it does.

Ernest Upton photographer

Some pretty big names have spent time on the Cactus stage including Natalie Maines, who became a member of the "Dixie Chicks." Caldwell said her father, Lloyd Maines, worked with him in the recording business from 1973 until five or six years ago when Maines moved to Austin.

Others who have performed at the Cactus include Michael Martin Murphey, Gary Morriss, Donnie Allison, Bill Haley's Comets, Buddy Morrow with the Tommy Dorsey Orchestra, and Guy Lombardo's Royal Canadians.

The typical annual schedule includes live concerts in the form of "Nostalgia Nites" (featuring music of the forties to the seventies), "The

Cactus Family Christmas Celebration," "Broadway Favorites," "Old Time Gospel Nite," and "Talent Search Concert Series." Other favorites are the musical productions such as *The Buddy Holly Story, Always Patsy Cline, Bye, Bye Love: The Everly Brothers Story,* and *West Texas Music! The Play.* They also do plays, many directed by popular radio personality of the area Jane Prince Jones, who was formerly the managing director for Post's Garza Theater.

While I was there, they were rehearsing for *Fiddler on the Roof,* and I met Tim McIntire, who played the lead role. He did me the favor of delivering one of my favorite lines. Talking to God about their hardships, the character says, "I know we're your chosen people, but sometimes couldn't you choose someone else?"

Caldwell likes to tell the story of two young Nashville songwriters in town for a clinic. They came over to take a look at the Cactus and were amazed to discover their idol, Sonny Curtis, was playing there. "We've been trying to meet Sonny Curtis for ten years in Nashville," they said. They finally managed it at the Cactus.

I suspect the Caldwells and other investors sleep better at night lately. The theater is making a profit while not only looking gorgeous, but having a comfortable aura about it as well. Best of all, Lubbock citizens have made a great audience for the performers the Cactus is launching. —*Joan Upton Hall*

For information:

Cactus Theater
1812 Buddy Holly Avenue
P.O. Box 2526
Lubbock, TX 79408
(806) 762-3233 or
(806) 747-7047
DonCaldProd@aol.com
www.cactustheater.com

Other attractions:

Buddy Holly Center, statue, and walk of fame
Historic Depot District
Amusement parks
Museums & Wind Power Center
Wineries
Breedlove Dehydration Plant tours
Lakes, parks, golf, specialty shopping

Annual events:

Buddy Holly Festival
Panhandle-South Plains Fair
Miss Texas USA Pageant

For details and accommodations:

C of C / Convention & Visitors Bureau
1301 Broadway, Suite 101
P.O. Box 561
Lubbock, TX 79408
(806) 747-5232 or
(806) 761-7000 or
1-800-692-4035
info@lubbockbiz.org
www.lubbocklegends.com

31
Mason: Odeon (1928)

Stacey Hasbrook photographer

Mason is obviously a town that cares about the meaning of community. After my tour of the theatre, I decided to stroll around the square to the Chamber of Commerce office on the other side. They were closed, but a small metal clip on the doorframe notified visitors why. Then I noticed nearly every business had the same kind of clip outside with the same notice: "Funeral Notice: Pearl Mary McWilliams, Age 105, Died July 4, 2001." I do not know who Pearl was, but evidently after that long a life, the whole town needed to know of her passing. That type of community explains why, when the Odeon was on the brink of extinction, the entire town rallied to make sure it didn't happen.

The name of this theatre comes from the term "odium," which was a small ancient Greek or Roman building used for public performances. It made perfect sense to save the theatre that premiered *Old Yeller* in 1957. The author, Fred Gibson, came from Mason, and it was a big deal for such a small town. Disney executives were flown into Austin and driven out for the premiere. Recently, the town held a huge *Old Yeller* celebration, which included the unveiling and dedication of a statue in front of the town library by Laura Bush on October 2, 1999. Disney allowed the movie to be shown again, and some of the cars in town still have the *Old Yeller* bumper stickers proudly displayed.

Thom Canfield, executive vice president of the Mason National Bank, moved to Mason in 1992 and quickly became a part of the life around him. In 1994 the owner of the theatre had decided to close down and turn the theatre into some kind of retail space. He had operated it for some seventeen years, and although it was still functioning, it did not run on a reliable schedule and no improvements were being made. He had converted the balcony into an apartment and was living there. He also had started leveling out the original floor so the town knew something was imminent.

A committee formed to determine what to do. The first step was a survey of citizen preference, and the overwhelming response was, "Yes! Keep the theatre." The owner was agreeable to selling, so a nonprofit corporation, the Odeum Preservation Association, was born. The bank loaned the money, and the townspeople filled out pledges to support with money, supplies, or labor, whatever would be needed. The association began hosting fund raisers from barbecues to garage sales.

When I asked Thom if his part was mostly business since he worked at the bank, he smiled and said, "Mostly no business." There were five people on the committee that agreed to buy the building and committed to raising the money. "It's been a labor of love." The public has been very involved all along, always a broad based support with no significant single benefactor. The only frustration has been the slowness of receiving grants to work on the building.

The renovations are ongoing, and over $200,000 has been raised in the last five years. The theatre has a new metal roof, and the building is totally paid for, which is way ahead of many renovation projects. The lobby had almost no restroom facilities, so most of the work was done in there first and the needed handicap access was added. The entrance has also been redone, the whole building painted, the water-damaged ceiling tiles fixed, and air conditioning added in 1998. Thom grinned when he commented, "When we got this place air conditioned and got comfortable seating, everybody thought they'd died and gone to heaven."

They looked into restoring the seats, but they were only eighteen inches in width and not as comfortable as the modern version with cup holders. The old seating was completely removed to work on the inside of the building, and for two or three years they showed movies "BYOC." The community knew that when the marquee said "BYOC" that meant, "bring your own chair," and the lawn chairs would line up. Then they put in about 200 new seats in 1999.

There has been great effort to make the theatre look like the original in spite of the fact that the theatre never had any particularly interesting features to preserve. Unlike many other old theatres, there are no little hidden cubbyholes or niches to crawl around in. The façade is the most interesting feature, and there are some sconces that will be redone. The main attraction involves the neon marquee. Thom reminisced, "When the inside was still horrible, we had that beautiful neon outside which sparked the town's interest. The night we turned it on—it probably had not been on for twenty years—people just drove around for hours to see it."

Stacey Hasbrook photographer

At first they continued the use of carbon arc projectors, which took two people to run smoothly. Thom swears it was a lot of fun. They finally decided to take it out in 1996 because it was difficult to operate and the parts were getting harder to find. Now they have new equipment and good sound. The theatre still houses a single screen, perfect for Mason.

Carbon arc machine retiring to museum. Stacey Hasbrook photographer

For the last two or three years Keven and Tennile Kothmann, who live in the area with their children, have managed the theatre. They had contacted the association earlier but were informed they could not make much money. About six months later they offered to do the theatre part time along with other jobs so they could live in the area. Since the project was designed to be nonprofit, the couple leases out the building. It pays enough to cover the operating expenses and insurance for the Preservation Association, and the extra is their income. According to Thom, "They are very attached to the theatre, and having managers makes it work much better than relying on volunteers."

Unlike some renovations, this one includes plans for the old equipment. The seats that were halfway salvageable were sold to the public.

Since there is no room in the theatre to display artifacts properly, two seats with a little art deco design on the end and the Motiograph projector when it is put back together will be placed in the Mason museum. And then it's into phase two, which will take another couple of years to complete.

The association hopes to raise the money to build up the stage. The people of Mason want to do live theatre and have chamber music. These two additions, however, mean more money than originally thought. Curtains will have to be placed in front of the stage, and more sound equipment will be bought. Since there is only an eight-foot space behind the screen, the association is looking into purchasing the property behind the theatre for changing rooms and storage. Killis Almond is helping with the plan and advising on stage renovation. His study will include a cost estimate to help determine what grant or fund raising will be needed. A slide projector will also be added for pre-show reminders that the theatre is nonprofit, and some art deco will be added but not carried out extensively.

For the past two years the theatre has managed to open four nights a week, and once a month they have a live country music show with different entertainers as well as other special events. Thom was quick to point out how human nature tends to take things for granted. "Now that it's up and running, nobody remembers that it almost closed. The children growing up now won't know how close we came to losing it." I think again about those small metal clips all over town for posting notices and smile.

Somehow I don't think the elders in a town of such community spirit will allow that to happen. —*Stacey Hasbrook*

For information:

Keven or Tenille Kothmann
300 Moody St.
Mason, TX 76856
(915) 347-9010
kkothmann@hctc.net

Other attractions:
Fort Mason
Mason County Museum
Seaquist Home
Fort Mason City Park
Comanche Creek Golf Course

Annual events:
Mason Roundup-July

For details and accommodations:
Chamber of Commerce
108 Fort McKavitt
P.O. Box 156
Mason, TX 76856
(915) 347-5758
masoncoc@hctc.net
www.masontxcoc.com

32

Midland: Yucca (1929)

photo courtesy of Midland Community Theatre, Inc.

"Keeping mum" was the last thing the Summer Mummers needed to do when they heard a demolition team was about to attack the old Yucca Theatre, vintage 1929. Economic development has a tendency to bulldoze historic structures unless somebody says, "Wait!" And that's what Midland Community Theatre (MCT), of which the Summer Mummers program is a part, did. They convinced the owner to grant them a long-term lease, and eventually they bought the building.

The Summer Mummers, a tenacious melodrama group, completed its 53rd season in 2001, despite a history of having to perform in everything from someone's backyard to a Quonset hut. At last the Yucca offered them a permanent home, and a Texas Medallion secured it. The group and the building have been featured in *Southern Living* and other magazines. By invitation, the group has toured Ireland. While movie star Kathleen Turner was living in Midland in 1971, she even played the villain in that year's melodrama.

So in the spring of 1981 MCT and volunteers rolled up their sleeves and went to work cleaning and restoring the old building. Considering it had been closed since 1974, the interior must have looked like the burial tomb of an Egyptian pharaoh. Sitting in the darkness all that time had been a wealth of gilded borders, scrollwork, Assyrian winged sphinxes, and bull heads atop pillars.

It took razor blades to scrape off the muck from the lobby tiles. They polished the golden details and repainted lions and pillars and re-stenciled

photo by Brian Hendershot and Bruce Partain for the Midland Chamber of Commerce

photo by Brian Hendershot and Bruce Partain for the Midland Chamber of Commerce

the designs on the papyrus ceiling and wall lamps. They brought in professionals to build a tiered floor for cabaret seating downstairs that seats 450. The balcony seats about 150. Today dinner theatre is an option at the Yucca, and it is sometimes rented out as such. The façade was restored to its original gothic style.

By July the Summer Mummers opened with their annual melodrama, *2001: A Space Oddity* or *The Sky's No Limit in Midessa, Texas*, written by Linda Bond and Bruce Partain. Each year, due to double casting, this all-volunteer group requires a cast and crew of about 120.

Every performance changes as the script incorporates news events and jibes at well-known Midland individuals. Also if a business treats its employees and customers to a showing, the actors make references to these. In *Texas Living* Gary Ford explained that people didn't "wear a coat and tie. In fact, many are dressed just plain weird. They've come to be kids again, to whoop and holler and throw popcorn." He also advised parental discretion for the PG rated shows, "just naughty enough not to be nice for children."

The Mummers Band sits in the orchestra pit. Between acts, there are olios, short vaudeville-style skits, songs, etc. Between other acts, they show *Movieola,* a Keystone Cops fashion video featuring familiar Midland landmarks and cameo appearances (George Bush was on it once while he was governor). Part of the fun comes earlier in the year when costumed actors appear unexpectedly with a cameraperson in tow, making clips to put in the *Movieola.*

In *M Magazine,* Mary Frances Beverly described the melodrama as "part Victorian morality play, part Three Stooges, and part barrelful of silliness." It must work.

Executive director Tim Jebsen says they sell about 12,000 tickets over the thirty performances (Friday & Saturday nights & some Thursdays). During a season they sell over $30,000 worth of popcorn to throw at the villain, about 1,000 sacks a night, not to mention cokes, beer, T-shirts, novelties, and raffle tickets. It's MCT's major fund raiser, and they love their rowdy crowds. Jebsen said, "It helps pay for our educational program and all other productions."

MCT owns the newer Cole Theatre too, which keeps a busy schedule. Both theatres are available for rental for public and private organizations (dance recitals are especially popular). Touring groups also frequent the theatres, and MCT produces its own musicals and dramas as well. Long-time member Dottie Fox recalls the Quonset hut years and a whole string of directors.

Everybody talked about Art Cole, after whom the newer theatre is named. He is also the founder of the International Association of Community Theatres. MCT director during the forties, he initiated many of the ideas that have become traditions. "We need a fund raiser," he said and along with others, he thought up Summer Mummers. It opened with the vaudeville classic *The Drunkard.*

Another of Cole's ideas was the belief that children should perform in children's shows. So MCT holds a theatre school for elementary through high school students. Students must audition to join the Pickwicks, and shows are presented to fourth and fifth grade students. No wonder Midland has such a theatre-hungry audience. They're brought up that way.

When I contacted Cole (now an artist living in Santa Fe), he said, "I had a plan: We would not sell season tickets. We would sell memberships with admission privileges to the plays and voting rights in the governance of the corporation . . . . I compared membership versus the season ticket as the difference between owning shares of General Motors stock and driving a Chevrolet. It worked."

He went on to say, "I explained my plan and my budget. The latter called for a three-month guarantee of $200 a month salary to me . . . 'If we don't have the year's money in the bank in three months, you owe me nothing.'

"'Hell, you can't live on $200 a month in Midland' came a booming voice from the back of the room, 'we'll pay you $250!'

"I hadn't gone to work yet and already had a raise!"

There is no shortage of theatre venues in the Odessa-Midland metroplex. Odessa College boasts an authentic replica of the original Globe Theatre in England, called the Globe of the Great Southwest. Shakespeare productions, national road shows, and local productions to please every taste are held there throughout the year.

Yet another venue for performing arts is a local nonprofit group called Texas Best. Linda Bond explained that each year they do an interactive show called "History in the House," performing in a historic house. Particularly relevant to this book, the subject for 2001 was about the momentous event in 1925 when former Montana Senator T. S. Hogan was touring all the towns involved in the gigantic Santa Rita oil strike. He decided on Odessa-Midland as the center of the oil industry, starting the city on its way.

Hogan hired Fort Worth architect Wyatt C. Hedrick to erect a twelve-story office complex, the Petroleum Building. Then in 1929 he had Hedrick build the Yucca, a 1,200-seat movie theatre constructed of cut limestone and black marble columns, both buildings in gothic style. Hogan built in dressing rooms and other facilities for live performances, because the Yucca began not only as a movie theatre but as a stage for vaudeville. Stars like Harley Sadler presented some of their last appearances in those days before giving up to movies.

Like other theatres, the Yucca served as an important rallying point during World War II. In the fifties through the seventies, movies began their long descent from popularity, displaced by television and other attractions until there was no reason to keep trying.

But the very man who started all Midland's economic good fortune could not have wanted his "pride of West Texas" to be razed. The city of Midland has MCT and the Summer Mummers to thank for reminding them that history is worth preservation. The Yucca has proven itself to be a nice complement for economic progress after all. The old vaudeville melodrama is alive and well. Besides, as Tim Jebsen said, "It puts the word 'fun' back in fund raisers." —*Joan Upton Hall*

For information:

Midland Community Theatre
2000 W. Wadley
Midland, TX 79705
(915) 682-2544
tim@mctmidland.org
www.mctmidland.org

Other attractions (Odessa-Midland):

Museums & exhibits
Professional sports & stadiums
Globe of the Great Southwest & Ann Hathaway's cottage
Music City Mall
Odessa Meteor Crater
Parks, golf, Putt Putt Golf & Games, amusement parks

For details and accommodations:

Chamber of Commerce / Convention & Visitor Bureau
109 N. Main
Midland, TX 79701
(915) 683-3381 or
1-800-624-6435
info@midlantx-chamber.com or
info@visitmidlandtx.com
www.midlantxchamber.com
or www.odessacvb.com

33

Mineola: Select (1920)

Don Hall photographer

Mineola may be called "the gateway to East Texas pine country," but when you step into the short stretch of old town, you feel like you're on an Old West movie set, complete with the roar of a train (albeit a diesel). The only thing that didn't look 1900s or earlier was the Select Theater (remodeled in 1948) with its neon-lighted tower and a marquee that proclaimed the same first-run movie advertised in Dallas.

Yet somehow Art Deco looked right here. After all, it's the longest continually operating theater in Texas, "and possibly the world," added executive director J.D. West. The building was a silent movie theater by 1918 (as far back as the courthouse records show). The Texas historical marker out front credits it as the Select in 1920.

Recognizing my husband and me as strangers, people stopped to tell us about their town. Within half an hour, we'd heard several tales. At least one of the hotels is haunted. A tornado in 1962 drove down this street rearranging buildings. Ladies of the night leaned over "that balcony yonder" waving to the drummers arriving on the train. Bonnie and Clyde once robbed a bank here. And the last of many gunfights happened in the sixties. The constable and sheriff shot it out across the street from each other. Then both mortally wounded, one crawled across the street to slit his opponent's throat.

It was hard to believe this now peaceful little town had such a wild and woolly history. It had been (and is) a railroad junction point, and there are three old hotels in sight. There had been saloons and an opera house early on, then several theaters at various times, including an air dome. Then the Select came along and outlasted them all.

In 1918 banker R.J. Gaston began building it as the best show in town. Finishing in 1920, he leased it to Mr. and Mrs. R. T. Hooks Sr. to get them to close their Star Theater. Through a long chain of events, they named it after the Select Motion Picture Company (owned by Lewis J. Selznick and son David O. Selznick until they sold to MGM).

Nobody knows what the Select was like better than former manager James O. Dear, who started working there in 1928 at the age of twelve. He cleaned floors, distributed handbills, and ushered. Through the years he moved up to projectionist, assistant manager, and finally manager. "The only time I didn't work there," he said, "was a three-year period while I was in the service."

He takes issue with the Texas historical marker in one respect at least. The marker reads, "In 1948 the Select was remodeled with such features as a gradually sloping floor and elevated stage." Dear says Mr. Gaston had originally built it with a sloping floor and stage where a curtain and scenery could be raised and lowered for vaudeville acts. Later talking pictures replaced silent films and live acts.

photo courtesy of James O. Dear and Sharon Chamblee

The changeable-letter marquee and the tower that stands twenty-four feet above the roof were added in the 1948 remodeling. Flashing neon strip lights make the tower seem to revolve, and the tiled front gives it a sleek appearance. Historian Sharon Chamblee, who operates the Lott House B&B, said, "The tower was visible for miles, and the 804-seat house charged forty cents for adults and nine for children."

Touring the building, director West showed me a separate door, right off the box office, where minorities had to enter and sit in the balcony. Today wardrobe and sound equipment are housed in the balcony and "cry room." West pointed out original features that remain from 1948 such as the candy counter and decorative tile in the restrooms. There had been an ice cream parlor in the lobby. You could ring a buzzer at your seat, and they'd take your order and bring it to you.

Mrs. Mattie Hooks was credited for the Select's success. Other theaters were failing during the Depression when the Hooks took over the lease from the outgoing owner. She was also the one who commissioned the remodeling in 1948. Though Mr. Hooks soon passed away, Mrs. Hooks continued to operate the theater until her health failed. Then her son, R. T. Jr., took it over.

After R. T. Hooks Jr. died in 1961, James Dear and Truman Thomas owned and operated it for the next two decades. Both are native Mineolans who had worked at the Select for years. Dear recalled the Saturday afternoon in 1962 when a tornado went through the middle of town. A matinee was in progress with a theater full of children. "I had stepped outside to see the strange-looking clouds, and I could see squares floating in the air. When they came down, I realized they were sections of a tin roof flying around like Frisbees."

The power went out when electric lines were ripped loose. They wrapped around the Select's tower but didn't damage it. Only the marquee and tile front had to be repaired. Other buildings sustained considerably more damage. A massive sheet of wood roof decking struck a brand new car parked nearby "and turned it into a convertible," but an old car next to it wasn't touched. The only fatality was an elderly man who had a heart attack after the storm was over and died the next day. The children in the theater were safe.

Dear and Thomas continued to run the Select until they retired in 1986, completing fifty-eight and a half years for Dear and forty-four for Thomas. They gave all the building contents to the Lake Country Playhouse, a non-profit organization that is run by a board of governors. LCP bought the building with the help of the Meredith Foundation, which Harry Meredith had set up as an endowment so that interest from it could fund the theater and other Mineola organizations. Dear has served as a trustee of the Meredith Foundation for thirty years and as chairman for twenty-five.

The foundation also funds J.D. West's executive director position, and he says they can petition for purchases. They are now asking for new seats to replace the uncomfortable originals (redone once many years before). "The new ones will be old-timey looking with lacy iron work at the ends where there will be a gold 'S'." They also want to go by photographs to restore the Art Deco wall paintings of red, gold, and black chevrons.

LCP showed movies with a thirties vintage projector and made popcorn on the original machine until both wore out. These items will go into a museum being developed in the former post office. West says they plan to display the items in a mini theater. Thanks to the Meredith Foundation, the Select now has a state-of-the-art projector and sound system, and they show the latest movies.

The only other change the LCP made was to enlarge the stage. At present, theater seats and chairs can accommodate 300. LCP had been performing elsewhere before they acquired this wonderful theater of their own. Today the versatile group presents plays four to six times a year. On weekends they show movies. Mr. Dear likes that. "That's the way it started, live acts sometimes and movies the rest."

The once wild and woolly town is all tame and friendly these days.
—*Joan Upton Hall*

 For information:

Select Theater
P.O. Box 827
Mineola, TX 75773
(903) 569-2300

Other attractions:

Museums
· Lakes
Antique & craft shopping

For details and accommodations:

Mineola Chamber of Commerce
101 East Broad St.
(U.S. Hwy 80)
Mineola, TX 75773
(903) 569-2087
Fax: (903) 569-5510
chamber@mineola.com
www.chamber.mineola.com

Don Hall photographer

Before the Paris Community Theatre (PCT) group acquired the vintage 1927 Plaza Theatre in 1985, they put a new spin on Shakespeare's immortal line, "All the world's a stage." They've performed at Paris Junior College, area schools, churches, and the Sixth District Courtroom. I've never seen a group having more fun, and they've been doing it for twenty-five years. When we visited to take pictures, an enthusiastic group of them met us. Heck! I was ready to join up myself if it hadn't been such a long commute from there to Central Texas where I live.

The group had its forerunner in 1922, and Dr. David Brock cited a review done on the Little Theatre's first performance. He said the reviewer spoke kindly of it, but concluded, "May future productions be ever striving toward the high goal of better plays and better acting." The group disappeared after the beginning of World War II but resurfaced as PCT in 1976. Volunteerism wasn't enough though; members had to pay five-dollar dues too. The current president, Bill Kennedy, recalled, "The first PCT cast only had three Parisians in it... but it brought together different people from different places."

Looking for humor in all the right places didn't mean they weren't serious. Some found new spouses, and whole families got involved. Brock even earned a Masters in Theatre and dropped his practice as a pediatrician. His thesis was "A Demographic, Anecdotal, and Personality Evaluation of Participants in a Rural Community Theatre." Most of the Plaza's set designs are Brock's.

Over the years PCT has only canceled a show twice, and they don't do so lightly. Kennedy said the show went on even when "Brock had to take over a lead role in *Life with Father* with one day's notice [and again when] an actor lost his false teeth on stage in mid-show."

In 1981 they rented the old Plaza Theatre building, but after extensive ice and water damage shut it down, they had to go back to their "all-the-world-stage" routine. They bought the theatre in late 1985 and began repair and renovations, all the while carrying on their regular performances.

Funding shortages alone would have broken a less dedicated group. Royalties for producing a musical start at $2,500. With that and the cost of constructing and painting a set, collecting props, and gathering or making costumes, the average show can cost $8,000 to produce. Hilda Mallory says people forget that, like any other business, they must pay utilities, note payments, promotions, and repairs.

"We barter for a lot of it," Ruth Thompson added. "The bug man and the plumber get four seats and an ad." During renovations, they replaced the seats, many of which were beyond repair. As a fund raiser, they sold the intact seats individually or by the row, so these mementos with a decorative "P" on the iron grills of each end seat are no doubt to be found all over town.

They have received a couple of TCA grants but haven't applied for others. "We have a twenty-five-year track record," historian Skipper Steely said, "What we need is a grant writer."

One thing in their favor was being able to employ prison labor from the Coleman Unit in Bonham. The men did good work for only the cost of meals and transportation.

Numerous contributors have helped out financially or otherwise though. Molly Grotjohn willed PCT a portion of her estate. Eighty-four-year-old Edythe DeWitt, long-time instructor of music and dance, gave $3,000 worth of costumes and accessories from her Detroit Studio as well as a set of original songs and dances for children ages three and up.

Director Jean Campbell especially appreciated this. One of her major thrusts is to involve area children in theatre experience. Children do the performing and schools bring in busloads of other children to see the shows. During the workshop, they put on five performances a day for four days.

"I insist the kids stay in their roles," Campbell said, and she told stories that proved the kids did. Once a pigeon flew in and settled in the middle of the action, but the kids acted like it was part of the show and never dropped a line. Another time, "Jack" waited in a jack-in-the-box to spring out. When another nervous young actor leaned over the box to look in, he threw up. "'Jack' never missed a cue," Campbell said, "but he didn't come back for two years."

They are bringing up a whole new generation of theatergoers who know how to behave and who love the shows. Many of the current adult patrons and PCT participants started at the age of three. Older patrons have remained loyal too, such as 100-year-old Molly Tankursley. At the end of last season, she said, "Now, don't you forget my season ticket for next year."

Paris had once been home to opera houses dating back to the 1870s. A huge fire in 1914 erased all traces of them, but the Plaza didn't open until 1927. Spanish-Moorish in style, it lit up the square with flashing signs and chaser lights. Its "Blizzard Cooling System" and plush interior made picture show viewing a treat. Children could go for a dime, one whole penny of it to spend at the concession stand.

In the seventies the movie theatre converted to a hall for country-western and later rock concerts, but its success was limited. The only other historical theatre existing in Paris today is the Grand, about a block away, bearing a "For Sale" sign. It had remained as a cinema until a multiplex moved to town.

At some point, the arched openings of the façade shown in photos were bricked in, but the exterior has been restored to the original appearance except for the missing star on top. Appropriately enough, the Plaza Theatre faces the beautiful plaza square in the heart of downtown. There you'll see a lovely white marble fountain, a gift from the Culbertson family after the 1914 fire.

photo courtesy Paris Community Theater

Renovation was completed in 1999 as part of the Main Street Program. Today the lobby of the Plaza Theatre welcomes visitors with a two-story-high ceiling, complete with chandelier. Elaborate carnival masks decorate the plaster walls of pale rose with burgundy accents. Iron grillwork railings mark the surrounding mezzanine. Inside the auditorium, the walls are a rich taupe and new light fixtures hang from the ceiling.

The day we were there, the PCT group told about the resident ghost they've named "Annabelle." Jean Campbell said Annabelle never did anything but playful tricks. Once Campbell had stacked books in a seat. When she went back, they were gone. They looked everywhere, and later the books were back where she'd left them.

Doing *Peter Pan*, they had a large ship as part of the set. A Navy man, the only one who knew how to tie sailor's knots, had spread the mast across the auditorium seats. Working alone late one night, he had tied three knots at the top of the mast and gone to the bottom only to find his first three knots untied. When the phone rang and nobody was on the line, he decided it was time to go home.

Don Hall photographer

Even the scientific physician David Brock had a story to tell. Working alone one night to design a set for *Camelot*, he heard a woman's voice making "an achy moaning sound" in the balcony. "I don't believe in ghosts," he said, "but I can't explain some of the things that happen around here."

So it seems even Annabelle has fun with the company of PCT. The group has at last established a warm and welcoming home, no longer having to rely on "all the world" for a stage. —*Joan Upton Hall*

For information:

Paris Community Theatre
Plaza on the Square
P.O. Box 913
Paris, TX 75460
(903) 784-0259

Other attractions:

Walking & driving tours
Museums & galleries
Evergreen Cemetery (site of many early Texas patriots' graves)
Sam Bell Maxey State Historic Structure
Lakes, parks, & specialty shopping

For details and accommodations:

Chamber of Commerce
1651 Clarksville St.
Paris, TX 75460
(903) 784-2501 or
1-800-727-4789
chamber@paristexas.com

35

Plainview: Fair (1923)

photo courtesy of *Plainview Daily Herald*

Good luck has had a habit of coming through the back door for the Fair Theater of Plainview. For starters, its champion, David Wilder, would much rather have watched a ball game than a ballet at the time a group of ladies approached him for help in buying the theater. There's even a baseball park named after him and his wife, Myrt. Still, he was a banker and the chairman of several civic committees and had a reputation for getting things done.

Historically the Fair (originally, "Plainview") played second fiddle to its neighbor, the Granada, built in grand Spanish Plaza style. Both were owned by C. E. McSwain, and like the younger kid who's been slighted on baby pictures, the Fair's early interior appearance was largely a mystery. It had hosted vaudeville and medicine shows; its stage trapdoor is still there. It also showed some of the earliest movies. An old ad from the *Plainview Daily Herald* had the theater offering "the very best and cleanest pictures."

In 1943 during WW II, Bill Weaks, then a high school freshman, sold tickets for ten and fifteen cents. He also manned the popcorn machine. He described a café that opened onto the lobby on one side and a barbershop on the other. Men waiting for a haircut would go watch Hopalong Cassidy while waiting their turn in the barber's chair. The worst thing that ever happened in the theater was when a man in the balcony choked to death on popcorn.

Every day except Sunday, Weaks, along with his friends Al Whittacre and Bobby Gentry, went to work at 1:00 o'clock and got off about 10:00 or 11:00, even later when there was a midnight special. For all this he earned $12.50 per week.

In the sixties through the eighties when other movie houses failed, only the Fair survived, though open intermittently and under a series of owners. It was just the right size, standing three floors tall with a split balcony. To this day it has its original 422 seats on the main floor and 150 in the balcony. Anything larger hadn't a prayer of filling up. At about that time, Mr. Luna bought it to add to his small chain of Spanish-language movies in the area. It may have been Luna who installed a dropped ceiling for energy efficiency, and through the years people forgot it had been otherwise. Finally the theater closed from 1997-99.

Jack Oswald, who owned a large antique business on the same block, bought the theater in distress. A man who respects preservation, he makes regular trips to Europe to buy and import fine antiques. Most of his clientele comes from out of town, and David Wilder said, "It's the only store in town where the customers come shopping in limousines."

In 1993 the Main Street Project prodded the citizens' group into action. By the next year, the city of Plainview bought the theater, leasing it to the governing Fair Theater Board (FTB) for a nominal amount. The board began to clean it up, thinking all they could afford would be painting and repairing. Wilder had higher expectations, and the Main Street architect drew out a plan.

FTB held fund raisers making enough to hold a Halloween Show for kids in '95 and '98, but restoration seemed impossible. Then they thought of using prison labor from the local Wheeler Formby Unit. When Wilder went to check into this, he found the labor would be free. The prisoners could work only four half-days a week, going to school the rest of the time. The only catch was the lack of a supervisor. "I had just retired," Wilder said, "so I said I'd do it. I didn't know it would take almost two years."

Wilder said the wiring was a mess and there were three kinds of heating and cooling systems that had been used by various owners. They had to gut the building and start over. By lucky accident they discovered what those dropped ceilings hid—beautiful pressed tin in good shape. They ordered molds from Chicago to restore parts of the decorative plaster molding on the twin balconies. Antiqued gold highlights applied to a dark base color finished it. Unsure what the color scheme had been, the ladies of the board selected gold, beiges, and burgundy. Again luck paid her backdoor visit when the Main Street restoration architect told them that was probably exactly what it had been.

photo courtesy of Fair Theater Board, David Wilder president

photo courtesy of Fair Theater Board, David Wilder president

According to Bill Weaks, the young prisoners weren't much more than kids and were trying to turn their lives around. Some of them showed real craftsmanship. Workers took the theater seats to the airport to sand, paint, and reupholster. FTB then "sold" seats to benefactors, entitling them to the first chance to buy a ticket for "their" seats at a given performance. The donation levels ranged from $500 for the "Clark Gable and Vivian Leigh" section to $100 for the "Abbot and Costello" section.

Grants to pay for the stage curtain, lighting and sound system (housed in what had been the movie projection room), air conditioning, and restoration of the concession and reception rooms came in from three foundations: the James and Eva Mayer Foundation, the Meadows Foundation, and the CH Foundation.

The barbershop and café that had opened onto the original lobby made the perfect solution to a need. The barbershop became their formal reception room. The café area became a concession room, especially handy for certain theme shows. For a fifties show done by the highly popular J.D.s out of Lubbock, they sold Coke floats. For Mary Hollan from Phoenix, they sold homemade cobbler. And for a Hee Haw show, they planted a few coupons from merchants for some really great prizes in popcorn boxes. Every box was sold when patrons heard what they might win. Wilder says they'll continue the theme idea—maybe with a car show or bike rally for the next fifties show.

Don Caldwell, general manager of the Cactus Theater in Lubbock, probably knows as much about acoustics as anyone. Wilder said he went all over the Fair auditorium checking it out and pronounced, "Not a bad seat in the house." The Plainview Symphony must agree. While it usually plays in one of Plainview's larger auditoriums, about five times a year for smaller audiences, it plays at the Fair.

Apparently, the working relationship between Wilder and the inmates was favorable. During the eighteen months he supervised the crew, some finished their sentences and were replaced, but for the grand opening, he contacted all of them and invited them to see how their efforts came out.

The program "Phantom of the Fair" was a variety show that, to Wilder's surprise, turned into a tribute-roast for him. Local talent presented music from all the decades the Fair had been open, some serious, some parodies aiming good-natured barbs at Wilder. One of the most popular came near the end of the evening when the "men in white" who had worked on the prison detail marched down the aisle chanting cadence drills about working with Wilder. They capped it off by singing, "David Wilder's Chain Gang."

That particular section of Plainview's Historical District looks quite sharp these days, and the city has even created Millennium Park across the street from the theater. As for David Wilder? Well, he might be one of the luckiest breaks that happened to the Fair. He's a theater man for sure now, president of the board and, "at least for now," director as well. The Fair Theater's a survivor, every piece of good luck that has come to it, well deserved. —*Joan Upton Hall*

 For information:

The Fair Theater
PO Box 1283
Plainview, TX 79073-1283
(806) 293-4000

Other attractions:

Historic Downtown District
Kidsville (unique wooden playscape)
Llano Estacado Museum
Abraham Art Gallery
Plainview Cattle Drive (45 fiberglass cows, stationed around town)
Parks, golf, hunting, specialty shopping

Annual events:

Texas Plains 2-Cylinder Club Show
Seasonal events
American Cancer Society's Cotton Barons Ball
Parade of Lights/Symphony Concert

For details and accommodations:

Chamber of Commerce
710 W. 5th St.
Plainview, TX 79072
1-800-658-2685
plainviewchamber@texasonline.net
www.plainviewtex.com

36

Port Lavaca: Port Lavaca Main Street (1936)

Stacey Hasbrook photographer

Some things lead the way by brute strength and others exist because they are quiet, determined survivors. The theatre in Port Lavaca is a survivor. Built in 1936, this building even refused to crumble before the force of Hurricane Carla in 1961 and served as a refuge for hurricane victims in both 1942 and 1945. The theatre thrived in the early 1900s and was known as Long's Theatre. The only enemy that nearly defeated it was neglect.

Then Port Lavaca native Russell Cain bought the building in 1983. He didn't do anything except paint the outside. When the Main Street Committee was formed in 1987, Russell donated it. "My hopes were that it would increase the quality of life in Calhoun County for the youth …because a person involved with the theatre becomes more positive about themselves, they gain more self-esteem."

Russell remembers coming to the theatre as a teenager and sitting upstairs. Like many small houses, Long's closed during the Depression and then reopened. Sometime in the late thirties, a fire partially damaged it. When the burnt area was redone, the theatre succeeded again, and many movie stars came here including Elvis in the early fifties. The doors finally shut for the last time in 1962 or '63, and the theatre lay dormant for over thirty years.

The project might never have gotten off the ground if the volunteers had realized what bad shape the fifty-eight-year-old building was in. It was structurally sound, but the roof had leaked and weakened the balcony. Juaniece Madden, Main Street secretary, pointed out, "If I had been in here and had seen what we were getting into before we got started, I would have said 'no way.'" A "mountain of trash" had to be thrown out including three soda machines from the time when Cokes were fifteen cents. Underneath the trash, however, they found floors and walls nearly as good as they were fifty years ago. They also found some original posters behind the projection room advertising vintage movies, the original *Von Ryan's Express* poster, and an older poster for *A Tale of Five Women*. These collectibles are now framed and displayed in the lobby. They also found the crawl space to the sump pump. Since the stage is lower than ground level, water used to collect down there, and they learned that the hard way.

Realizing that the theatre was probably one of the finest buildings in the area in its day, the committee did not give up. It seemed to be a most promising "make-over." By December 1993 Main Street Incorporated had received over $22,000 in grants and donations and needed about twice that to complete the project, yet they proceeded.

The first major task was to add a new roof. After the addition of the roof, the building was gutted except for several rows of chairs, and then they set to work on the interior. The "buzzard roost" or balcony was rebuilt without the original partition down the middle that segregated the blacks to the right side. They junked the old equipment, which couldn't be used at all. The floral carpet is new, but the design matches the old style. The walls were painted a soft pink and 263 new red chairs were added. A donated 1890s piano itself cost $7,000 to restore. Overall, about $80,000 was spent to put in a stage, refurbish the balcony, replace the seating, and add air conditioning. The Meadows Foundation gave half of the money and the rest came in small donations and community support.

The seats were a special research project. Each one is a donor chair. The first three rows in the balcony, eighty-four chairs, bear the names of eighty-four former local fair queens. The research to find and track down these queens or their families was tedious. Each of the other seats in the balcony and on the lower level is inscribed with the name of the person who donated the cost to buy the seat either for himself or to honor someone else. A few of the old seats were salvaged and can be found at the Davila Shoe Shop.

Except for one contractor, the restoration was completely done by volunteers. In late November 1993 members of the Coast Guard spent time scraping paint from the walls. A local hospital, scheduled for partial demolition, donated parts such as acoustical tiles, restroom furnishings, light fixtures, and doors. If volunteer hours were considered, the restoration cost would have been more like $200,000.

The first event held in the theatre since restoration was a Christmas tree judging contest in December 1993. Businesses decorated the trees and people paid twenty-five cents to vote for their favorite to raise money for further renovations. This project raised over $300. When the time came for the opening gala, the only renovation left was the outside of the building.

On September 29, 1994, the gala grand opening was a black tie event. The elegantly dressed crowd enjoyed a champagne reception in the Fay Bauer Sterling Park and spent the evening reminiscing about what the old theatre had been like. In attendance that night, Cain remembered seeing *Hopalong Cassidy* as a child, and Madden recalled the lights of the marquee. "When I was a young girl, I thought that marquee was the most beautiful thing."

Then the crowd strolled a block's walk to the theatre and, according to the newspaper report, "stepped through the doors and into a piece of the city's past." They found the "classic downtown movie palace" had turned into a live performance stage glowing with a soft pink light. Local talent put on the first play, *The Night of Jan. 16*, which was special for Cain because it was the first play he had done in high school. It was the debut of the city's first acting troupe in fifteen years, and it played to a sold-out house with a standing ovation.

The Port Lavaca Main Street Theatre group, a nonprofit organization, believes it is one of only three acting groups that own their own building. They put together five or six productions a year, plus special events. The most popular productions are comedies. The group now has about a hundred members involved in performing who believe they are a vital element of education for the area. Additionally, they know that the arts are essential to the long-term economic development initiatives of any community.

The theatre continues to improve. Large murals across the side and back by Houston artist Kati Ozanic were completed in 1996 and paid for with money earned by the theatre. The building behind the theatre has

Stacey Hasbrook photographer

1,800 square feet of space and two restrooms. Plans are for it to be donated and renovated to serve as storage of props and costumes and for dressing rooms.

In the process of becoming new, however, the theatre will not forget its survivor's history. In the lobby hang two pictures in recognition of service. One is of Fay Bauer Sterling, the VP of the Main Street Committee, who Cain says was "really the main power behind the renovations." The other is of James I. Denham, who managed the theatre from 1936 to 1943. Cain concluded, "Main streets are from a nostalgic era...[and this theatre] is going to be a useful part of our community instead of a silent reminder of the past." —*Stacey Hasbrook*

 For information:

Port Lavaca Main Street Theatre
P.O. Box 1614
315 E. Main St.
Port Lavaca, TX 77979-1614
(361) 552-4082
jweaver@tisd.net
www.plmainstreet.org

Other activities:

Parks, wildlife and bird sanctuaries
Hatch Bend Country Club
Calhoun County Museum
Halfmoon Reef Lighthouse
La Salle Monument

Annual events:

Bull in a China Shop

For details and accommodations:

Chamber of Commerce
1-800-556-7678
(361) 552-2959

37
Post: Garza (1916)

Ernest Upton photographer

When Charles William Post created his utopian town, his vision included a theatre. Unfortunately, he didn't live to see it. Fortunately for people of the area, they have one now, and the Garza Theatre, Inc. players are doing their best to make Post the ideal hometown their founder dreamed of.

C. W. Post had already made a fortune on the coffee-substitute "Postum" when he visited the OS Ranch in 1906. His next invention, first called "Elija's Manna" but more popularly known as "Post Toasties," came later, but seeking a more healthful environment, he chose West Texas. He bought over 27,000 acres of land to build his city on, a model of morality and sanitation. He couldn't have picked a prettier spot, a river valley right off the edge of the caprock.

He formed the Double U Company and offered homes to prospective buyers at thirty dollars down with payments of fifteen dollars a month interest-free. The catch was you had to furnish three references and be approved. Mr. Post used his influence to bring railroad connections to town, but until that was finished, mule trains brought in supplies to build stores, a "state of the art" hospital, and a hotel (complete with French chef). He did not build saloons.

As if one icon of high standards were not enough for the area, Garza County was named "in honor of Leonardo de la Garza, prominent rancher and businessman of San Antonio, who was a staunch supporter of the Texas Revolution," states the Texas historical marker outside the Garza County Museum (originally the hospital). "He minted the first money in the state of Texas, and was the first to use the Lone Star emblem. The brand of the Garza family was recorded in June 23, 1762."

These high standards have influenced the present. Mr. Post's original Double U offices are now occupied by the OS Museum, which shows an ever-changing art exhibit that any city might envy. This display comes from Giles McCrary, who served as mayor for many years and who collected art during his extensive travels. On the day we went there, we met McCrary himself, sporting a big "OS" belt buckle.

The Garza Hotel is one of the most pleasant bed & breakfast hotels anywhere. As for the theatre, it won an Action Award from the West Texas Museum Association in Lubbock for its "outstanding contributions to the enrichment and culture of the Southern High Plains."

Back in 1916 the town had gotten its theatre, the Palace, which showed mainly movies. Naomi Matsler, the present theatre office manager, remembers going to the Saturday afternoon matinees as a young girl while her parents sat around visiting with friends. She especially liked sitting in the balcony.

Opening night. Photo courtesy of Garza Theatre, Inc.

The Palace closed its doors in 1955, but vandals broke in and set a fire that seriously damaged the stage area. After that the building was boarded up for the next thirty years. Citizens wanted a theatre for the performing arts but lacked know-how, so in 1986 a group decided to contact native son Will McCrary (no relation to Giles) in New York. He had acted and danced on Broadway and in such highly acclaimed films as *An American in Paris* and *Mr. Roberts*.

Mayor Giles McCrary helped fund the playhouse, the group renamed it "the Garza," and Will McCrary agreed to take advantage of his forty-one years of professional theatre experience in a new capacity. For the next six years he was, according to a program flier, "the director, designer, producer, actor, and driving force behind the theatre project."

In 1987 the town received a "Main Street City" designation. The Garza has also received financial backing from TCA, the Caprock Cultural

Association, and a very generous actress, Dina Merrill, granddaughter of C. W. Post.

Support comes from private citizens too, and each year businesses can purchase a poster-size ad for fifty dollars. These are hung all around the stage, similar to vaudeville days. Each year some of the businesspeople write another check to "Just put up my poster again."

Nevertheless, repairs and seven or eight productions a year require a lot of cash and effort. Every summer Garza Theatre, Inc. can count on one show as a sell-out for their 238 seating capacity. It's their Harley Sadler Tribute. Sadler had been a West Texas traveling showman who performed in a tent from the twenties through the forties. The Garza stages the old Sadler scripts and has sometimes hung banners on the walls to suggest a tent-show atmosphere.

Naomi Matsler says they add to the mood by selling bags of saltwater taffy. The bags all have some kind of little prize inside, and if you have a colored coupon, you get to come up on the stage and choose a gift from those donated by local businesses. She also showed me the Serendipity Shop next door where patrons can buy snacks and cold drinks for other performances. "For a melodrama," she said, "we hand out bags of wadded up paper for the audience to throw at the villain."

The aim is to give the audience a good time, and tricks like having Dracula vanish from the stage keep them guessing. (I won't give away the secret, but it's an old Shakespeare trick.)

Other aims are to buy a stage curtain and to "do something" with the ceiling. In the front and around the edges in the auditorium, you can see what's left of pressed tin, but most was ruined and won't hold a paint job. "We have no funds for restoration," Matsler said. "We feel fortunate just to keep going."

Will McCrary seemed to have been unanimously loved. The first thing I saw on the wall on entering the theatre was a framed picture of him with Harvey, a six-foot-tall white rabbit that the hero imagined. (Or did he?) McCrary had acted in the well-known play *Harvey* the first time it was done at the Garza. The whole area grieved when McCrary died in 1991 after forty-five productions, but he had taught them the show must go on.

Jane Prince Jones, a popular radio personality, took over the reins of managing director until 1995 and now does directing at the Cactus Theatre in Lubbock. Christy Morris, who has been involved with the Garza from the beginning, is the current director.

The group continues to have the gala each year that McCrary started. There they present the Willy Awards. The different production directors nominate cast and crew. Then at the end of the year, a committee selects the winners of each award. Each winner earns a trophy inscribed with his or her name. "It's a very big deal and everybody looks forward to it," Matsler said. They have a catered dinner and wear formals and tuxes, though one year everybody came in costume.

Theatre's late mentor, Will McCrary, poses with Harvey, courtesy of Garza Theatre, Inc.

Further encouragement can be seen by anyone walking past the theatre. Actors from each season have their handprints immortalized in concrete. Inside, the tall exposed brick walls are adorned with photos of past performances, each production individually framed along with its playbill. When you look around at the number of them, you can't help being impressed.

I think C. W. Post would smile if he's looking down on the theatre. The Garza Theatre, Inc. players have contributed a lot to the utopia Post dreamed of. —*Joan Upton Hall*

For information:

Garza Theatre Office
226 E. Main St.
Post, TX 79356
(806) 495-4005
nrmatsler@juno.com

Other attractions:

Tower Theatre (live music)
Museums
Old Mill Trade Days (once
a month)
Lake, golf, specialty
shopping
Trade Days

For details and accommodations:

Caprock Cultural
Association
P.O. Box 37
127 E. Main St.
Post, TX 79356
(806) 495-4148
ccarts@door.net
www.posttexas.com/
main.htm

38

San Antonio: Majestic (1929)

Stacey Hasbrook photographer

I remember the first time I walked into the Majestic Theatre in San Antonio. At the end of May, all of us fifth and sixth graders who had served as safety patrol members during the school year were treated to an all-day-Saturday series of movies and cartoons complete with drinks and popcorn as a reward. Imagine several thousand kids ages ten to twelve contained within one building. I'm sure we were noisy and rambunctious, but when the lights went down, we sat trance-like, watching the screen come to life while stars twinkled high above. I don't recall what we watched, but I can still feel the hushed excitement of knowing we must be special to get to experience such a place. But as I grew older, like most of us who take special places in our hometowns for granted, I didn't appreciate the full wonder of it. Not until I began to do research for this book did I realize how close we came to losing the "Queen of Houston Street," and how she arose over and over again to survive in glory.

Designed and constructed by Eberson and Hoblitzelle and built on land leased from J. M. Nix, "The New and Greater Majestic" replaced the original Majestic at the cost of $3 million in 1928-29. With nearly 4,000 seats, it was the largest theatre in the South, the second largest in the nation. The opening on June 14, 1929, marked the beginning of "Prosperity Week," a chilling irony so close to the infamous stock market crash on Black Friday. Over 500,000 people attended the citywide celebration that included General Jose M. Tapia representing Mexican president Emilio Portes Gil, and Texas governor Dan Moody.

The September 1929 edition of *Motion Picture News* reported the event. "That most daring exponent of the romantic in theatre architecture—the so-called atmospheric theatre—was submitted to a new test, and . . . came through with flying colors when the opening of the new Greater Majestic Theatre in San Antonio was made the occasion of an International celebration." Hoblitzelle intended to capitalize on the lack of vaudeville type entertainment in the southwestern United States and insisted that his establishments would "provide clean, wholesome entertainment and pass the inspection of the watchful eyes of the local churches."

It was too late for the typical silent films of the twenties, but vaudeville was popular and movies were developing. The celebration did not last long however. Black Friday hit just weeks after the theatre opened. It closed in 1930 for a couple of months and then reopened with bare bones scheduling. Movies began to be an escape to get through a time of tough national struggle.

The extravagance contradicted the times. At the top of the eighteen-story building was a penthouse apartment and private roof garden. The vertical marquee was higher than any other in the South. It rose seven floor levels to 76 feet, was 14 feet wide at the top, and was lit with 2,400 lamps. The double-sided sign on top of the building could be seen for 50

1929, photo courtesy of the UT Institute of Texan Cultures at San Antonio, *The San Antonio Light* Collection

miles in any direction. The building had its own well, which could produce 3,500 gallons per minute, and a tank with 35,500 gallons was stored on the roof. City water was also piped into the building for emergencies.

The theatre was placed sideways on the block, and the foyer tunneled to the left giving no indication of its size. The "L" shaped lobby was cave-like, with inlaid tiles, copper lanterns, vaulted ceilings, painted murals, and latticework. It opened into a two-story area with an encircling balcony decorated with columns and Spanish Baroque features. At one end was a huge aquarium, and throughout the area, a fountain, tapestries, red armchairs, a seventeenth-century walnut table, wood, silver, and bronze candlesticks and torches were strategically placed. An imitation cave alcove in the lower balcony lobby had stalagmites from which water trickled into a pool of goldfish. A canopy over the entrance protected the patrons from sun and provided an outdoor café for the upper-level balcony. It was one of very few theatres that provided elevators for the theatre patrons, and other amenities included public telephones and telegraph service.

Eberson concentrated on creating the illusion of the outdoors within his theatres' interiors. "We visualize and dream a magnificent amphitheater, an Italian garden, a Persian court, a Spanish patio, or a mystic Egyptian temple yard, all canopied by a soft moonlit sky." For the Majestic, the illusion put us in an outdoor courtyard of a castle in Spain. Real birds flew around the lobby and perched on balconies alongside stuffed birds. The most beautiful in the collection was a white peacock with a spreading tail that measured more than ten feet across and stood more than ten feet high.

Specially treated Spanish cypress trees grew in the upper levels with azaleas, oleanders, magnolias, blooming cactus, rose bushes, and South American palm trees. A 3D-village scene formed the side walls, and the ceiling created an immense domed sky with floating clouds and a blue night sky with small twinkling bulbs for stars positioned correctly according to experts at *National Geographic*. A cloud machine gave the effect of sitting beneath a rolling sky. The theme aimed at creating a setting "more beautiful than a castle in Spain" with boxed seats on either side. The smaller second balcony above the projection booth was used for segregated black audiences, and a separate entrance with box office and elevator was located on College St. behind the theatre.

Melinda Doster photographer

The Majestic was the most popular movie house in the area from the thirties through the sixties. During the last days of regular stage performances, many stars performed for the five major military installations operating at full strength during WW II, many giving their final war performances at the Majestic. The organ, a 24 rank Marr and Colton and one of the largest ever, was dismantled and the pipes donated as a contribution to a scrap metal drive during WW II. Called the MagicStick by some, the Majestic is one of the finest examples of the atmospherics surviving in the U.S. today.

In 1973 the theatre had to be closed for a day due to fistfights and vandals, and by the summer of 1974, films were restricted to black action movies and Spanish language movies. Finally, on the last day of December 1974, the great theatre closed, but office space continued to be occupied. Luckily in 1975 the theatre was placed in the National Register of Historic Places, and then in 1976 the Hoblitzelle Foundation donated the Majestic Theatre and building to Downtown, Inc. In 1978 it briefly opened as the Grand Majestic Music Hall with star Arthur Godfrey but failed.

Boarded up for several years, the Majestic lay dark until 1981 when Pace Productions of Houston brought in Broadway's *The Best Little Whorehouse in Texas*. The response brought a million-dollar renovation complete with the sale of plush suites and new name, the Majestic Performing Arts Center. The number of seats was reduced to 2,486, each being totally restored, but again the losses grew. In 1987 the lights threatened to go out again. It would require $5 million to fix the essentials and another $2.5 million to re-create the original glamour.

Last minute salvation came again with funds mostly from private sources and the city's $2 million commitment. In 1988, as part of a downtown revitalization program, the city bought the building and leased it for fifty years to Las Casas Foundation. Restoration began in January 1989. After a $4.5 million dollar restoration, the Majestic reopened as the home of the fifty-year-old San Antonio Symphony and venue for Broadway shows and concerts. It proved a great example of effective public, private, and nonprofit effort. The Majestic Tower that soars above the theatre has apartments, bringing life to the downtown area.

An article in the now defunct *San Antonio Light* truthfully pointed out that "To see the Majestic is to understand it." Three days before the deadline on this book, I attended *Phantom of the Opera* in this incredible place. It has the same overwhelming elegance of its beginnings, and the grandeur takes your breath away. I could close my eyes and be that child who sat in quiet awe so long ago. Today, the comment by Michael Spies of the *Corpus Christi Caller Times* in 1976 still holds true: "Imagine the inside of a Fabergè egg and you're almost there."

Other San Antonio Oldies:

The Majestic may be the most well-known theatre restoration, but San Antonio has a wide variety of other old theatres still thriving as well. The oldest is the Alameda built in 1904, which is currently undergoing renovation so that it will become a "cultural zone for the arts that reflect San Antonio's diverse history." Then there is the Empire Theatre built in 1914 now recognized as the Charlene McCombs Empire Theatre. This theatre, with its extremely steep balcony, holds live performances in a gold-leaf accentuated Romanesque setting. Another live stage is the Josephine Theater from the 1940s that draws a crowd for live music as well. And, if that's not enough, you could always check out the Mission Drive-in, one of a handful left in the country, a reminder of bygone times of family outings when simple pleasures meant the most. —*Stacey Hasbrook*

 For information:

Majestic Theatre
212 E. Houston St.
San Antonio, TX 78205
(210) 270-8748
1-800-447-3372
Visitor's Center
(210) 226-3333

Other attractions:

Museums, historic sites, parks, missions
Lakes, golf, ranches, art centers, gardens
HemisFair Institute of Texan Cultures
King William District
La Villita
RiverWalk
Retama Park (horse racing)
El Mercado

Annual events:

Fiesta de las Luminarias
Fiestas Navidenas in El Mercado

Holiday River Parade Lighting Ceremony
Las Posadas
Regional Christmas Lighting Tour
Texas Folklife Festival
Livestock show and rodeo

For details and accommodations:

Chamber of Commerce
602 E. Commerce Street
P.O. Box 1628
San Antonio, TX 78296
(210) 229-2100

39

Snyder: Ritz (1921)

Ernest Upton photographer

Snyder's community project, "Puttin' on the Ritz," was aptly named. It's a class act all the way, and everybody involved seemed to have totally immersed themselves in the long, arduous process. The theatre group handed me a written statement listing four purposes: "to ensure quality entertainment, to implement activity of the Ritz Community Theatre, Inc. (RCT), to renovate the Ritz building, and to rejuvenate downtown business to promote tourism." All high goals, but how could one little group attain so much? Let's start with the theatre's history.

The adobe Cozy Theatre, as the Ritz was first named, had already been operating a few years as a movie house when T. L. Lollar bought it in 1921. Then he built another one. Modern Snyder resident Jayson Limmer, while attending the University of North Texas, wrote that Lollar installed the very best equipment in the Cozy, such as "a Wurlitzer Electric Motion Picture Orchestra... that included, not only the traditional organ effects, but also a doorbell, horse's hoofbeats, and a bird whistle." Lollar also installed a top quality screen "to eliminate all eyestrain." After he died, his wife bought two more theatres, all in downtown Snyder. In the course of time, their son-in-law, N. R. Clements, became the sole owner.

Snyder was in the middle of an oil boom in 1950. Clements renamed the theatre the "Ritz" and completely rebuilt the whole thing of concrete, even the ceiling. It had a soundproof cry room, the latest in projection and sound equipment, forced air heat, and washed air cooling, as well as all the plush accoutrements of carpet, velour stage curtains, and upholstered seats. According to Limmer, since there weren't enough places for an oilfield worker to find a bed, it made sense to buy a theatre ticket and sleep in air-conditioned comfort.

Interest in movies fizzled out, and by 1970 the Ritz was the only theatre left standing. It closed, becoming more and more dilapidated. The oil business dwindled, and roof damage was so extensive no one even wanted to turn it into another kind of business. Eventually it was condemned.

Ellie Dryden and Mike Thornton were knocking around the idea of starting a theatre group and trying to acquire the old Ritz in early 1991 when they came up with the idea of "Puttin' on the Ritz." A group of volunteers organized to form the Ritz Community Theatre, Inc.

Demolition of the building had already begun when the Lollar-Clements descendants bought it and donated it to RCT. As if renovating a building weren't enough, the group decided to prove themselves and raise public awareness by launching a regular schedule of productions. Dryden said, "That meant gypsy-like traveling from stage to stage at a school, Western Texas College, and the Martha Ann Woman's Club. Successful membership drives each year made it possible to produce three plays a year for three years, operating "slightly in the black."

Phase I was to replace the roof and restore the original storefront and neon marquee. Phase II was to gut the interior and start over. Help came from many sources such as having prisoners from the Price Daniel Unit do much of the cleanup work.

RCT knew the movie house needed a lot of changes to make it a live-stage venue. Obviously it needed an expanded stage, dressing rooms, and storage for props and costumes, but the part patrons use had to be different too. For live theatre instead of movies, larger areas are needed in which people can gather and visit before a performance and at intermission. How was this to be accomplished?

Mike Thornton, by then the board president, had another brilliant idea. He contacted Dr. Michael Jones, Associate Dean for Graduate and Research Studies of the College of Architecture of Texas Tech University. The question regarded whether a student might be able to design an interior for this as a project. Dr. Jones liked the idea and in the spring of 1992 brought not one but five senior design students to look at the building. They came out several times, measuring and listening to what the board wanted. In May each student submitted a set of plans. After much deliberation, RCT chose the one done by David Schall.

The community was highly supportive. More than a thousand people showed up at the culmination of Phase I when the old Ritz sign was lit again after more than twenty years of darkness. N. R. Clements, one of the first owners, was on hand to see it, and as quoted in the *Snyder Daily News*, he said, "I didn't think I'd ever see it look like that again. I don't think you can fit this many people in it though."

Michael Endy, drama instructor at Western Texas College, not only worked with the RCT in a theatrical capacity but also provided electrical plans. The East Side Church of Christ donated the 120 seats that were needed. Hosts of well-wishers and volunteers donated materials, time, and/or money. A chandelier in the upstairs mezzanine came from Owens Dress Shop, which had closed.

RCT had bought one key item at auction with the help of the Scurry County Historical Society and kept it in storage, planning a special place for it. It was the old marble soda fountain from a no-longer-existing Stinson drugstore. This they use for a "ver-ry ritzy" concession stand. They have the brass rail and stools too, but these would be in the way at a concession stand. They *have* used them as props.

Ernest Upton photographer

The wall decoration behind the counter is part of the original, and the silver figures at each side are of the mythological huntress Diana, accompanied by hounds and carrying her bow. Ellie Dryden said people have remarked, "I don't remember those naked ladies at Stinson's." Dryden said that was probably because the ladies had been clothed in tarnish.

Beautiful metal wall sconces, in the lobby and at each side of the proscenium, are among the few things original to the old movie house. They were the only ones among many that weren't too far gone for repair.

Inside the auditorium, you get the effect of stadium seating in a steeply "raked" (and tiered) floor. This is accessible from both the first floor lobby and upstairs through the second floor mezzanine. Visibility of the stage is excellent anywhere you sit.

Before all this beauty was in place though, the Ritz hosted its first production on October 1995 to coincide with the annual White Buffalo Festival and Cowboy Chautauqua. Though not finished, the facility was close enough and they used folding chairs. This gave the audience a chance to see what was to come and to be aware that the theatre would be available, not just for RCT productions, but all kinds of community functions. To a full house they presented a melodrama, *The Shakey Tale of Dr. Jakey.*

Dryden said they feel fortunate to have such a talent pool of actors and stage technicians to choose from in the immediate area. Part of this she credits to schools. Snyder High School Drama Department has been dubbed the "winningest school in Texas" for its University Interscholastic League One Act Play competition. Jerry Worsham, who headed the department for twenty-four years, is on the RCT board (and planned the interior decoration of the Ritz). He points out that drama is not the only fine art at which Snyder students excel, noting musical accomplishments too. Several SHS students have succeeded in show biz. Perhaps most notable is Emmy Award winner Powers Boothe, but several are names and faces you would recognize if we had space to post them here.

It appears oil isn't the only resource Snyder has struck it rich on. With the kind of talent growing up and the RCT group's energy and expertise, this little city is sure to continue "puttin' on the Ritz." *—Joan Upton Hall*

For information:

Ritz Community Theatre, Inc.
P.O. Box 943
Snyder, TX 79549
(915) 573-8880

Other attractions:

Scurry County Museum
Towle Memorial Park
(including prairie dog town)
Historical courthouse & landmarks
Lakes, specialty shopping

Annual events:

Cowboy Chautauqua and
White Buffalo Festival

For details and accommodations:

Chamber of Commerce
2302 Avenue R
P.O. Box 840
Snyder, TX 79550
(915) 573- 3558
snychcom@snydertex.com
www.iitexas.com/gpages/
snyder.htm

40

Taylor: Howard (1929)

eclectic — a choice of the best from diverse sources, systems, or styles; someone who uses an eclectic system or method (*The American Heritage Desk Dictionary*).

This one word pretty well sums up not only the Howard Theatre, but its twenty-five-year-old owner Jason Steiniger, as well. Jason believes it is the diversity that will make the theatre successful and long-lived. He makes his home in a tiny apartment space above the first floor with his cat Jerry and has worked hard to "re-create the magic of the original."

Where else can you find first-run movies, WWF-style wrestling events, Saturday music concerts, VIP seating with couch, loveseat, over-stuffed chair, and table, and have Domino's pizza delivered? Even refreshment refills are only a dollar.

Like many small towns across Texas, Taylor has begun a downtown restoration plan, and new inhabitants such as Jim and Ace Tobak imagine artists, writers, and musicians living and working in shared retail spaces of downtown Taylor, occupying and renovating what are now empty, unkempt buildings. They have started a nonprofit cultural organization, the Artists' Coalition of Taylor, which is hosting regular Saturday concerts at the theatre.

The original Howard was built in 1929 directly across the street from today's building. Taylor had three movie houses at the time: the Howard which ran "A" movies, the Rita (the building the current Howard occupies) which ran the "B" movies, and the Don to the south and around the corner for the Spanish movies. When movies no longer were identified by "A" and "B" status, the Rita closed, and the Howard moved across the street and reopened on May 8, 1959, with *The Shaggy Dog*. The original ticket

Stacey Hasbrook photographer

booth separated the main entrance and the entrance to the balcony so minorities could go directly up to their seats. The theatre remained segregated until sometime late in the sixties or early seventies.

The theatre has changed ownership five times in the last eight years with Jason at the helm twice. He and his wife first leased it from March 1998 to June 1999, but when they divorced, he got rid of it. The original owners, Howard Bland and eventually daughter Betty Cromwell ran it from 1924 to 1993. When the fourth lessee gave up, Jason approached them to purchase rather than lease the building so he could "do what needs to be done, not put money into someone else's building." They liked what he had done with the theatre before, and they weren't really interested in improving, so Jason bought it from their son, Frank. When I asked if he got a good deal, Jason smiled, "Oh yeah...I always get a good deal." It's a good tax deduction and has made him a profit almost every month. He just keeps the cost as low as he can yet maintains the atmosphere and service.

Jason purchased and began renovating the entire theatre in the original fifties style in May 2000 with new floors and aesthetic touches like the original ticket counter and a display of antique movie memorabilia that he found stashed away in the numerous niches hidden in the building. Even the bathrooms are fun, identifying which to choose by pictures of Marilyn Monroe and James Dean.

When I asked Jason why he bought the Howard, he smiled and admitted it was not for romantic attachments to movies. He's a businessman with many investments and trading under his belt. In fact his parents, who live in Pflugerville, had considered buying and running it, but both were working full time so they suggested it to their son.

But it is obvious to anyone he speaks to that some magical transformation has occurred. His eyes sparkle when he talks nonstop about the theatre, and it is difficult to keep up with him when he's running around in the theatre. He is the everyman at the theatre: he takes tickets, sells refreshments, runs the films, does all the maintenance, and is the bouncer.

The bouncer? Yep. Often making it a gang hangout, kids were running wild in and out of the Howard. Steiniger won't allow it. He talks to the problem individuals, and if the behavior continues, he bans them. He doesn't believe they have been taught how to act in a theatre, and so it has become his job to educate them. That, and it's his business, which he won't allow them to destroy.

photos by Stacey Hasbrook

In a very short time Jason has learned the ins and outs of running a theatre. He followed the equipment repair guy around and learned how to thread film and run platters in one day. When he needs to fade the music, he reaches over and has to turn the volume knob to the left manually. He smiled mischievously as he did so, obviously enjoying getting to show off the neat stuff he gets to play with.

Figuring out which movies to bring in took a little practice too. He chose *Hannibal* to reopen the downstairs screen and *Save the Last Dance* upstairs. *Hannibal* bombed. That's when he learned to read his audience. "When you're from a small town, the last thing a teenager wants to do is stay in town for dates on weekends, so my audience is primarily middle school kids, upper elementary, and usually families." Thus he runs as few "R" ratings as possible.

He has also discovered Taylor is not too fond of anything that smacks of Sci-Fi as evidenced by the small showing when I was there for *Tomb Raider*. Upstairs *Shrek* seemed to fair better. Classics don't do well either. When he first reopened the upstairs screen on June 23, 2000, he played *Gladiator* and *Ben Hur* back to back. The classic didn't fly.

The theatre has two screens, the upper being the converted balcony. Upstairs has 118 seats while the downstairs seats 350 (original seats). Jason runs each film usually two, sometimes three weeks. Depending on the popularity of the film, the first week (or two) is downstairs and then the film moves to the upstairs screen.

Concerning good stories about the place, Jason prefers to recall a more recent one. The largest crowd up to that point was sixty. When *Titanic* opened in May 1998, however, the line was around the block, and the theatre sold out. It was also May with a temperature of 92 so it was the first time they had needed to use the air conditioning. When the 1950s air conditioners refused to work, the temperature inside the theatre rose above outside heat. Opening all the front and back doors he could for any sign of a breeze, Jason discovered his problems had just begun.

Suddenly the sump pumps went out and water started seeping out from the restrooms. It was clean water, but pretty soon two rivers about two feet wide and an inch or so deep were pouring through the lobby as fast as they could like currents, down the theatre aisles and toward the drains at the front where the screen is. Before Jason could completely panic, the patrons coming out for concessions simply jumped the water to the counter and with big smiles commented on how cool these unexpected special effects were. "They didn't even care." Jason finally located the spot behind the theatre to turn the water off and furiously mopped up the remains. Of the 350 customers, only about 50 decided to leave.

My experience kept me there too. Exploring around this theatre is so much fun.

Upstairs behind the balcony seats is a catwalk of a hallway painted in psychedelic, glow-in-the dark images. In this area are the tiny apartment and the original ladies' and men's restrooms, which are now Jason's bathroom/shower and Jerry the theatre cat's room. They are all separate, and to get to them you have to go out into the hallway. I think the cat must be kind of spoiled with a room all to himself.

Up more stairs and we are in the projection room, which looks much like the old fire hazards in archive pictures complete with metal doors that slam shut to contain the flames. This room does not use the old dangerous equipment though, so the threat of fire is gone, but all of it lies around the floor like a 3-D collage, including an original twenties film rewinder that still works. The room is dark, mostly wood with a low ceiling, and cozy with innumerable old and somewhat newer gadgets (forties) to investigate, including an old phone that would ring if the projectionist didn't notice the movie was messing up. And it's a little hot in the summer.

To the left of the projection room is the "Bird Room." When Jason bought the theatre, the window in this tiny room had been broken, and fifty or so pigeons with all their babies were living there. Jason's brother cleaned them out and painted and repaired the area into a bedroom for the time he was helping with the renovations. Today a stuffed black gorilla sits on the bed as a scarecrow until someone needs to stay there again.

Next, we climb up again thorough an incredibly narrow, short passageway where even short me has to duck to crawl up onto the roof where the view is incredible. I think Jason got a little nervous when I leaned out over the sidewalk to take a picture of the neon sign that now works exactly as it is supposed to for the first time in twenty-five years. The only big project left is eventually replacing the roof and painting over the leakage stains on the ceiling inside.

As I drank a new version of an old favorite, vanilla-Coke, I talked with Jim who did some of the renovation labor and helps out when he can as a volunteer. Watching happy patrons exit, I realized that for half the price of a big city movie, I can drive a shorter distance and get a fun and unusual flashback to another time. That's my plan and I'm sticking to it. —*Stacey Hasbrook*

 For information:

Jason L. Steiniger
308 N. Main St.
Taylor, TX 76574
(512) 365-2995
platinum586@hotmail.com
www.howardtheatre.com

Other attractions:

Museums, golf, parks, historic districts
New Canaan Farms
Nofsinger Home
Visitor Center
Williamson County
Sheriff's Posse Rodeo
Granger Lake

Annual events:

Rattlesnake Roundup

For details and accommodations:

Taylor Chamber of Commerce
1519 North Main Street
Taylor, TX 76574
(512) 352-7374

Terlingua: Starlight (late 1930s)

Stacey Hasbrook photographer

When you first step into the Starlight, you have to stop for a moment to get your equilibrium back. Three major attractions try to grab your attention. In the center on a raised platform midway between the front dining area and a thirty-foot-wide stage is the semicircular bar handmade of mesquite. Above the bar hang cow skulls with eyes made of ornamental Christmas balls. When asked about the skulls, proprietor Angie Dean admitted she changes them out fairly often as "I don't like to be boring." Not a chance!

Then there's the mural, "The Spirit of Terlingua," painted by Stylle Reed. It portrays a nighttime scene of a dozen miners and residents gathered around a campfire with the Chisos Mountains and Big Bend country in the background. "Picture the artist," Dean says, "a cowboy over six-foot tall, in black high-heeled boots, black shorts, black hat, and holey shirt up on scaffolding. It was hot, and he painted from nine until about six, as fast as he could go. It was like watching ghosts materialize." It looks like you could step right into the campfire scene.

And then there's Angie Dean herself, a small, muscular, but very dignified woman who is also the bouncer and refuses to have a gun in the place. Her weapon of choice is an orange plastic clown bat like rodeo clowns use. "I've escorted a lot of people out, and of course there are some folks that have been just excommunicated. Period."

The Starlight has only been called by this name since about 1979. Originally the building was the Chisos movie theatre when Terlingua was a mining town of 2,000. It was built in the late thirties. The long, narrow building (90 x 30 feet) was constructed to provide Spanish movies for the miners and their families. The original tin roof was domed, and the walls were made of adobe. According to the custom at the time, a little white picket fence framed the front of the theatre.

When the mining business slowed down in the mid-forties, Terlingua began its descent into ghost town status, but the movies ran until sometime in 1952. The front entry had a horseshoe shaped lobby rather than a rectangular entry. Finally, in 1955, the mining operations completely stopped and everything closed. Tin roofs, including that of the Chisos, were sold as scrap.

Sometime between closing and the late seventies, the building was sporadically used as a dance floor just as it was, roofless and falling apart. Thus, the new name "The Starlight Theatre." By 1990 it had stood roofless nearly forty years and was in a terrible state of deterioration and neglect.

"Those were the wet years" according to one of the bar patrons the night we visited. "Yeah, when they started cleaning it out, there were several feet of water standing down by the stage, and frogs were living there and beer cans were just floating around." Sam Richardson, editor of *The Lajitas Sun*, confirmed the circumstances when we talked to him the next day. "Just a couple of more gallons in there and you could go swimming. It was no glamour spot, certainly no tourist attraction."

The history of the theatre is interconnected with that of Angie Dean. She first came to the area from Galveston for a river trip in 1983 and couldn't believe her eyes. "The first night we camped out at the river, I was looking at the stars and said 'gosh, too bad that cloud is in the sky,' and someone said, 'Angie, that's the Milky Way.' Right then I knew I hadn't been living in the right Texas." It took a couple years to make her way to Terlingua, working as a river guide, bartender, waitress, or cleaning houses. She even had a little shop in Lajitas called Crazy Angie's Flying Circus.

In October 1990 the Ivy family, who owned the ghost town, had to add a layer of concrete to the top of the walls to level it off before a roof could be added. The top edges were only about five inches wide and were caving in. Finally, Angie and her husband leased the building and began the complete renovation of the Starlight. At that point it was just a dirty, dark, filthy building with no electricity, no water, no anything. Finishing took almost a year.

The original walls had to be filled in where necessary and were a "baby poop yellow" from years of being washed down. When Angie started scraping with a wire brush, she discovered the lovely pink plaster, so they shifted to sandblasting in July. "We had to be very careful; the walls are not very thick. It took a light touch." The entire front was gone. They had to rebuild the stairs that led to the projection area above the entrance, which now serves as Angie's office. And they sprayed the ceiling with black acoustical material for the music that would eventually be performed here. The bar opened December 31, 1991, and the restaurant in '92. By September '93 the Deans were divorced, and Angie has been in charge ever since.

The stage is used by the school drama club and for Christmas productions. Terlingua also has had a local theatre group who performs. Local singers and songwriters are highlighted regularly such as Butch Hancock, part of the Flatlanders band out of Lubbock. Well-known performers like Jerry Jeff Walker have also appeared there. "Not too much country music, but a lot of rock and roll," Angie said. There is even a donated piano that is kept tuned, and occasionally someone gets up and plays. Joan volunteered me, but I politely refused.

Some movies were shown when they first opened, but they had to have a huge satellite dish to get anything to watch like games and specials on TV. Every once in a while they have "Video Daze" where local folks bring in their home videos to entertain. "Mr. Barnes, the old coot over there, films everything," Angie said, intending for him to hear her. "He's the local paleontologist, geologist, surveyor of everything prior to seventies, and the one who discovered the swimming reptile site."

The largest crowds tend to gather for the New Year's Eve party with a band out of Austin, and one year they crammed 300 people inside. Angie describes that scene as "a--holes to elbows. It was just awful."

Proprietor and barkeep Angie Dean spins a yarn for Joan Hall. Stacey Hasbrook photographer

Every few years movie stars come to town to make a film, but "most of us are so hokey we don't know who they are," smiles Angie. Kenny Rogers did one of the Gambler films here. A favorite was Sam Shepherd who, while filming *Streets of Laredo*, a sequel to *Lonesome Dove*, came in dressed in his costume, complete with teeth browned out, "looking real seedy, and we didn't know who the heck he was." Angie's favorites have been James Garner and Sissy Spacek. "He's just as much a star in person, and she is such a nice woman."

Over the years it seems not much has changed in Terlingua—not the laid-back attitude nor the casual conversation. The hot topic of discussion this night concerned the only major change in the place recently. "What happened to your hair?" each person asked as they entered. Eventually all agreed Angie's new short haircut looked pretty darn good. Angie leaned close to whisper, "People from all over the world come out here, and I frequently feel that this bar is right out of the first *Star Wars* movie; you remember?" Indeed I could visualize the aliens at the bar scene, and her comparison seemed apt. —*Stacey Hasbrook*

For information:

Angie Dean
Starlight Theatre
P.O. Box 287
Terlingua, TX 79852
(915) 371-2326

Other attractions:

Hallie's Hall of Fame Museum
Big Bend National and State Parks
Rio Grande float trips, camping
Big Bend birding expeditions
Scenic drives
Rio Grande Village
Lajitas Resort

Annual events:

International Good Neighbor Day
Original International Memorial Championship Chili Cookoff
Terlingua International Chili Championship

For details and accommodations:

Big Bend Area Travel Association
P.O. Box 401
Alpine, TX 79831
(915) 837-2326

42

Texarkana: Perot (1924)

photo courtesy of Horace G. Shipp, Historical Resources

Two blocks farther east and Texarkana's Perot Theatre wouldn't be a Texas theatre. State Line Avenue runs north and south down the middle of the city connecting with Arkansas, and the theatre serves not only these states, but Louisiana and Oklahoma as well. The Perot's Neo-Italian Renaissance interior is the very definition of "classicism": the philosophy that art *and life* should emphasize order, balance, and simplicity; seeking what is universally true, good, and beautiful.

Architect Emil Weil is said to have designed his grand theatres to suit the character of the community, as he did in Shreveport and New Orleans. Going into this one is like entering a Greek or Roman palace. One legend says the faces of angels and babies that appear in the laurel leaf motif were sculpted on the likeness of the architect's child.

Shortly after the grand reopening in 1981, Hal Holbrook appeared there. Quoted in *Texas Highways* (June 1983), he stated "I'll bet an awful lot of people in this town don't know what they've got." Well, maybe they do. Volunteers continue to serve in key roles, and the theatre operates in the black with the majority of its funding coming from the general public: 61 percent commercial proceeds and 23 percent individual contributions.

From the outside, a prominent sign embossed in the masonry identifies the large brick building as the Saenger Theatre. Only when you approach the entrance to the lobby, do you see the tasteful brass plaque, "Perot Theatre."

Texarkana boasted eleven opera houses at one time, and the Saenger Amusement Company had three of them. One occupied what is now a parking lot across the street. A mural honoring native son Scott Joplin spreads across the wall next to the lot. In 1924 Saenger built this, their finest, to bear the company name. It opened as a venue for both motion pictures and stage performances such as vaudeville acts. One woman remembers as a child going with her grandmother to see a show. A tightrope walker balanced on a line strung from balcony to stage.

The city is located not only at a juncture of states, but along a major railway route too. Performers and patrons often stopped off for the night en route between one large city and another. Performers frequently made unscheduled appearances at a Texarkana theatre, and the Saenger was the best. Once Will Rogers along with Ziegfeld did a benefit for the drought-stricken farmers in the dustbowl of Oklahoma. Through the years celebrities such as Annie Oakley, Douglas Fairbanks Jr., and Orson Welles graced the stage.

photo courtesy of Texarkana Regional Arts and Humanities Council, Inc.

In 1931 as silent film and vaudeville declined, Paramount-Publix Corporation bought and renamed the theatre the Paramount. Through the Depression it flourished despite failed businesses around it. Nita Fran Hutcheson, director of marketing and development, says her parents told of a typical Saturday night treat during their courting days. For twenty-five cents, they could dance at the rooftop garden of the Grim Hotel nearby (now vacant) before going to the midnight show at the Paramount. About that time the movie houses started offering dishes for a nickel apiece, and Hutcheson's parents collected a set of green "Depression glass."

During the war years, newsreels kept people informed, and patriotism ran high. To conserve on electricity for the "war effort," some of the massive chandeliers were taken out. Free passes went to firefighters and police officers. Ushers remember the crowds as the rowdiest ever, and when news reported the end of WW II, people made a human chain leading from the auditorium aisles up through the balcony.

Saturday was a favorite for children. Popcorn cost a nickel and two people could share a Coke. Horace Shipp, chairman of the Historical Resources Committee, liked the matinees and cartoons, but it cost fifteen cents to get into the Paramount, and he could afford it only on special occasions. Most of the time he went to the Strand across the street for only nine cents. Sometimes he could even pay with R.C. Cola bottle caps.

But times changed after the war. The Paramount went to second- and then third-rate movies. Ushers were said to have bagged up the leftover popcorn each evening to take to the police station in appreciation for their help in dealing with the ever more frequent patron disturbances. By the end of 1977, the theatre shut down.

The city of Texarkana sought funds to purchase and restore what had been declared a National Historic Treasure. Individual contributions came in as well as several grants, but this wasn't enough. They presented their plight to the family of H. Ross Perot, who had grown up here before becoming famous as a successful businessman. The family had gone to the Paramount frequently, and H. Ross and his sister, Bette, along with other family members decided it would be a fitting tribute to their parents. They gave their backing. In fact Bette worked closely with the organization to recapture the theatre's original grace and beauty.

Texarkana contractors Lacy Enterprises, Inc. formed a team with the Austin firm of Bell, Klein, and Hoffman, specialists in historic preservation design. Work on the outside of the building was completely structural except for removing the old Paramount marquee. On entering the outer lobby, you see the black and white checkerboard marble floor, worn from countless feet where people bought their tickets. A huge beveled mirror with gold leaf frame hangs at one side, flanked by historical pictures. An inner lobby, lit by crystal chandeliers, leads patrons to their seats. Dark blue draperies have replaced the concession stand.

In the mezzanine hangs a portrait of Bette and H. Ross's mother, Lulu May Perot, but their father, Gabriel Ross Perot, disliked having his picture made. According to a quote in the *Texarkana Gazette*, H. Ross said his father claimed "he only wanted to be hanged once."

As of April 2001, the likeness of another family member also stands in the mezzanine. H. Ross and Bette never knew their brother, Gabriel Ross Jr., born in 1924. He had died at the age of three due to a sudden stomach illness, but the parents told many stories about him. One story related how the family liked to meet friends in front of the theatre on Saturday nights and listen to music played by the Salvation Army Band. Little Gabriel would "dance his heart out, and they would give him a tambourine to play." The child's statue depicts him smiling, dancing, and waving.

photo courtesy of Texarkana Regional Arts and Humanities Council, Inc.

Bette Perot spared no effort to keep restoration details authentic. Fifty-seven years of spilled Coke, food, and gum had ruined the carpet, but one undamaged area was found under a stairwell. This sample was sent to the original London manufacturer for matching and weaving. It was worth it. The blue and gray leaf design set the color scheme for the entire theatre.

Intricate designs in relief molding decorate everything—proscenium columns, ceilings, and arches. Most was intact, except where they pulled out the concession stand. Heat and grease had ruined it there, and it crumbled. For this reason and the carpet damage, they no longer allow food and drinks in the theatre. The molding had been painted one flat color before. Now backed with blue, the reliefs stand out in shades ranging from brown to ivory. Gold leaf highlights the moldings. Executive director Ruth Ellen Whitt added, "At a cost of $14,000 in 1977."

I could have spent an evening admiring the ceiling alone with its inlaid designs. Light fixtures with iridescent light bulbs hang from large medallions. When the company that made them went out of business, Whitt said they bought all the bulbs they could get. Many of the chandeliers and wall sconces remain. The ones that had been removed were replaced with close matches from the Baker Hotel in Dallas after it was demolished.

The Perot accommodates 1,606. Downstairs the seats have been replaced, but the original aisle standards, bearing a gold "S" for "Saenger" were kept. Seats in the three-tiered balcony have been refurbished. As in most other theatres, minorities had to buy their tickets at a separate booth, enter a separate door, and sit in the highest tier of the balcony. "Yes, we had our days of infamy," Whitt said.

Appearance works in harmony with modern comfort and functionality. However, the original movie projector has been totally restored to give audiences an authentic experience when viewing classic films. The Perot is listed as a Texas Historic Landmark and is on the National Register of Historic Places.

The grand reopening in 1981 fostered a two-day party of street dances, picnics, and gala dinners. The Dallas Symphony performed, and big names have been coming ever since: Cary Grant, the Vienna Choir Boys, Burl Ives, Blood Sweat and Tears, to name but a few. The Paramount has been the site of several movie premieres such as Jackie Gleason's *Papa's Delicate Condition*.

The theatre had originally used a large pipe organ, but at some time it was moved backstage in bad shape. Whitt, showed it to me, explaining that experts estimate moving it back and refurbishing it would cost $500,000. "It's my goal," she said, "to see that happen by the year 2003."

She pointed to a photo (circa thirties) in which a band is seated on the awning roof at either side of the Paramount marquee. For safety reasons, they can't do that anymore, but Whitt adds, "My other goal is to get an orchestra on that roof."

As we toured, Whitt now and then picked up a tiny scrap of paper or ticket stub. "The end of school is a busy time for us," she said. "Dance studios schedule their recitals one after another."

Programs for school children are a major emphasis. "Kids today don't know how to present themselves in a theatre, so we have to teach them." Whitt said. "We show them how sound carries in these acoustics, which have been favorably compared to Lincoln Center. We offer some tickets for as little as five dollars in an effort not to exclude anyone. About 13,000 kids a year come through here now."

Later Nita Fran Hutcheson spoke about the fun of leading kids' tours. They're always interested in spirits they've heard rumors about, so she tells them, "Everyone who comes here leaves something. Now that you've been here, a part of your spirit is here too."

And she knows a thing or two about spirits. While the old stage boards were being torn out, tap strip, trapdoor and all, she and theatre director Terri Stepan were at hand. She kept glimpsing images behind her and from the corner of her eye, but she didn't want to mention it. Who would believe such a thing? Then once, she jumped enough to make Stepan ask what happened. She confessed, and Stepan said, "Oh, I've been seeing them for two weeks."

Hutcheson surmises, "We had disturbed the spirits. Once the stage was laid, we never saw them again."

She also related an experience that happened to Jim Stuhlmiller. He was on the catwalk working with lights when he lost his balance. He felt someone grab his shirt and pull him back to keep him from falling. He turned to say thank you, but no one was there.

Hutcheson doesn't worry about it anymore. She accepts spirits as part of inevitable change saying, "Treasure the past, participate in the present, and plan for the future."

Did architect Emil Weil have the town pegged right in choosing a classical decor? The definition fits. The most successful periods for the Saenger/Paramount/Perot have brought together common ideals for art, man, and his surroundings. —*Joan Upton Hall*

 For information:

Texarkana Regional Arts & Humanities Council, Inc. (TRAHC)
P.O. Box 1171
Texarkana, TX 75504
(903) 792-8681
Fax: (903) 793-8510
artsinfo@trahc.org
www.trahc.org

Other attractions:

Post office & Justice Center (on state line)
Scott Joplin mural
Theme parks
Oaklawn Opry
Regional Arts Center
Museums & exhibits
Union Station

Annual events:

Quadrangle Street Festival
Four States Fair & Rodeo
Junior League Mistletoe Fair
Stranger Bluegrass Festival
Jump, Jive & Jam Fest

For details and accommodations:

Chamber of Commerce
819 State Line Ave.
Texarkana, TX 75501
(903) 792-7191
chamber@texarkana.org
www.texarkana.org

43

Uvalde: Opera House (1891)

Stacey Hasbrook photographer

Esther Trevino, managing director of the Opera House in Uvalde, doesn't mind if the elevator comes all the way down, opens, and then closes because that could be an electrical issue. If, however, it stops on the second floor, "I refuse to go up there and check," she whispers. Ghost stories have circulated for a long time. No one knows who the ghost might be, but strange things do seem to happen, and people have even left the theatre in the middle of work because of strange feelings.

A night picture taken by the *San Antonio Express News* ten years ago further promotes rumors of a ghost. The photographer and staff made sure that everything in the windows of the theatre lined up perfectly and that the tops of a row of cabinets in the background, which could barely be seen from the street, were cleared of clutter so the light from the windows would show perfectly. When the picture came back and the article was printed, there in the window of the cupola was an unidentifiable figure on top of a cabinet that the photographer swears was not there when the picture was taken.

Another ghostly example involves the times when staff have made sure to turn out all the lights to go to an evening meeting or reception. When they return they find the lights in the men's restroom are on again. As we climbed to the first landing, Esther stopped on the stairs to clarify, "The funny thing about it is if you're up there walking around alone and you feel something, it's not scary. The atmosphere is actually very calming."

Built in 1891, the Opera House is Uvalde's oldest standing public landmark. The records show title transfers from city founder Reading W. Black to FA Piper, the first mercantile occupant, and then to John Nance Garner in 1916. The Uvalde Real Estate and Building Company, a pioneer civic group, provided for construction of the building to "dazzle the townspeople and ranch folk of the area as well as travelers directly across the plaza on the thoroughfare once known as the Old Spanish Trail."

The scene of many melodramas, The Opera House was once considered the "center of cultural activity in southwest Texas," and during performing seasons, professional traveling groups would arrive. The theatre was an early day tourist destination, and groups would travel by train north of Uvalde and then come down from the station to the theatre by wagon. In 1907 the grand opera *Faust* was presented. In 1908 the Methodist church brought in the *Mikado* for a benefit, and many believe it was the most lavish ever presented in the theatre's history.

The ground floor has always been for commercial business, but the upstairs was the town's only place for large social gatherings. It has been used for a variety of events including church meetings, service clubs, and wedding receptions. They even showed a few silent movies until it was turned into an office building in 1916.

Original stores operated on either side of the theatre entrance on the first floor to help maintain the building. The bottom floor made money to support the theatre above, which was "built to bring the arts to the frontier." The roof was made of copper, and it had a copper-plated corner bay with a steeple topped by an ornate weathervane, Poof the drunken dragon.

Esther said the story of the dragon is that the builder wanted a weather vane on top of the cupola. He went drinking with the architect, and "that's what he came up with. It has bullet marks, the tail's gone, and it never would turn." In 1993 Poof was brought down, and a bronze replica of it was designed to replace it. The original Poof lives in the small museum next to the reception area for the theatre. For its size, this museum contains an incredible amount of historical information and artifacts.

Stacey Hasbrook photographer

Governor Dolph Briscoe and his wife were major supporters of the Opera House. The Garner family donated the building to the city in 1979. A commission was appointed to plan the restoration, which began in December 1979 with a grant from the Texas State Historical Commission and matching city funds. The Opera House reopened October 1, 1982.

After Mrs. Briscoe died, the city council made a motion to change the name of the Opera House to honor her. When it came out in the paper, Esther called to inform them that it would cause problems since the Opera House is identified as a historic place with a marker. The city owns the building and could have made the change but decided to place her portrait in a prominent place on the rise of the stairway instead. They had to move the original painting of John N. Garner further up on the side wall to do it. His portrait dated from when he was the vice president of the United States. People often tell Esther, "See how he looks at you. He's mad at you for moving him." But the two portraits make a big impression on people climbing the stairs.

Up above to the left, the White Room, named for the benefactors whose portraits hang there, is the reception area where the ghost figure shows up in that newspaper picture. The three wooden drop leaf tables, originally from Garner, sit side by side to form one long meeting table. The windows and wood are all original, as is the glass in the windows and in the beautiful bay window area.

The floor inside the theatre was originally flat and the stage slanted forward sharply. "How the actors stayed on there, I have no idea," Esther commented. Now the seating area slants down toward the stage, which had to be raised on one end to make it level. The trusses and alternating steel beams are all original, and the columns have never been repainted, just cleaned with wood cleaner. Most of the 370 seats came from a nineteenth-century theatre that was being demolished. They were reupholstered in 1981. The stenciling up and over the stage was copied from an original piece.

Originally a kerosene chandelier was lowered and raised from the ceiling to light the theatre, and a small kerosene lamp lit each window, creating a smelly but very beautiful effect. The stage was also lit with little kerosene lamps lined up across the front.

The large, elaborate dressing rooms below theatre level are in their original locations, but electricity and showers were added. This area is kept very cool because it gets so hot between the floors, and the actors get their exercise going up and down the flight of stairs between the dressing rooms and stage.

The front part of the theatre is three stories high, with the two-story auditorium on the second floor, but on the back wall the hallway and dressing rooms are up only a little over half a story (between the first and second floors) so opening the escape hatch above the hallway puts you on the roof behind the building, which is only two stories high.

To really appreciate the aura of the Opera House, one has to sit dead center in the balcony and enjoy the peace that settles there. One of the special benefits is that the atmosphere creates concerts that are more intimate than in other places. Esther pointed out that the younger ones "have to learn how to act, but they don't seem to mind that it's a true concert the way it's supposed to be."

Rumor has a trap door located somewhere on the stage, but it has never been found. The balcony was closed down for twenty-eight years until the roof could be replaced, but the ceiling suffered little damage and has the original paint. The first stage curtain had local advertisements and a floral design, but it has also been replaced. The use of long yellow pine throughout makes the acoustics perfect. Professionals don't even need microphones to project well.

The most famous visiting performer was probably Lillie Langtry, but Uvalde produced its own actors with Dale Evans and Dana Andrews as well as more currently, Matthew McConaghy.

Currently the 370-seat theatre has community and professional performances and a concert series. Every six weeks or so there is a new performance, but musicals take a little longer to prepare. Planning the show schedule is done about a year in advance.

In addition, sometimes art displays line up the stairway leading to the balcony where all of the stained glass except four small panes is original. Community awareness programs are held each season to benefit all citizens. There is also a Celebration Fund where individuals make a donation in honor of a special person.

Just to make the point it seems, when we were on the second floor walking toward the back of the sitting area, suddenly Esther said, "See. These are the things I'm talking about." She reached in to move the wooden wedge door jam and close the ladies' room door. "I came to the bathroom this morning, and this door was closed. So I won't go in there the rest of the day. I'll go next door." We can't vouch for whether or not this is true, but the look on Esther's face was clear—she knows who had opened that door. —*Stacey Hasbrook*

For information:

Esther Trevino
104 W. North St.
Uvalde, TX 78801
(830) 278-4184
esther@peppersnet.com

Other attractions:

Museums, parks, golf, forts
Scenic drive
Briscoe Art and Antique Collection
National Fish Hatchery
El Progresso Memorial Library
Pioneer Cemetery
Alamo Village

Annual events:

National Soaring Competition
Sahawe Indian winter/summer ceremonial dances
Wings Over Uvalde (sailplane)

For details and accommodations:

Chamber of Commerce
300 East Main Street
P.O. Box 706
Uvalde, TX 78801
(830) 278-3361
Victoria@uvalde.org

Uvalde Convention & Visitors Bureau
300 E. Main St.
Uvalde, TX 78801
1-800-588-2533
(830) 278-4115
Kimbra@uvaldecvb.org
www.uvalde.org

44

Victoria: Victoria (1910)

Stacey Hasbrook photographer

When Sheila Westerholm, development/marketing director for the Victoria Community Theatre, and I walked into the beautiful home of Rubin Frels, the owner of the Victoria Theatre, we knew we were in for a treat. In addition to the house and furniture, throughout were pianos and organs of various ages. When I close my eyes now to try to count them, I see two grand pianos in the living room and at least three other instruments in the dining room. These are the keys to the legacy passed down to the son of movie history in Victoria.

Rubin Frels Sr. moved to Victoria from Palestine in 1924 and was one of two families who controlled the movie industry in town. In five years he

245

built a movie dynasty of sorts in central and south Texas, and at one point he probably owned seventeen different movie houses. He was the last of ten children and set up his entire family in the theatre business. An article written in the late twenties reported Frels' purchase of a lot near the square where he would build a modern Victoria Theatre predicted to be a "great credit and serve the city for many years to come." It was to include all the modern devices including the installation of a Vitaphone for talking pictures. This site would open as the Uptown Theatre in 1931. At this time he operated the Victoria and Princess theatres in Victoria and had theatres in Cuero, Goliad, Yorktown, Columbus, Yoakum, Sealy, and Bellville.

photo courtesy of Rubin S. Frels

Rubin Frels was a man in charge of his business. In the late thirties and early forties the senior Frels had a tiff with the Central Power and Light Company. He thought their rates were too high so he built a shelf of concrete over the alley and supported it with big steel rods. There he put some engines and generators to make his own electricity. That way he wasn't connected to the city, and in the '42 hurricane, the theatre was the only place that had lights.

Frels had one of the two theatres that were air conditioned at the beginning of WW II, and he had to learn to fix the compressors himself. As the war intensified, the building was closed as a theatre and turned into a beauty shop. After the war Frels leased the building again and took out the concrete floor so the original showed. At that time the arched front entry got straightened out, and the Victoria sign was destroyed.

There must have been quite a bit of prestige involved with the control of the local movie industry as one photo in *Historic Victoria* shows a black and white picture of Mrs. Frels riding in a touring car with Mrs. Franklin D. Roosevelt.

Frels's son Rubin has a favorite story, but he wasn't there when it happened. In 1926 the theatre had a small pipe organ, and at some big show the organist showed up drunk. Rubin's father fired him on the spot. Frels had heard about a young lady working as a telegrapher at the Western Union at the end of the block, so he went down there and asked if she would like to play the organ at the Victorian. When she answered, "I don't play the organ, just the piano," his reply was, "Well, you're going to play one tonight." Soon after that they fell in love and married, and "then a little later I came along," Rubin chuckled. Ah, a movie love story.

When Gene Autry came to town, he stayed in the family home. Rubin remembers Autry's horse on the stage. He also remembers that when Autry and his sidekick Smiley Burnett dined in the Frels' home, they "ate fried chicken like crazy." When the Frels later visited Smiley's home in California, Rubin's mother became sad when she saw an organ there because her husband had gotten rid of the organ from the theatre.

Rubin has become an expert craftsman, builder, and renovator of organs. He was more than a little surprised when he went down to A&I (now A&M Kingville) to help the music department. They had a little practice organ that he took in trade not realizing it was the original one from the theatre that his mother had played. It didn't look the same even though the main parts remained. He hasn't decided what to do with it, "though it wouldn't be hard to re-create it." In addition to the organ, some of the original furniture is also in Rubin's home.

In an article by Vince Reedy, a former editor with *The Victoria Advocate*, Gary Dunnam explained why so many of the old theatres went under to the multiplex concept. Multi-screens that are located in one area can run with about the same staff as a single screen, but they pull in much more in ticket and concession prices. The heydays were the fifties, and it was a booming business with double features, a midnight showing on the weekends, and different shows every week. Before economics killed off the downtown theatres though, fire destroyed two of them.

The Victoria Theatre is the last and oldest movie house left standing in town. Vince Reedy reminisced in an article, "New theatre harkens back to the heyday of movie houses."

Today's multiple shows are a far cry from the nostalgic days in old downtown Victoria, back when they sold tickets and popcorn to folks lined up all for the same program...no PG-13 or R ratings to contend with, just a movie for everyone on the only screen in the house.

An article dated December 3, 1983, in *The Victoria Advocate* relates a history of the Frels theatres in Victoria. Eddie Reyna began with the Frels' movie chain as a popcorn boy on December 4, 1938, wearing a suit he had borrowed from his brother. Yes, even the popcorn vendor had to wear a suit to work in a theatre. Reyna worked himself up to booking agent at a time when the studios produced up to 650 films a year. Now they only do about 200, but programs don't change four times a week anymore.

The schedule changed every two days with a different show for Saturday only. The theatres used to buy movies in blocks of fifty or sixty directly from the companies. Now the multi-screens keep one show anywhere from two to twenty weeks at a time. During Eddie's time prices were a nickel for children and a quarter for adults, and a date cost about sixty cents for two tickets and two bags of popcorn. But around 1941 it went up to nine and thirty-five cents respectively. Reyna's only complaint about the movie business concerned the sex and violence. "Remember the nice fade-outs [on bedroom scenes] they used to have?"

Today the colors of the theatre are deep reds, yellows, greens, and blues, which match the tiles on the wall outside. The Victoria Theatre is strictly for live performances, not movies, and houses the Victoria

Community Theatre, which was chartered in 1977 but can be traced back to the fifties. It is the largest arts organization in the area and is a nonprofit, tax-exempt educational organization. Soon, however, a new performing arts center will be built, and the fate of the Victoria Theatre is once again back in family hands. It is certain that Rubin Frels, the son of Victoria's movie man, will continue the music in some form, and he is determined the theatre "will not be demolished!" —*Stacey Hasbrook*

Sound and light booth. Stacey Hasbrook photographer

For more information:

Sheila Westerholm
P.O. Box 1365
207 E. Constitution St.
Victoria, TX 77902
(361) 576-4744
1-800-677-5696
sheilaqotj@yahool.com

More attractions:

Parks, camping, golf
Texas Zoo
East Texas Oil Museum
Fannin Battleground State
Historic Site
Rangerette Showcase
Coleto Creek Reservoir
Mustang Wilderness

For details and accommodations:

Chamber of Commerce
Victoria Convention &
Visitors Bureau
P.O. Box 2456
Victoria, TX 77902
(361) 573-5277

45

Waxahachie: Chautauqua Auditorium (1902)

Don Hall photographer

On seeing Waxahachie's Chautauqua Auditorium for the first time, I had the impression of a wooden circus tent, including the spire on top. No wonder: it started as a real tent in 1900, a design that carried over when the auditorium was built in 1902. It survives as the only Chautauqua in Texas today.

Chautauquas were originally a summer training retreat for Sunday school teachers. Their purpose eventually grew into an educational and cultural movement. Similar assemblies were established throughout the country, and traveling circuits or "tent Chautauquas" sprang up, continuing through the 1930s. The Indian name "Chautauqua," comes from Lake Chautauqua, New York, where the idea originated in 1874.

Interestingly, some scorned the traveling "show people," despite the high standards expected of them. The *Chautauqua News* of Waxahachie's Preservation Society quoted a story from Theodore Morrison's *Chautauqua: A Center for Education, Religion and the Arts in America* (University of Chicago Press, 1974). It happened at a little town just north of Abilene, whose population has since dwindled, but it was once a candidate for a Chautauqua of its own.

> [This] association [of immorality and performers] led to a remarkable dispute described by Marion Scott. In Tuxedo, Texas, it seems the Methodist minister wanted a Chautauqua, while the Baptist minister considered Chautauqua depraved. The town divided behind the two champions, and all factions came together, first to argue then to pray. Failing any manifest answer to prayer, the two ministers agreed to fight, the town shut its businesses and rallied to watch. Before squaring off, the two contestants prayed again. Then they set to, the Methodists won, and the town got its Chautauqua.

Waxahachie got its Chautauqua in 1900 and built the auditorium. Each year at the end of July it held a two-week-long assembly. Families traveling by wagon, on horseback, or on foot came to hear such notables as William Jennings Bryan and Will Rogers. People set up tents under the towering trees in what is now Getzendaner Park. Records report 200 tents in 1905 and over 3,000 attendees in 1913.

According to Kirk Hunter and Maureen Moore, the auditorium literally overflowed with participants during the most popular presentations. Buggies would pull up next to the windows to provide extra seating, and at least once, tents were erected there to shade the crowds. Attendance was estimated to be 5,000 to 7,000 at times.

In the early seventies the Chautauqua Auditorium had fallen into such disrepair the city considered tearing it down. Shannon Simpson, of the Ellis County Museum, recalls as a boy, being able to get inside easily and "walking across exposed floor joists, where boards were missing."

Citizens pitched in though, and by 1974 it was restored, complete with a small-scale replica built out front as a ticket office. It had also earned a Texas historical marker and placement on the National Register of Historical Places.

courtesy of Shannon Simpson, Ellis County Museum

Restored today as it was in 1902, the octagonal structure (patterned after the Institution in New York) has a seating capacity of 2,500. Wooden garage-like doors can be raised to make it an open-air building. John Smith, Parks and Recreation director, pointed out the craftsmanship and ingenious design of the building. A key feature is the cantilevering mechanism of the wooden door and window panels that makes them glide smoothly into the upper portion of the wall, discreetly hidden. The original stage floor, many times refinished, is intact. We tend to think such a building would require modern engineering and steel framing, but the main structure has stood for 100 years. Those carpenters of bygone days knew a thing or two.

Inside, the beauty and warmth of varnished wood surrounded me. I sat on one of the long, park-style benches and took it all in as the stage curtain billowed in the wind. My gaze was drawn to the beaded board ceiling that peaks in the middle and the pie-shaped wedges that radiate out from a center supporting post.

original beaded board ceiling, Don Hall photographer

Under-stage dressing rooms, accessible by twisting, narrow stairs, have now added restrooms. A large water tank furnishes drinking water. Ceiling fans, electric lights, and heaters provide more comfort than earlier patrons enjoyed, but the building could have worked without them. I could see myself settling in for a two-week-long retreat in this peaceful place. However, tent living for two weeks, especially if it rained, may have tested the patrons a bit.

Today a typical Waxahachie Chautauqua Assembly is a one-day affair. It continues to offer programs that entertain while they teach, and it doesn't have to bring talent in from New York to do it. Sessions for a recent assembly were as follows: "From Celts to Cowboys" (finding the roots of familiar tunes), "Chemistry Alive" (humorous style combined with scientific demonstrations, just as it was done 100 years ago), "Journeys into

253

Folk Art" (what it is, how it comes to life through examples), "Shakespeare: Revised & Alive" (experience *Romeo & Juliet* with a surprise ending in a tradition that harkens back to the earliest examples), "Comanche Land Forever" (names in modern-day Texas celebrating the Comanches' sense of place and need for preservation), "Rescuing Texas' Legendary Courthouses" (examples of these historic "temples of justice" of which Texas has more than any other state), "Celebrating Bach — What's in a Name?" (lets you in on some of the fascinating extras from the mind of the composer), and "Conversations with Will Rogers."

Other organizations make use of the auditorium as well. The Multi-Cultural Arts Center recently hosted a performance of African dances. The Fort Worth Symphony gives a concert each year. The Waxahachie Community Theatre presents a play each spring using elaborate costumes and sets. They recently performed *The King and I.* Surrounding towns hold dance recitals there. Smith adds, "But the most popular bookings are for weddings."

Just what makes the Chautauqua idea different from that of vaudeville? I had a hard time distinguishing it at first. For one thing they both appeared and grew popular during the late 1800s and very early 1900s. They both depended on traveling circuit performers, and both suffered a loss of popularity in competition with movies and radio. But miles apart were their approaches.

Chautauqua programs, originally designed for Sunday school teachers for religious and educational purposes, were then broadened to include culture and entertainment. So how could anybody object to that? Well, remember that fight between the two ministers in Tuxedo, Texas? What the negative faction objected to were the more extravagant or sensational programs. Apparently they operated on the idea that if you're having fun, it must be "depraved."

The Chautauqua Preservation Society of Waxahachie explained it best in their January/February 2001 newsletter. Early vaudeville had a different approach. It was geared toward a mostly male working-class audience looking for slapstick and bawdy laughs. As society changed, Chautauqua became more liberal and vaudeville more refined. If vaudeville still wasn't cultured, at least respectable people could watch its songs, dances, and comedy routines. By the twenties both venues were vying for the same audience and succeeding only on a superficial level. People decided to watch picture shows and pay less money.

Other Chautauquas disappeared completely during this period when they forgot what made them different. Thirty other towns in Texas once had Chautauquas. Due to the vision of the town's citizens, Waxahachie's found new life. At the rededication ceremony of 1975, speaker Dr. Ernest Connally from the U.S. Department of the Interior said a historic building like the Chautauqua Auditorium was "a link between generations bearing a message in three-dimensional, tangible form of human aspirations and endeavor."

Kirk Hunter adds, "That was twenty-five years ago. Since then, one more generation has come of age and become part of the link. We are all fortunate recipients of the legacy of the Chautauqua Auditorium and the messages it brings to us." —*Joan Upton Hall*

For information:

Kirk Hunter
Chautauqua Preservation Society
1112 West Jefferson Street
Waxahachie, TX 75165
(972) 937-8887
khmm@hpnc.com

Other attractions:

Ellis County Courthouse
Texas Theater & Courthouse Video (on square)
Ellis County Museum
Nicholas P. Sims Library
Lakes, parks, specialty shopping

Annual events:

Scarborough Faire
Renaissance Festival
Gingerbread Home Tour
Bethlehem Revisited
Motorplex races
Classic Bike Rally
Seasonal events

For details and accommodations:

Chamber of Commerce
Convention & Visitors Bureau
102 YMCA Drive
P.O. Box 187
Waxahachie, TX 75168
(972) 937-2390 or
(972) 938-9617
www.waxahachie.com

46

Whitewright: Odeum (1914)

Don Hall photographer

Remember the line "If you build it, they will come," from *Field of Dreams*? Well, it seems *re*-building is exactly what Pat Hubbard is doing with Whitewright, a little town sixty miles northeast of Dallas, a little town that didn't even appear in the *Texas Travel Guide*. "There was nothing to keep the youth from leaving," Hubbard said. Although houses and stores showed evidence of an affluent past, most of them were boarded up and/or run-down, and that went for the Odeum Theatre too.

That's what Martha and Mack Woodruff of Trenton were used to seeing when they revisited it a couple of years ago. They were amazed to discover the wonderful little secret of a restaurant named Coffee & Pie Oh

My! and a theatre the equal of any in Dallas. But it didn't stay secret for long. "Now," Martha says, "We have to call ahead for a reservation for dinner."

What a difference it makes when good will, imagination, and money come together! Success and hard times, however, had given Whitewright a roller coaster ride through the years.

Around the early 1900s the town thrived as a major railroad and agricultural center. It boasted Grayson College and early forms of theatre (shown in tents and the school). Then in 1911 a massive fire swept through town. Twenty or thirty Victorian mansions and the whole main street were destroyed except for the First National Bank (a fine old corner building now being transformed into a B&B). Most of the buildings except the college were later rebuilt.

Time was ripe in 1914 for a proper theatre, so Morehead & Mangrum built the Odeon, a variation of the present name "Odeum."

As reprinted from the *Whitewright Sun*, the grand opening announcement read:

> Without making any rash promises, we feel confident that our comfortably seated and well ventilated fire-proof show house and our arrangement with the film companies for the best pictures representing the favorite talent and costly production, will meet your approval. Our contract with the General Film Company insures us the best Vitagraphs...and other companies that employ high-priced talent in the production of pictures.
>
> *The Perils of Pauline*, a popular serial picture that is now holding the center of interest in Dallas and other large cities, will be a regular feature at the Odeon every Monday night until we catch up..., then every other week until this popular picture serial is completed....Come Friday night...and see what we have prepared at great expense for your amusement and edification.

A later edition again assured a "practically fireproof" building, and went on to promise the following amenities: "free ice water and a telephone," "fans now in transit," "a player-piano...the latest that could be purchased," and "a clock placed where the time may be ascertained."

All this for a ticket price of five or ten cents. How could anyone refuse?

In the early twenties a partnership that owned several other area theatres bought the Odeon but sold it in 1926. This began a series of new owners, renovations, and renamings: "R&R," "Linda," and "Palace." Despite precautions, the Palace did burn in 1943, and during wartime it was almost impossible to get building materials. The owner had to install used seats. To make matters worse, after the war, the general loss of public interest in picture shows caught up with the Palace too, and it closed down.

Then came Pat Hubbard, mother of seven children, who had moved out of Dallas, then Plano, and then Allen. Finally, about twenty years ago, she and her family settled on a 500-acre ranch near Whitewright. "This is as far north as I'm going!" she declared. Experienced at restoring houses, she turned one of the downtown buildings into a restaurant so she could get a good piece of pie whenever she wanted it. Next a nice dress shop like her grandmother had owned. Then, missing the fine old movie houses she had grown up with in Dallas, she said, "I never restored a theatre, so I decided it would be fun."

By that time the theatre's seriously leaking roof had taken its toll, and all they could save were the side walls and the original lobby floor. Since there was no way to tell what the theatre had originally looked like inside, Hubbard decided to go with her favorite theme, Egyptian. Having traveled extensively in Egypt and Africa, she knew her subject well. She hired a Pennsylvania company that specialized in restoring theatres, and the man in charge was Jim Mustard.

Mustard's credentials are impressive. He's done restoration on the largest flagship palaces and the small town beauties. In addition to theatres in other states, he either fully restored or did remedial work on such Texas theatres as the Lincoln in Houston, the Majestic in Brownsville, the Grenada in Dallas, the Aztec and Alameda in San Antonio, the Victoria Theatre, and the Inwood in Dallas. It may tell us something that he stayed on at the Odeum as the manager.

Hubbard said, "The managers I've hired for my businesses are in their late sixties, and it's working out really well."

One of these managers is Ben Jones of Hubbard Galleries (and, yes, you should expect quality art when you visit the shop). Jones' uncle by marriage was the Morehead who built the theatre, and he has family portraits to go in the museum (close to completion when I was there). He also showed me a book by Billy Holcomb, *Theatre Row: Movie Palaces of Denison, Texas*, that demonstrated the area's love for fine old movie houses. There were thirty of them in that one town and only one remains. Hubbard Galleries was a major benefactor in publishing the book, and the editor, Mavis Anne Bryant, is now researching Whitewright buildings.

Hubbard changed the theatre's name one more time to the "Odeum" and decorated according to inspiration from tombs of the pharaohs, using authentic looking reproductions—a sarcophagus here, hieroglyphics there,

a goddess atop a pillar, anything that carries patrons to another time and place via imagination. Stained glass depicting Egyptian designs surrounds the front door. "Cleopatra's Throne Room" and "Tutankhamen's Throne Room" signs identify the restrooms. The atmosphere of the 154-seat auditorium is plush.

Manager Jim Mustard showed us the inner workings of the Odeum. When he demonstrated his top-of-the-line equipment, it's to his tribute that, as technically challenged as I am, he was nevertheless able to make me understand—and be fascinated. I now know, for example, why special layering of walls perfects the sound. Why a seamless, special screen will pay off when movies on digital disks become the norm. Why you'd buy a $3,000 Schneider lens from Germany when you could use a $495 one from Kodak.

Don Hall photographer

"Of course there's a need for cheaper equipment too," Mustard added. "If you're running a twenty-screen theatre, you need sixty lenses."

Runco, "the Cadillac of the business," plans to bring its new equipment and use the Odeum for demo purposes because they realize this theatre can do justice to their product. It's ready for digital disk and satellite delivery systems.

"The only other theatre in this country," Mustard said, "that equals our sound and picture quality is the George Lucas Theatre at Skywalker Ranch in California, where I've been many times."

In short, the Odeum isn't just a pretty face. Once people attend a movie there, they bring their friends next time for a surprising experience of sight and sound. They tell Mustard things like, "We've found a little golden jewel on Grand Street in Whitewright!"

Pat Hubbard downplayed her mentorship, saying, "Anyone can make a difference, and it's contagious."

I recalled driving into town and being struck by the number of people I saw repairing their houses or doing landscape work. It seems Hubbard's aim to rebuild Whitewright and "they will come" is working on many levels. —*Joan Upton Hall*

For information:

The Odeum Theatre
114 W. Grand St.
P.O. Box 864
Whitewright, TX 75491
(903) 364-9939

Other attractions:

Museum
Art gallery
Lakes, specialty shopping
Walking and driving tours

Annual events:

Mother's Day Rose & Garden Tour

For details and accommodations:

Visitors & Information Center
125 W. Grand Street
Whitewright, TX 75491
(903) 364-2000

47

Wichita Falls: Wichita Theatre and Opera House (1908)

Ernest Upton photographer

The idea of balancing respect for a historic building and making a profit is like walking a fiber-optics-thin tightrope, but the Wichita Theatre and Opera House seems to be accomplishing the feat. "And it only took us five years of experience and a million-dollar investment to come up with a workable plan," laughed Dwayne Jackson. He and his wife, Lisa, are co-directors as well as president and vice president respectively of Stellar Art Group.

The Texas historical marker tells that the Wichita Falls Opera Company was formed in 1908, with land and funding donated. According to a 1938 article in the *Wichita Daily Times*, "Those who built it did not expect it to make money, and they were not disappointed on that score." It was a much finer theatre than you'd expect for a population of only 6,500, and since it wasn't on a well-traveled route, theatrical companies demanded high guarantees for coming. Committed to bringing culture to the city, the company brought in such celebrities as William Jennings Bryan, Anna Pavlova, Lillian Russell, Ernestine Schumann-Heink, and Evelyn Nesbitt. In 1913 *Ben Hur* was presented there because the Opera House had the only stage in Texas that didn't have to be altered to accommodate it.

When motion pictures came in, the owner remodeled the interior for film presentation and brought in a mechanical piano to accompany the silent films. Competition, however, proved to be too much when several other movie houses sprang up and a municipal auditorium was built. The Opera House closed in 1926.

1908, photo courtesy of Dwayne and Lisa Jackson

In 1938 a series of articles in the *Times* lamented the fact that the building was about to be razed. It held many memories for old-timers who remembered it as a gathering place for events like the "Liberty Bond Follies" of World War I. This aroused interest, and the building was reopened in 1939 as the Wichita Theatre.

A group of attorneys bought it in 1980 for musical concerts. Shows like the Light Crust Doughboys and Sons of the Pioneers brought back the audience. Encouraged by success, they did a huge promotion of a superstar singer, but the star failed to show up. The loss of money and reputation was too much to bear, and again the theatre closed. Another business leased it for a while, but from 1985-1995 it stood empty.

That's when hometown-grown Dwayne Jackson got an idea for using it. While at Branson, Missouri, he decided the old 1,000-seat Wichita Theatre and a Branson-style production were made for each other. With the financial backing of his parents, Jeral and Rowena Jackson, Dwayne and Lisa established a family corporation, Pro-Voice, Inc., and bought the building. Untold amounts of sweat equity went into it as they cleaned, restored plaster and paint, and replaced the carpet to give the old girl a face-lift. Totally new air conditioning, sound and light installation, and a sixteen-foot stage extension made her the envy of newer theatres.

They put together the Texas Gold Country Music Show, made up of the Texas Gold Rush Band, comedian "Chester Drawers," and emcee Danny Kirk as regulars. In each production, they hosted top country and gospel entertainers as guests. They found this to be most successful as an offering every three or four months.

"We thought people, starved for entertainment, would swamp us," Dwayne Jackson said. "We were in for a rude awakening." It takes time and publicity to attract the public's attention.

For instance, with coverage from the media, 450 people came to a screening of the film classic *Casablanca,* the first time shown since the seventies. But when repeated a couple of years later with minimal media attention, only about 125 showed up. People will support a historical institution only if they have a deep interest in it. Jackson said younger generations, accustomed to watching their favorite performers on TV, don't have that motivation, so he appeals to other interests.

Today the Wichita Falls Theatre and Opera House presents various kinds of musical productions, plays, and a regular series of classic and family-oriented films. Also private and public groups often rent the theatre. When the Jacksons bring people in to see a movie, they inform the audience there's a whole stage behind that screen. Also they tell patrons of either stage or screen venues, "When the lights are up, you see a historical facility. When the lights are down, you see a modern, state-of-the art production."

Mike Helms photographer

Jackson said if he could tell beginning theatre groups and managers anything it would be this: "If you can't support it as a business, you better be careful. Don't get lost in the history." He advises any group to give people entertainment they'll return for, and publicize, publicize, publicize to bring in out-of-town patrons. A local audience alone will not keep a theatre operating in the black. Even nonprofit groups have constant expenses, and donations might play out. The biggest continuing challenges to nonprofit groups are bringing in new blood and getting publicity. "They can't *make* money if they have no money for promotion."

He cited information from the Chamber of Commerce: Wichita Falls has a population of 106,000. Widen the radius to 50 miles, and it's 320,000. Widen it to 150 miles and it's 7 million. If families, church groups, and tour groups know about it, they might not just say, "Let's go to Branson," or "Let's go to Granbury." They might also start saying, "Let's go to Wichita Falls." At the time we were there, Jackson was working on a marketing video. He has started a new publication, the *Texoma Monthly*, available as listed at the end of this chapter.

Remembering another attraction for potential patrons, ghost rumors, I asked Jackson if there were any such stories. He told me plenty. People say that many years ago a stagehand fell to his death from the balcony, and some have reported encounters with the poor fellow's ghost. One story came from the time the attorneys had the theatre leased to a stagehand who stored his equipment there. This renter (being a kindred "spirit" I suppose) had regular conversations with the dearly departed.

Lisa and Dwayne Jackson hadn't paid much attention to the rumor until they began renovation. Working together one night, they heard the crash of a metal bar hitting the wood floor. When they checked, the only bar was the one lying right where they had left it. They had to admit they were "spooked" other times as well. Once when working late at night as they often did, Lisa was walking up the grand staircase to the balcony. She heard her name whispered behind her clearly and repeatedly. Assuming it was Dwayne, she went back down to catch him at it, only to see him in the middle of a task way down on the stage. They have no explanation for these occurrences.

Chris Jackson and his friend Landon Mack described an encounter of their own. For Chris's thirteenth birthday, he and several friends spread their sleeping bags around in the mezzanine for an overnight ghost vigil. Most of the boys gave up and went to sleep, but not Landon or Chris. Five years earlier they had been convinced the rumor was true when both saw eyes watching them through a vent. On the birthday night, they lay in their sleeping bags talking. Landon saw a figure standing in the men's restroom doorway. Then it dashed across the upstairs lobby.

So it seems the Jacksons are better at tightrope walking than ever. They balance not two but three goals in their business. Besides paying tribute to their historical building and making it profitable, they also must coexist with something that claims squatters rights at the theatre. To their credit, they're accomplishing all three. —*Joan Upton Hall*

For information:

Wichita Theatre & Opera House
924 Indiana Ave.
P.O. Box 8142
Wichita Falls, TX 76307
(940) 723-9037
Dwayne@WichitaTheatre.org
www.wichitatheatre.org
* Same contacts for inquiries about *Texoma Monthly*

Other attractions:

Wichita Falls waterfall and river trails
River Bend Nature Works
Museums & art galleries
Berend's Landing, Elevator Rock
Graham Central Station (5-club musical complex)
Backdoor Theatre, ballet, symphony, Studio Brazos
Red River Speedway
Lakes, parks, golf

Annual events:

Red River Rodeo
Arts Alive!
Zephyr Days
Texas-Oklahoma Fair
Seasonal festivals including Christmas Magic

For details and accommodations:

Chamber of Commerce
P.O. Box 1860
Wichita Falls, TX 76307
(940) 723-2741
wfbci@wf.net
www.wichitafalls-commerce.com and
www.wichitafalls.org

48

Denton: Campus (1949)
The New Kid on the Block

photo courtesy of Denton Community Theatre

When we started this project one criterion for selection was for the theatre to have been "born" no later than 1940. With a birth date of 1949, the Campus could hardly have started at a more inopportune time—just when public interest in movies was beginning to wane. The Campus, however, is outstanding proof that newer theatres can also serve as rallying points for a community.

It is to manager J.P. Harrison's credit that the Campus succeeded during the fifties and sixties. Harrison's career "in show business," as he called it, began when he did promotionals for vaudeville shows. He came to Texas as Interstate Theatres' city manager then was transferred to Denton to manage four theatres, the youngest of which was the Campus. He went to great lengths to promote the opening of any new movie. For Cecil B. DeMille's *Greatest Show on Earth*, he decorated the front of the Campus as a circus tent and hoisted a mannequin on a trapeze. For jungle movies, he'd put out tropical décor. For *Gunfight at the O.K. Corral*, he created a western look.

photo courtesy of Denton Community Theatre

From all accounts, everybody loved him for the children's shows he presented on Saturday mornings. Except once when he gave the kids stray pets.

Harrison was one of only two men in the theatre industry who had twice won the Quigley Award, and for the movie promoter this was equivalent to an Oscar. He retired in the late sixties at the age of eighty-two.

The height of glory for the Campus came in 1966 when *Bonnie and Clyde* premiered with Warren Beatty attending. However, its glory faded after that. Julie Glover, Main Street manager, remembers when the Campus cheapened to $1 movies. The last time she went there, it smelled moldy and had an audience of about ten people. Soon after in 1986 they locked the doors.

By 1989 the courthouse was the only building downtown that didn't look dilapidated. It had received a generous grant for renovation. Denton's population was too large to qualify for the Texas Main Street Program, so a coalition of citizens organized their own to revitalize the area. Private money paid for the independent program, but the following year Denton was able to join a newly funded urban Main Street partnership. The Main Street Program encourages property owners to make improvements, offering free architect's assistance and low-interest loans co-sponsored with local banks. Denton even offered a 50 percent tax abatement over ten years to anyone who purchased a locally designated historic building.

The Greater Denton Arts Council bought the Campus Theatre and assigned management to the Denton Community Theatre (DCT). Because of a generous foundation grant from Ben E. Keith, DCT named the auditorium after him. An additional grant was awarded by the Meadows Foundation. Scot Wilkinson, executive director, explained that DCT is made up of 300 to 500 volunteers, some of whom once made careers in drama while others are simply willing and able to develop their theatrical talents.

Months before the grand opening, these volunteers put on their work clothes to do cleaning, painting, and toting. They were tired of holding performances anywhere they could, constantly having to erect and tear down sets. The promise of a permanent home spurred them on. As quoted in a special grand opening edition of the *Denton Record-Chronicle*, Bill Kirkly, assistant manager of DCT, said, "The greatest hardship any theatre faces is burnout.... Community theatre depends on volunteers, and you just can't continue asking that much of them and expect to maintain morale."

In 1995 the Campus reopened as a venue for live performances and since then has had a huge impact on the town. Booked over 300 nights a year, the Campus brings in audiences that stimulate nightlife and development of the downtown area. It has helped Denton in another way too by serving as a catalyst to unite the various arts groups, each of which used to try to go it alone.

The grand opening involved the whole town. To accommodate the three-day celebration, one street was closed so they could pitch an enormous tent. Area musicians and other entertainers, even jugglers, kept up the pace. Wouldn't all of this circus atmosphere have pleased J.P. Harrison? Since the old Campus had been a movie theatre, the Greater Denton Arts Council called in members of affiliate groups to produce a show called "A Salute to Movie Musicals." For the first season, DCT scheduled plays that had also been movies, launching it with Neil Simon's *Barefoot in the Park*.

Alan Nelson, restoration architect, did an exemplary job. Articles about the Campus Theatre have appeared in *Texas Highways*, *Mainstreet*, and *Texas Architect*. The old Campus used to crowd in 1,187. Nelson opted for a more intimate configuration. A magnificent thrust-style stage and a large backstage area eliminated about fifteen rows of seating. The balcony is used for lights and sound equipment, with offices, and prop and storage space behind that. Most importantly for patrons, the builders also opted for more legroom and more comfortable seats. That left room for 300 seats, but at that mark the royalties for DCT productions go up. Smart planning led them to install 299 seats with room for handicapped accessibility.

Before I even entered the auditorium, I admired the Art Deco beauty of the lobby. A floral wall motif leads up the stairs. Julie Glover and Scot Wilkinson told me the mural had been there originally but had faded. Texas Woman's University art professor Gary Washmon agreed to the project of repainting the designs. According to the *Denton Record-Chronicle*, Washmon and fifteen students spent more than a hundred volunteer hours of their weekends restoring the work. At Washmon's request, the Arts Council made a $500 donation to an art scholarship fund and let the students write "TWU Art Department 1995" beneath the mural.

Don Hall photographer

Wilkinson said DCT produces about five main shows and three summer musicals a year. With such a large talent pool, including college students and some children, patrons don't see the same actors over and over. Other groups such as Denton Light Opera Company and numerous musical groups also perform at the Campus. The Music Teachers Association holds its annual concert there. DCT is proud of its children's theatre, Pied Piper Players, in which they teach classes leading up to a production three or four times a year.

I liked Wilkinson's concept of a concession stand. He wants it to both evoke nostalgia with the usual movie fare (popcorn and Junior Mints) but also to tantalize with modern favorites (cappuccino and desserts). Whether he has carried this out, I didn't find out.

DCT doesn't do its marketing and promotion by decorating the theatre anymore. It coordinates its efforts with that of the Convention & Visitor Bureau, and the theatre's website is a model worth following. This "new kid on the block," the Campus Theatre, and the city of Denton could teach the "oldies but goodies" a few new tricks. —*Joan Upton Hall*

For information:

Denton Community Theatre, Inc.
Campus Theatre
214 West Hickory
P.O. Box 1931
Denton, TX 7620-1931
(940) 382-7014 or
1-800-733-7014
dct@campustheatre.com
www.campustheatre.com

Other attractions:

Museums & Art Galleries
More performing arts theatres
Historic driving & walking tours
Parks, lakes, golf, specialty shopping
Texas Motor Speedway

Annual events:

Seasonal events
North Texas State Fair
Blues Festival

For details and accommodations:

Convention & Visitor Bureau
414 Parkway
P.O. Drawer P
Denton, TX 760-7895
(940) 382-7895 or
1-888-381-1818
cvb@discoverdenton.com
or
info@denton-chamber.org
www.discoverdenton.com
or
www.denton-chamber.org

Resources That Have Helped Theaters

Action Award - West Texas Museum Association
Actors Equity Association
Association of Theater Owners
Ben E. Keith Foundation
Bridwell Foundation
CH Foundation
Dodge-Jones Foundation Golden Nail Award - Amarillo C. of C. for West Texas Theaters
Dunnigan Foundation
Harry Meredith & the Meredith Foundation
Hoblitzelle Foundation
International Association of Community Theatres
James and Eva Mayer Foundation
Jeanne R. Blocker Memorial Foundation
King Foundation
LBJ Foundation
League of Historic American Theatres
Main Street Program
Mabee Foundation
McDermott Foundation
Meadows Foundation
National Alliance for Musical Theatre
National Association of Theaters
National Historic Treasure National Register of Historic Places
National Trust for Historic Preservation
Playwrights Festival at Claude
Rockwell Fund
Ruth Lester Award
Texas Commission on the Arts (TCA)
Texas Historical Foundation
Texas Nonprofit Theatre Drama and Design Competition
Texas State Historical Commission/Landmark/Marker/Medallion
Texas Touring Artists
Texas Tourist Commission
Thomas Foundation

Glossary

ad drop - A colorful and attractive drop curtain on which are painted advertisements for businesses supporting the theater.

> **Example:** The Anson Opera House possesses one of four such curtains surviving from the opera house era. Restored by the same company that made it, it is an outdoor scene surrounded by local advertisements.

Adler letters & glass - When lighted marquees with changeable letters came in, it saved managers a tremendous amount of time from painting signs. The Adler company invented the milky glass of the background as well as cast aluminum letters. While they also sold plastic letters, they guaranteed that if the aluminum ones broke, the company would replace them.

> **Example:** The Majestic of Eastland still uses its full set of cast aluminum letters.

air domes - Outdoor spaces that showed motion pictures. They had walls (sometimes make-shift) to shut out nonpaying patrons but no roof. These went out of fashion when patrons began to demand more comfort.

> **(No known examples survive.)**

art deco (also called "art moderne") - A style of decorative art beginning in the latter 1920s that was most prevalent in the 1930s and 40s; marked by the use of geometric designs and bright colors. Eastland's 1987 souvenir program, regarding restoration, characterizes: "futuristic art deco style [as that which features] sweeping curves and rounded corners..., scalloped proscenium arch..., curving walls, and recessed lighting."

> **Examples:** Because most of the theaters in this book flourished during the art deco period, their restorations reflect this.

atmospheric - An elaborate decorating style that evokes the effect of an exotic setting. It employs such architectural devices as the façades of buildings and softly lit alcoves along side walls with back lighting. This suggests sunset fading to night when the house lights go down, with stars twinkling on the ceiling. Of his trademark illusion of outdoor space inside the auditorium, Eberson said, "We visualize and dream a magnificent amphitheater, an Italian garden, a Persian court, a Spanish patio, or a mystic Egyptian temple yard, all canopied by a soft moonlit sky."

Examples: The Majestic in San Antonio, a castle courtyard in Spain; the Majestic in Dallas, a Roman garden; the Paramount in Abilene, Moorish castles in a Spanish plaza (designed by David Castle).

"bicycled" - Managers sometimes shared movies between theaters. **Example:** When Clifton's Cliftex couldn't hold the audiences, the owner opened the Gem nearby. He staggered the times of the movies so that when the first reel at the Cliftex was finished, it was "bicycled" to the Gem to start there, each reel following until the movie was over.

Black Friday - On Oct. 29, 1929, stock market prices fell below the previous year's gains. That day was the beginning of the Crash when public confidence in the American economy was shattered bringing on the Great Depression. Many movie theaters were forced to close, but the ones left became an escape during a time of tough national struggle.

Example: San Antonio's Majestic opened on June 14, 1929, ironically, the beginning of what was called "Prosperity Week." It closed in 1930 briefly and then reopened with bare bones scheduling.

"buzzard roost" - A slang term for the highest balcony in a theater.

Example: During renovation, Port Lavaca's Main rebuilt its balcony (and dropped the derogatory reference) without the original segregation partition down the middle. The balcony sections of many theaters have served as the source of undamaged carpet, painting details, etc. that provided copies for restoration.

carbon arcs - Basically two carbon rods, one slightly larger than the other, are inserted into the sides of a machine until the points nearly touch in the middle. When lit, they burn somewhat like a welding torch. The intense light is reflected off a bowl-shaped mirror in the back of the machine out the front through the film, thus projecting the image on the screen.

Example: Until 1998, Lambert Little projected films at the Texan Theater in Hamilton "the old way, striking carbon arcs."

cry room (also called **"monkey room"**) - Karl Hoblitzelle originated the idea of building small, soundproof cubicles with only a few seats. The room had speakers and a glass wall. Mothers with noisy babies could go there to keep from bothering other patrons and still keep up with the movie.

Example: People remember when even small-town theaters like the Llano Lantex was remodeled, providing one of the greatest "what-will-they-think-of-next?" topics, the cry room. Many theaters still have them.

combustibility in projection rooms - In the early days, nitrates in film made it highly combustible, a dangerous combination with carbon arc projectors.

To keep the fires from spreading, owners learned to make the room a concrete cubicle with steel doors. Even over the projector ports, there are steel traps held up by an easily melted substance, which will release the traps to keep flames from escaping out the ports.

Examples: A large number of the theaters in this book were damaged or completely gutted at one time or another by fire. A fire in the projection room of Canadian's Palace was reported to have "blown the projectionist out the door!"

depression glass - During the Great Depression, movie theaters that survived used promotional giveaways to keep the audiences coming. One tactic was to give patrons an inexpensive dish, and people could collect whole sets. Surviving pieces have become valuable as collectors' items.

Example: A Texarkanan I spoke to still possesses a set distributed at the Perot (then named Paramount) and collected by her parents.

"hemp house" - A theater that used a pulley system of sandbags and hemp ropes to raise and lower the curtains.

Example: Galveston's Grand Opera House still has some of the original 1894 ropes. The curtain system has never been electrified.

love seats (also called "sweetheart" seats) - Extra wide seats at the ends of alternate rows to offset the lineup of seating and improve viewing.

Example: The National at Graham has a beautifully restored set, on which owner/manager Pam Scott painted details by hand.

Motiograph - A type of early movie projection equipment.

Example: Unlike some renovations, Mason's Odeon includes plans for the old equipment. The Motiograph projectors will be put back together and placed in the Mason museum.

nickelodeons - Any building, usually a store, where early motion pictures were shown; chairs, benches, and barrels were pulled up for any patron who could pay five cents. **(No known examples survive.)**

odeum/odeon - In ancient Greece and Rome, a building used for public performances of poetry or music; the term has come to mean a contemporary theater or music hall.

Examples: Two of the theaters in this book took the name: Mason's Odeon and Whitewright's Odeum.

olios - Vaudeville kept audiences entertained with short skits, songs, etc. between main acts. Also **"moviola"** - a Keystone Cops fashion video featuring familiar local landmarks and cameo appearances.

Examples: Midland's Yucca does this for its melodramas, never leaving a moment for the audience to become bored.

platter system - Most old-style projection rooms have a commode and sink because the projectionist had to watch the film too closely to leave. The platter system helped. Even today, film comes in cans of twenty-minute reels. Originally the projectionist had to switch between two projectors at the end of each reel. Today to prepare a film for showing, the projectionist winds it onto an enormous platter, splicing reels together as he goes. For every hour of a movie, the film is about a mile long and all of that has a complicated journey from one platter, through the projector, and back onto another platter, ready for the next showing.

raked floor & tiered floor - Sloping the floor in the audience can provide better visibility of the stage. On a pronounced slope, each row may also be "tiered" (horizontally level in graduated levels, like steps).

    Examples: The Snyder Ritz auditorium floor is raked and tiered steeply enough that it looks like stadium seating. Most auditoriums are gradually sloped (raked). At Uvalde's Opera House, the floor inside the theatre was originally flat and the *stage* raked forward sharply. Now the seating area rakes down toward the stage, which was made level.

"rat run" - A passageway allowing actors to move from one side of the stage to the other or front to back of the theater, unobserved by the audience.

    Example: In making a partition along the side walls for the rat run front to back, Dalhart's La Rita got the idea to incorporate several box seats to conceal it beautifully as well as functionally.

"road house" - In vaudeville days, this was a slang word for a theatre that had traveling acting troupes to perform.

shutters in grooves or **wing and grooves**; also **travelers** - mechanisms of the Victorian theater or a shallow stage.

    Example: For historically correct shows, Bastrop's Opera House utilizes wing and grooves (or shutters in grooves) for at least four staggered pieces of flat scenery to develop the illusion of diminished perspective. It also uses "travelers," scenery on curtains that go back and forth, while painted drops can go up and down.

Vitaphone - An early attempt to convert to sound; something like a large phonograph record that produced dialogue and sound effects. Synchronizing the film and the sound must have been a very tricky business.

    Example: The Rialto was the first theatre in Denison to convert to sound, using a Vitaphone system.

Index